A Border Within
National Identity, Cultural Plurality,
and Wilderness

D1550816

A Border Within addresses the question of English Canadian identity by exploring how unity is possible in the presence of a plurality of discourses. Ian Angus examines the relationship between globalizing social movements and the particularities of identity politics by extending the theories of Harold Innis and George Grant. Grant and Innis, argues Angus, provide a critique of homogenization that is the key to meeting the challenges of developing a new relationship with the natural world and of forging a new multicultural society.

Angus breaks down the superficial oppositions that have been the traditional touchstones of discussions of Canadian identity – the Garrison and the Wilderness, colony and empire, Canada and the U.S., the Self and the Other – in favour a view that does justice to the complex intertwining of identity and difference. In doing so he not only opens the way to a new understanding of the politics of identity in English Canada and the creation of a theory of Canadian social identity as postcolonial, particularistic, and pluralist, he also makes an elegant and passionate plea for reintegrating philosophy into public discourse.

IAN ANGUS is associate professor of sociology and humanities, Simon Fraser University.

A Border Within

National Identity, Cultural Plurality, and Wilderness

IAN ANGUS

McGill-Queen's University Press
Montreal & Kingston · London · Buffalo

© McGill-Queen's University Press 1997
ISBN 0-7735-1652-2 (cloth)
ISBN 0-7735-1653-0 (paper)

Legal deposit fourth quarter 1997
Bibliothèque nationale du Québec

Printed in Canada on acid-free paper
Reprinted in paper 1998

This book was first published with the help of a grant
from the Humanities and Social Sciences Federation of
Canada, using funds provided by the Social Sciences
and Humanities Research Council of Canada.
Funding was also received from Simon Fraser University.

McGill-Queen's University Press acknowledges the
support of the Canada Council for the Arts for its
publishing program.

Canadian Cataloguing in Publication Data

Angus, Ian H. (Ian Henderson), 1949–
 A border within: national identity, cultural plurality,
and wilderness
 Includes bibliographical references and index.
 ISBN 0-7735-1652-2 (bound)
 ISBN 0-7735-1653-0 (pbk.)
 1. Canadians, English-speaking. 2. Group identity –
Canada. 3. Canada – Relations – United States.
4. United States – Relations – Canada. 5. Multicul-
turalism – Canada. 6. Human ecology – Political
aspects – Canada. I. Title.
 FC97.A47 1997   971.064'8   C97-900264-8
 F1034.2.A69 1997

This book was typeset by Typo Litho Composition
Inc. in 10/12 Palatino.

*For Tom, who thought the human condition and
embraced the wide world from the island of Eire*

Contents

Preface

This is a little book that I had thought would be much longer. Perhaps it is so because of the size of the task or perhaps it is only my limited abilities. In any case, much of the work remains undone in the sense that the argument of this book requires further application and extension. But at least part of the reason is the changed circumstances between the first formulation of the task and its preparation for publication. The notion of "English Canada" that I believed could be brought to philosophical articulation has in recent years come upon its historical limit in a manner that can be referred to, but not completely explicated, by mentioning the success of the Free Trade Agreement and the North American Free Trade Agreement. Globalization has finished the English Canadian left-nationalist politics to which the more philosophical project with which I aligned myself was bound. To this extent the book is a swan song. This is said as a fact, and it is one that I take no pleasure in stating. Thus the philosophical project has had to incorporate this sense of end into its own self-conception. It can suggest a new beginning, through an immanent critique of the discourse of left-nationalism and English Canadian social and political thought, but it cannot bring into being the coalition of social forces that might make such a beginning a historical factor. This weakness of philosophy cannot be overcome by the strength of one's desire.

My work on the interpretation, critique, and development of the work of Harold Innis and George Grant has been ongoing for about fifteen years. Along the way several people and organizations provided necessary support for my task and encouragement regarding its worth. I would like to thank Viviana Angus, Roman Onufrijchuk, Rowly Lorimer, Robbie Schwarzwald, Arthur Kroker, Manoly Lupul, Bill Leiss, Michael Dorland, Brian Shoesmith, Myrna Kostash, Andrej Zaslove, and the Association for Canadian Studies. Some of the chapters in this book have been through earlier drafts that were published in other contexts. However, the current argument is, I believe, one upon which I have settled. Acknowledgment of prior published versions is extended to The Edwin Mellen Press, *Continuum: The Australian Journal of Media and Culture*, *The Massachusetts Review*, *Canadian Issues/Themes canadiens*, the *Journal of Canadian Studies*, *Canadian Forum*, and the *Canadian Journal of Political and Social Theory* (vol. 13, no. 1–2). I would like gratefully to acknowledge financial support for the project from the Social Sciences and Humanities Research Council of Canada (grant no. 410–91–0051), the Association for Canadian Studies (Canadian Studies Writing Award, 1990), and the 5-College Canadian Studies Program (Faculty Research Grant). Intellectual work, like any other, cannot be done without resources. The organizations and publications that have supported and encouraged work in Canadian Studies have been a key aspect of opening an intellectual space for dialogue about the formation and destiny of Canada. The assistance that this work has received has enabled me to make my own small contribution to the task.

A Border Within

CHAPTER ONE

The Possibility of Public Philosophy

The politics of identity is a familiar theme in English Canada. Throughout the period since the end of the Second World War until recent changes in both political culture and intellectual orientation that may be associated with the Free Trade Agreement and the North American Free Trade Agreement, "identity" was the key term through which the will to maintain, or develop, an independent Canada was expressed. Not that there were not critics. Liberal continentalists dismissed the concern as mere parochiality. Marxist and some dependency political economists often discarded the term as an ideological reflex, in favour of the supposedly more material concerns of economics, class, the mode of production, or imperial power. Yet the assumption that cultural concerns, such as that with identity, can be simply counterposed to material ones is itself a relic of a base-superstructure distinction between ideology and material conditions that has received its own share of deconstructive energy in the last two decades. Culture should be understood in an inclusive anthropological sense to encompass both ideology and material conditions insofar as they are united within a form of life or a style of practical involvement. Indeed, this wider conception of culture displaces the distinction between base and superstructure and renders it rather useless as a starting point for social philosophy and political criticism. The main tendency of English Canadian left-nationalism understood this fact well and synthesized dependency economics and concerns with cultural autonomy in a discourse whose main political intervention was oriented around the term "identity." This concern had a public resonance far beyond those who would consider themselves left-nationalists. It became a defining feature of the cultural landscape. Now that the politics of identity have become pervasive throughout the world, it is wondered in English Canada whether the

concept can be of any further service here. In part this change has
come about because of the destructive turn that the politics of identity has taken towards ethnic nationalism and various forms of fun-
damentalism in other parts of the world, though we can see signs of it
here as well.

Today the dangers of the politics of identity are all too evident.
"Identity" is a relational term: a group self is defined in distinction
from an other group. The politics of identity thus contains within itself the permanent possibility of degenerating into exclusion, scapegoating, and violence. This is the historical lesson of fascism that is
returning to haunt us. If one's identity is feeble or threatened, it can
be shored up by lighting upon an imagined cause, a supposedly fifth-
column group that undermines all one's efforts. Identity is in this
way constructed through a rebound. One avoids the uncertainties of
self-examination by constructing a presumed superiority in project-
ing a debasement of the other. Especially in times of rapid change,
when established groups are on the decline, this option emerges with
a vengeance. Nationalism, in particular, is a form of social identity to
which violence towards the other seems a permanent possibility. Ethnic identity contains the same threat, and when the two are combined
in ethnic nationalism, there seem to be no limits to the terror that can
erupt. Fundamentalisms of all kinds are proliferating, by which
groups attempt to put their multiple and sloppy origins of identity
into an unquestioned, presentable form.

Many thinkers today are in retreat from the politics of identity for
this reason. Nationalism should remain a civic nationalism, it is
claimed. All ethnic or non-civic forms of belonging should be
shunted aside into the private realm. This renewal of liberalism has
the advantage of defending shared values of citizenship that can perhaps overreach ethnic or local divisions, but it does not consider that
this private-public separation may itself be implicated in the renewal
of group hatreds. Basically, it assumes that what is common or shared
can only be reached by setting aside differences – putting them out of
consideration. There is a similar reaction in English Canada with regard to multiculturalism. It is now suggested that multiculturalism
ghettoizes immigrants and forcibly keeps them out of the mainstream
of Canadian society. It is claimed that "special consideration" for any
group itself leads to sexism or racism by making these social differences criteria for differential treatment. The only reasonable response,
it is said, is to relegate social differences to the private realm and to
implement policies of difference blindness. It is supposed that any
form of public recognition of difference initates the slippery slope
that leads to violence, the ghetto, and ethnic cleansing.

In addition to these destructive tribalist tendencies of the politics of identity, we are pressured by forces of globalization that are primarily driven by corporate economic power. These forces are the basis for the pervasiveness of the language of fate in contemporary life. We are repeatedly told that we must adjust to this or that tendency, that we must scramble in order not to lose out and redesign ourselves to fit the imperatives of the new world system. The system that economic globalization proposes is now visible in its main features: an increased intensity of work as a result of fierce competition and the fear of unemployment, dispossession and marginalization of increasing populations who have no place in the global economic order, and rampant consumerism as a way of life among those who "make it." Independent decision making within the system shrinks to marginal spaces without resources and isolated, private consumer choices. Globalization presents itself in terms of necessity and fate as if it were a natural force with which there can be no reckoning. Yet there is a contradiction here. On one hand, it is supposed to be a necessary fate, but on the other, we are also enjoined to accept it and to mould ourselves in its image. The language of fate diminishes, but cannot entirely eclipse, the importance of action in human life. It attempts to shrink action to mere reaction, to simple adjustment to the so-called forces of necessity. This language of fate has also infected the politics of identity, which is presented as if it were necessarily bound by a fate of devolution into intergroup conflict.

Our path seems blocked in both directions – on one side by the destructive tribalism that assertion of one's identity seems to encourage, on the other by the blind forces of necessity to which we apparently must adjust. We live in a time stunned by fate. It is not a felicitous era in which to speak of political vision and common goals, even less of a philosophy oriented to the destiny of a people. English Canadian social and political philosophy had always to criticize the apparent forces of fate. Since the motive force for modernization in a dependent colony came from decisions and exigencies originating elsewhere, it was necessary to criticize their apparent necessity in order to open up a space for an independent future. "Technology" was the main term through which the analysis and critique of modernization, industrial society, and liberal individualism were articulated. In this way there came into being one of the decisive features of the English Canadian intellectual landscape: the close connection between the conservative critique of modernity and the left-nationalist critique of capitalism. The liberal centre was left to advocate continentalism, free trade, and modernization, thereby abandoning the specific characteristics of English Canadian social and intellectual history for an international discourse that had no place for the critique of dependency. English Canadian thought is thus a struggle with fate and specifically with the idea that modernity constitutes a fate.

Contemporary public discourse is blocked by both the tribalizing devolution of the politics of identity and the globalizing forces of corporate political economy. They erase commonality through a reduction to self-interest, consumerism, and the depressive adjustment to fate. It is therefore not sufficient simply to begin to speak as if the commonality that the public intellectual would like to address were simply intact. There must be a preliminary construction of the possibility of commonality itself. At this point the public intellectual becomes a public philosopher. A philosophy centring on the possibility of public discourse needs to reach into the socio-historical formation of the polity in order to construct the commonality through which the polity may confront its destiny. This is a daunting task. Edmund Husserl called the philosopher the "functionary of mankind" to indicate the standing apart from one's merely personal interests and the straining towards the universal that philosophy demands.[1] It is hard to muster such arrogance, or such courage, today. To turn one's philosophizing to the destiny of the peripheral formation that is English Canada is no less humbling, though the task is haunted by the even greater worry that there may be nothing of universal significance to be found. Articulating a marginal philosophy thus requires a risk that is summed up in one of William Blake's *Proverbs of Hell*: "If the fool would persist in his folly he would become wise." I must leave it to the reader to decide how far the current attempt has progressed.

Addressing the contemporary impasse ultimately depends upon crafting a public philosophy that can speak to the historical attempt to preserve and project an English Canadian identity in America and that can move outward from identity towards an embrace of diversity. Identity and difference is one of the oldest questions in philosophy. Now our common fortune requires that it be given a formulation that will speak to our historical formation and our destiny. Philosophy must break through both exclusively tribal loyalties and mere necessity to reinvent the possibility of action and the ideal of self-knowledge. To so do, it replaces the language of fate with that of destiny. The destiny of English Canada was spoken of through the concern with our identity, and current doubts about the politics of identity seem to require an abandonment of such sweeping, magisterial terms as "destiny." But destiny is not fate.[2] We may speak of fate when human projects are overwhelmed by the uncommunicating gods or by the impersonal forces of nature, but not when the future seems lost by the inarticulate fumbling of our own hands. We may be caught within a destiny that we cannot sufficiently shape, but this is not the iron necessity that rules fate, only an inability to further a project whose human provenance carries no guarantee of either failure or success. We live in a time of stumbling, and the recovery of terms such as "destiny" is necessary to place our intellectual and political efforts in the reflected light of their honourable origins and pressing tasks. The politics of identity is ineluctably tied to the concept of destiny – the forging of the future of a people out of its past – and to those human virtues that are sufficiently rooted in the history of our nation to rally another attempt at grasping it. It is the responsibility of philosophy to clarify this public task and thus to think together identity and destiny.

The construction of commonality takes place through an interpretation and deconstruction of the historical formation of English Canada. By decomposing it into its elements, the crucial features of its formation can be defined and given expression. The retrospective reflection thus opens up the possibility of a prospective definition of a social and political philosophy for English Canada. It is in this retrospective-prospective thinking that the destiny of a people or nation is articulated.[3] The articulation of such a destiny grounds the possibility of public philosophy. A task such as this emerges in a time of transition from one settled period into another. We are currently in the midst of the dismantling of the welfare state and the social contract of the post-war period, which guaranteed a minimum social safety net for most citizens and the transfer of wealth between regions through the federal government. Thus the people and the regions were wedded to a social goal through a centripetal federal force. It was certainly not perfect, but, as is often the case, the negation is most instructive. The globalizing economic forces that are destroying the capacity of the nation-state to articulate a social goal raise the spectre of widespread social injustice and the breakdown of any common goals. At this juncture, we are forced to look into the past and anticipate the future in order to articulate a public philosophy. The politics of identity to which this process might give rise will have to counter the language of fate and to show that, as *self*-examination and *self*-criticism, it can avoid devolution into scapegoating the other and construct itself through an inclusive social goal.

The possibility of greater injustice forces us to articulate the ground of a new public philosophy.[4] The politics of identity has shifted in recent years from a national identity oriented centripetally towards a plurality of social identities connected to social movements that appear to have a centrifugal force. In the language of postmodernism, it is all "difference" these days. The most general formulation of such difference is the question of the relation to the other, especially the extent to which an ethics of respect can replace a denial of difference. Such respect for the other involves an abjection of the self. Only two cases are take up explicitly in this work: respect for the other ethno-cultural identity that is the best side of multiculturalism and accep-tance, rather than domination, of the other of nature that the ecology movement proposes. The ethic of respect for the other that is the underlying philosophical issue pervading the new social movements can be contrasted with the defence of "one's own" that was given philosophical expression in George Grant's reflections on national-ism. In this book I develop the term "particularity" from his work. This direction of inquiry provides a sounder philosophical basis for the rethinking of the relation between specific identities and human universality than the concept of difference, which tends towards a blindness to, or even outright rejection of, the notion of universality altogether. In a similar fashion, I extend Harold Innis's concept of "monopolies of knowledge" to open a space for the marginalized, emergent knowledges that social movements invent. In this manner I attempt to construct a new beginning for the politics of identity in English Canada.

This new beginning stems from an alignment of the philosophical task with the new social movements and their varied critiques of con-temporary society. A defence of the other is the point at which these movements might coalesce as a counter-hegemonic force. Many related issues have recently been pursued under the headings of post-modernism, post-colonialism, and the globalization of culture. In the coalition of social forces opposing the FTA in the "free trade election" of 1988, the new social movements and left-nationalism could be held in alliance. Recently a polarization has been set up between new and exploratory concerns and the older tradition of left-nationalism.[5] Often, left-nationalism is criticized as patriarchal, industrialist, Anglo-centric, and so forth, as if it were ever a hegemonic force in Canada that could be blamed outright for the course of events. Nonetheless, the suspicion that the defence of one's own requires an internal homogenization – of regions, classes, genders, and the like – is not entirely without foundation. However, proponents of the new social movements have thus far failed to answer the question of how they could forge an integrated social alternative instead of a merely exter-nal plurality of differences. Such a polarization has the effect of evacu-ating the space of the nation as a site of social struggle. It is either defined a priori as a conservative issue and abandoned or reaffirmed in a static left-nationalism that becomes increasingly estranged from the current reformations of social movements.

Overcoming this polarization on the political level will be the major task for the forces of social change in the next decades. It is a task with which this book is aligned but, obviously, one that no book can achieve. The concern here is to pose the issue at the level of social and political philosophy and, it is hoped, thereby achieve some generality of articulation. This text remains, in the tradition of left-nationalism, oriented to the level of the nation (though conceptualized as *English* Canada), even though it attempts to displace any implication of homogenization. It seeks a unity that is not homogenizing, that is to say, a hegemonic totality rather than an empirical or structural one.[6] Through an immanent critique of left-nationalism, it attempts to define the issue of new social movements in a manner that resonates with the history, politics, and philosophy of the struggle for Canadian independence. Only through the forging of a historical continuity such as this, it is supposed, will the newer project gain deeper roots and the surpassed project regain contemporary relevance.

All social and political criticism, as well as philosophy, has a universalizing component,[7] but it also never cuts the link that binds it to its provenance. A thinking oriented to transforming a given situation must be especially concerned with this link. The link to national identity is the basis for the unity of English Canadian social and political thought and its relevance to the particularities of the situation whose transformation is at issue. The qualifications that must be introduced into this term "national identity" are a main theme throughout this book. I specifically exclude, for example, First Nations and Quebec in order to focus on the definition of English Canadian identity. Also, I resist the temptation – introduced mainly by the postmodern turn in the human sciences – to regard all references to national identity as necessarily repressively homogenizing, and I develop the internal plurality that it requires to avoid this consequence in relation to multiculturalism and ecological diversity. Some such term as "national identity" must be maintained in order to theorize the link to provenance that assigns political relevance. Moreover, this link has been a main theme within English Canadian social and political philosophy because of the necessity of defining its situation and independence. That it is so need not cut one off from universal concerns. Parochiality is not a necessary consequence. This is another unnecessary polarization that needs to be rejected. English Canadian thought is, of course, permeated on all sides by influences from elsewhere. But to be interested in the situation in and of Canada is to be more interested in the particular formation of such influences as they enter "inside" than in their original articulations. Such are all national traditions, permeable and yet with a certain unity – a unity that does not precede the tradition but is formed through it, just as the situation of thought is not merely external to it but is defined and elaborated through the thinking. Nonetheless, in the contemporary context, such a unity of one's own must be placed alongside a respect for what is, and remains, other. This work thus engages with a tension between particularity and abjection. It is suggested that through this tension a new formation of universality may emerge. This is the philosophical expression of the political continuity between left-nationalism and the new social movements that I attempt to articulate. It is by no means a completed task.

This book begins from the notion that the concepts of identity and difference are intertwined and that it is superficial to put them into a simple opposition. I defend here the view that the public recognition of diversity is constitutive of the historical formation of English Canadian identity through the critique of technology and modernity as homogenization. Such a view could revitalize the public realm and counter the stunning force of fate. This context is a vital resource for overcoming destructive tribalism and globalization. The new centrifugality of contemporary social movements is a valid critique of the absences in previous centripetal federalism. It is in these movements that the destiny of the critique of technology and modernity that has formed English Canadian philosophy is to be found. Their centrifugality can be incorporated into a national identity only if that identity is itself thoroughly re-examined in order to make way for a new articulation between identity and diversity. Contemporary social movements have rediscovered the perennial possibility of human action to create new visions of the future. They have been influential beyond the numbers of their activists because they engage in an alternative form of identity formation that counters the productivist tension, marginalization, and consumerism of globalization. Any new politics of national identity will have to start by gathering these openings into its centre.

This book begins by analysing the project of left-nationalism that was the major alternative and critical discourse in English Canada between the Second World War and the FTA. It digs beneath this project to uncover the radical aspects of the thought of George Grant and Harold Innis that centre on the critique of technology and modernity which did not enter into this project, and it attempts to extend these aspects further in dialogue with contemporary social movements. It is an engagement with the constitution of English Canadian identity and the light that it may shed on the human condition.

CHAPTER TWO

The Social Identity of English Canada

Human society has not always included the nation-state. It is a distinctly modern form of social organization that came into being in Europe during the eighteenth century. While the terms "nation" and "state" are often treated as equivalent, they are conceptually distinct. The "state" refers to institutions, forms of government, and social forms of regulation and control. It is concerned with the external side, as it were, of the modern nation-state as expressed through the social organization of power and influence. The classic formulation of this concept was by Max Weber, who, following Trotsky, defined the state as "a human community that (successfully) claims the monopoly of the legitimate use of physical force within a given territory."[1] The state thus refers to the apparatus of ruling that, at least in the final analysis, depends upon violence. The "nation," on the other hand, refers to the extent that a human group feels itself as a unity in relation to this "external" state organization. Weber noted that this relation was not based on any empirical characteristics that such members of a group might have in common, but on "a specific sentiment of solidarity in the face of other groups."[2] The feeling of belonging to a group, and of having this feeling in common with other members of the group, is the core of national identity. In general, a feeling of belonging to, or identifying with, a socially defined form of human organization may be called a "social identity." This book is about the social identity of English Canada.

WHAT IS A NATION?

What, then, are the specific characteristics of national identity? The emergence of national identity alongside the modern form of the state in the eighteenth century was possible because of the wane of several previously powerful factors of social integration. Benedict Anderson points to the loss of religious communities based on sacred languages (usually written), in which there was a fusion of language and the world – unlike the modern conception, in which we assume that there are many languages for the same thing and that, as a consequence, any particular sign system is in this sense arbitrary. A second and related factor was the loss of the hierarchical dynastic political system in which the power of the king was divinely, religiously legitimated and in which all social organization radiated "downward" from this high centre.[3] The loss of the divine anchor that the king's body provided instituted, in Claude Lefort's words, a "society without a body" or a "purely social society" in which "neither the state, the people, nor the nation represent substantial entities."[4] Such a purely intrasocially constituted and legitimated power necessarily has these two characteristics mentioned by Anderson – the creation of arbitrary, or non-worldly, signs and the de-substantialization of social identities – and thereby opens up the possibility of democracy, which is instituted and sustained, according to Lefort, by "the dissolution of the markers of certainty." For exactly the same reason, it also motivates a nostalgia for a society at one with itself, as a substantial unity, which constitutes the totalitarian impulse in modern societies. It is for this reason that modern nationalism has often become a substitute religion.[5]

Modern society, and thus the modern nation, emerges from a transformation of space and time. The loss of divinely inspired hierarchy concentrated in the king led to a conception of territorial sovereignty that was equally present over all the area which it claimed. This conception arose alongside a correlative of "homogeneous, empty time" based on the clock and calendar, which gave rise to new forms of communication, especially the novel and the newspaper.[6] Anderson concludes that three main factors converged in the creation of modern national consciousness: a new capitalist system of production, a new print technology of communication, and a new recognition of the significance of linguistic diversity.[7] With the emergence of the modern nation-state, a new form of social identity emerged which is based on horizontal social relations equally significant across a given territory and which faces other similarly constituted groups. The territorial division of the earth is no longer simply accidental, but becomes a significant factor in the constitution of human identities, though, as Lefort reminds us, this significance is no longer merely natural or substantial, but pertains to the capacity of a given national group to render meaningful its spatial location. It thus is constituted within the realm of social power, which is ultimately enforced by the monopoly of legitimate violence.

Every discussion of nationalism includes a survey of the various factors that may become symbolic for national identity. Most often mentioned are ethnicity, blood, race, religion, language, cultural values, history, geography, and psychology.[8] All these and more have been proposed as the content of nationhood. None can be said to apply to all cases. In a thorough summary of studies on the topic, Eric Hobsbawm has noted that "there is no way of telling the observer how to distinguish a nation from other entities *a priori* ... All such objective definitions have failed."[9] The diversity of contents of nationhood is thus a significant part of the phenomenon. The feeling of belonging to a nation is ineradicable from the definition of the nation, and the symbolic markers that may express this feeling of belonging are diverse and often unpredictable. In Ernest Renan's classic words, "a nation's existence is ... a daily plebiscite, as the individual's existence is a perpetual affirmation of life."[10] This feeling, as Weber's definition points out, is often manifested in distinction to other groups of a similar sort. In other words, there is not only one nation but a plurality of nations, and one's national identity is most visible in contrast to the different national identity of others. Such feeling may fix upon one (or more) elements in elaborating a sense of belonging.

The association of the nation with the people, or the citizens, is more well founded, especially since, in a modern society, there is no definite centre (such as the body of the king) and this openness, or "empty space" (Lefort), implies that a social identity such as the nation is only meaningful through the social actors who belong to it. But this interpretation is not adequate either, at least not in a static sense. In the first place, some people resident in a nation may not be (or feel themselves to be) part of the national group, but more important, nations come into being and pass away. A people may press for its own national state. A state may be divided by the secessionist claims of a "nation" within it. At this point the definition of the nation and national identity tends to pass over into the issue of nationalism, which has been defined by Hobsbawm as "the body of citizens whose collective sovereignty constituted them a state which was their political expression."[11] This view includes the notion often held by nationalists that the nation is, or should be, the primary and overriding form of identification and social identity. Interestingly, critics of nationalism also tend to define it through its purported exclusivity, claiming that it is, in Michael Ignatieff's words, "a fiction of identity, because it contradicts the multiple reality of belonging."[12] From this definition comes the temptation to conflate nation, state, and the territory that it commands. In this vein Abraham Rotstein has

diagnosed in Canada a tendency that he calls "mappism," a conflation of national identity with territory, which reacts viscerally whenever territorial integrity appears threatened and at other times seems
entirely dormant.[13] Natonalism created the modern nation-state, and
in turn, modern nation-states often promote nationalism to solidify
their power internally and sometimes in order to enlist support for
external territorial expansion. Thus, I argue, while it is possible to
regard the nation as constituted through the social actors who feel a
belonging to its territory (as a consequence of the de-substantialization of social identities in modern secular societies), one must overlook neither the changing nature of nations nor its coexistence with
other forms of social identity. One of the predominant characteristics
of both nationalists and anti-nationalists is the tendency to regard the
nation as an exclusive form of identification. However, national identity, certainly in distinction from nationalism in its exclusivist forms,
coexists with other forms of social identity, such as region, class, and
gender, to name only a few. The tendency to conflate national identity
with nationalism tends to occlude this important point. There is no
basis for defining the nation, or even nationalism, as generically and
by definition exclusivist. I will argue throughout this text that one of
the main valuable aspects of English Canadian national identity has
been to propose a non-exclusive form that is amenable both to other
nations and to its own internal diversity.

While a nation may select any of a number of symbolic rituals and
everyday practices to regard as definitive of national identity, there
needs to be some account of why and how the division into separate
national identities was established. The creation of national languages that are distinct from other national languages and that
homogenize dialects within the state was important in the period of
European nation building. Anderson refers to the birth of administrative vernaculars in the previous period as a factor influencing new
nationally oriented forms of communication.[14] These were originally
"state" languages, languages of administration spoken by elites, but
they became the basis for the national European languages through a
gradual and unplanned evolution. Why should this be the case? Karl
Deutsch has claimed that the constitution of a social group as a group
depends upon the nature of the internal communications within it as
compared with those towards the outside. "The community which
permits a common history to be experienced as common, is a community of complementary habits and facilities of communication ... In
the age of nationalism, a nationality is a people pressing to acquire a
measure of effective control over the behavior of its members ...
Whatever the instruments of power, they are used to strengthen and

elaborate those social channels of communication, the preferences of behavior, the political (and sometimes economic) alignments which, all together, make up the social fabric of the nationality."[15]

Deutsch does not focus on the *contents* of the symbols of national belonging, but instead on the means of communication whereby these symbolic forms are circulated – a change of focus comparable to Harold Innis's theory of media of communication, which will be discussed in chapter 3. While one cannot account for the formation of the nation as such through a specific symbolic content (since such contents change from time to time and are different in different nations), it can be described through the means by which such symbolic content is made pervasive throughout the nation. Any social group is constituted as a group – that is to say, it takes on specific definable characteristics that distinguish it from other groups and is attached to distinctive symbolic contents – through a lesser development of the means of communication with "external" partners than with those internal to the group; or, to put it the other way around, through an intensification of intragroup communications. In fact, it is the relative degree and quality of the means of communication that brings into being the distinction between an internal and an external group. National identity thus presupposes a heightened degree of communication between members and a relative slackening of external communication with non-members. The rise of the nation-state involved such an intensification of internal relations and the coincident constitution of external groups. This intensification constitutes the national feeling of belonging, and the attachment to specific symbols of nationhood is based upon the prior distinction of an inside and an outside inaugurated by a new configuration of the media of communication.

A feeling of belonging such as constitutes national identity might well lend itself to manipulation and propaganda, to enlisting support for territorial expansion, even to distorting and obfuscating the interests of the members of the nation itself. This possibility, which is inherent in the fact that a feeling of belonging can attach itself to an indefinite plurality of symbols of nationhood, is the basis for the connection that many people make between national identity and aggressive nationalism. The Marxist tradition of social analysis has been sceptical of the claims of nationalism for the reason that it obscures intranational divisions between classes and fosters intraclass conflict in place of the international solidarity of the working class. Louis Althusser, for example, considered the political and communication forms of the modern nation-state *solely* as "ideological state apparatuses," thereby defining as necessarily ideological all feelings of belonging to a nation and conflating them with the power of the state.[16] In a similar vein, Eric Hobsbawm coined the term "invented tradition" to refer to "a set of practices, normally governed by overtly or tacitly accepted rules and of a ritual or symbolic nature, which seek to inculcate certain values and norms of behaviour by repetition, which automatically requires continuity with the past."[17] Modern nations, indeed, have often invented such rituals of symbolic participation in order to mask and soften the coercive practices upon which the state depends. Hobsbawm remarks that invented traditions are particularly characteristic of the nation's "exercises in social engineering."[18] There is no doubt that this is a widespread aspect of the nationalism of contemporary nation-states. It is important to decide, however, whether it can stand as a general view of the nature of national identity, or even of nationalism.

There are certainly many cases in which fascism and imperialism have enlisted nationalism as a self-justification. However, there are also many cases in which nationalism has been a potent anti-imperialist force in struggles for national liberation. National identity, and even nationalism, enters into other political issues in diverse ways and cannot be either condemned or accepted in a blanket fashion. Moreover, it cannot be equated with the more obvious forms of nationalism. National identity is often perceived and effective even when no political issues are pending. It is a form of social identity that bears comparison with other forms, such as gender, personal, regional, neighbourhood, and social movement identities, not simply a political ploy that can be accepted or rejected at will. While it may be characteristic of nationalism – or rather, a certain type of nationalism – to promote this as the exclusive or overriding form, national identity itself is one among an overlapping plurality of social identities.

Nationalism itself is, then, an elusive and contradictory phenomenon. National identity often coexists with other social identities and may be a form that is not solely the product of ideological manoeuvres by the state. Its character and importance as a contemporary form of social identity can only be rejected if one *assumes* the more fundamental reality of another social identity. Some (probably most) Marxists, such as Althusser and Hobsbawm, for example, simply assume that class is the only non-illusory form of social identity. From this assumption it is easy to fire salvoes at the more obvious forms of manipulation to which national identity and nationalism are prone. But doing so obscures two key issues: how class itself is formed as a social identity[19] and how national identity might interact with class, and also other social identities, in a manner that cannot simply be reduced to manipulation. There are other examples of this dismissive attitude to national identity from outside the Marxist camp. Feminists, for example, have sometimes argued that issues of national identity are a diversion from, and intensification of, the oppression of women.[20] In general, this is a key problem in contemporary discussions of social identities. If one such identity is *naturalized*, or assumed as fundamental so that its constitution is regarded as unproblematic and therefore left uninvestigated, it can be used as a site from which to launch barbs at all other identities as *constructed* within the system of social power. It is characteristic of the pervasive liberalism of contemporary societies that "the individual" social identity is naturalized and is the predominant ideological basis for taking pot-shots at all other social identities as somehow more constructed and less "real." National identity often seems to be a target in this context. Its misuse by aggressive or repressive nationalism usually serves as an excuse. But we must keep in mind that *all* social identities are constructed within the field of social power, and thus no social identity could ever be immune to manipulative and dominating uses: not class, not women, not the individual – none. The issue is then not to defend or attack national identity or even nationalism in a general fashion from some vantage point that is assumed to be unassailable. It is to investigate the specific conjuncture under which a formation of national identity brings into being a collective sense of belonging and a political project that can resonate with, and perhaps fuse together, other critiques of the social order.

This conception of national identity is what Antonio Gramsci called "the formation of a national-popular collective will."[21] In his view, the national-popular brings together the "elementary passions of the people" with intellectuals who share these passions and give them form and leadership in order to propose "intellectual and moral reform."[22] Gramsci elaborated his concept of "hegemony" in order to clarify the way in which social power is not simply imposed from above but relies upon the consent of those governed. The means of obtaining this consent are not neutral, however, but are themselves dependent on the effectiveness of ideas and the means of their propagation and reception. He proposed this conception in opposition to the bourgeois form of the modern nation-state. However, it has the important implication that the current bourgeois form should also be understood as a coalition of passions and interests united under a leadership, albeit a capitalist one. The capitalist nation-state could not continue to exist if it did not have roots in the passions and interests of a large section of the population. Without this grounding it would be able to maintain its position only by the continued use of violent repression. Such repression is always available should the legitimacy and power of the state be called into question, but it must be explained why repressive instances are the exception rather than the rule. The incorporation of the people into the nation is accomplished by the activity of expressing and forming popular desires, which is the formation of a "historic bloc" that is the historical actor formed through this hegemonic process. The specific "bourgeois," or nowadays "consumer capitalist," form of this world-view is what ties national identity to class society. However, an alternative national-popular will is possible through the uniting of all the subaltern classes under a different world-view articulated by a different intellectual leadership and constituting a new historic bloc. The main point here is that social change does not occur by rejecting out of hand, in an Althusserian fashion, the national identity in which the passions of the people are expressed. It occurs through accepting the feeling component and entering a struggle over its formation and destiny.

Gramsci's work represents the part of the Marxist tradition that accepts the "Weberian" point about the nation as a community based in a feeling of belonging. Weber pointed out that this feeling of belonging is present in any type of communal action. Even class action involves a feeling component and a knowledge component in order for the members of the group to act as a group.[23] I am not arguing that the Marxist tradition as a whole has ignored these components of feeling and knowledge in the formation of class; rather, I am arguing against the deep-rooted economist reductionism in the Marxist tradition that would demote the question of national identity to naught, or to an unfortunate mystification. From a Gramscian point of view, social identities and actors are not simply classes, but are the historic blocs formed from the welding of classes, groups, and interests together through a process of building hegemony. Engels had already clarified this component in a manner very reminiscent of Weber when he argued that in any actual political struggle, the divisions between different segments of the subaltern population can never be entirely overcome. "The 'people,' therefore, will always appear divided." Thus political struggle is required to produce a "moral effect."[24]

A second and parallel point against the Marxist reduction of social identities to class can be made in this regard. The point that national belonging is generally regarded by Marxists as merely imagined and artificially constructed was made above with reference to Hobsbawn and Althusser. It is also characteristic of Marxist approaches to regard the state as simply a reflection of economic power. In the *Manifesto of the Communist Party*, Marx and Engels defined the executive of the state as "but a committee for managing the common affairs of the whole bourgeoisie."[25] Following this lead, Leo Panitch has argued that a contemporary theory of the Canadian state has three main requirements: it must show the complex of state institutions, it must demonstrate the linkages between state power and class inequality, and it must specify the state's functions in the capitalist mode of production.[26] I have no argument that the state does indeed function in the manner described by these three requirements, but the question is whether this is all it does. The claim that the state's function is only to reproduce and fortify the economic power of the capitalist class over the working class simplifies considerably the nature of the contemporary national state. This simplification is already evident in the terminology used – in the occlusion of all issues connected with national identity through the exclusive use of the term "the state," thereby implying that there is no (legitimate) form of identification with the nation-state. By way of contrast, since the appearance of the capitalist market economy, there have been attempts by various social groups to respond to and limit the restructuring of society around the capitalist market and mode of production. These attempts have often, though not exclusively, expressed themselves through the nation-state.

The classic account of this point was made by Karl Polanyi, who described modern capitalist society as a double movement, "each of them setting itself specific institutional aims, having the support of definite social forces and using its distinctive methods. The one was the principle of economic liberalism, aiming at the establishment of a self-regulating market, relying upon the support of the trading classes, and using largely laissez-faire and free trade as its methods; the other was the principle of *social protection* aiming at the conservation of man and nature as well as productive organization, relying on the varying support of those most immediately affected by the deleterious action of the market – primarily, but not exclusively, the working and the landed classes – and using protective legislation, restrictive associations, and other instruments of intervention as its methods."[27] The Marxist account of the state is concerned with only one side of this double movement and thus is blind to the basis of identification with national identity. The movement of social protection from the ravages of capitalist society also passed through the nation-state. One might cite legislation governing the length of the working day, the minimum wage, medicare, welfare, unemployment insurance, transfer payments, and so forth as examples of this effect of the protective response on the nation-state.

In a similar manner, Marxists often describe multiculturalism as a state policy designed to tame and obfuscate the history of repression of ethno-cultural groups. Again, this is only half a truth. It ignores the history of multiculturalism as a policy proposed by subaltern ethno-cultural groups in order to alter their status. The point is not that it is one rather than the other, but that these two are both present in tension. The state is thus a site of contestation between the two sides of the double movement described by Polanyi. To the extent that forms of social protection were institutionalized by the nation-state, it is not hard to see that the identification of "the people" – of a mixture of classes, but especially the subaltern classes – with "the nation" is an identification with the gains that the movement of social protection made against the capitalist forces through using the power of the state. In other words, it is not just false consciousness. In the contemporary situation of the attack by market-identified forces on the social protective power of the nation-state, the strong identification of English Canadians with medicare, for example, is an important indication that the "feeling of belonging" that historically has constituted this nation is identified with the institutional processes of social protection and will be an important element of any "historic bloc" that might play a counter-hegemonic role in the future. An important part of the constitutional conflict of the last decades is the fact that in Quebec identification with forces of social protection is associated with the Quebec nation-state, not the federal one, and with the sovereignist political project.

In summary, we may distinguish three aspects of national identity as it is constructed within the modern nation-state. First, there is a formation of the means of communication such that an inside is distinguished from an outside and communication within the inside is intensified. This may be called the *institution of a nation*. Second, there is selection and propagation of the specific symbolic markers that define the content of a given national identity. This may be called the *rhetoric of national identity*. Third, there is the historic bloc who identifies with the national-popular will and acts on behalf of the national identity. This may be designated the *national actor*, which is often called "the people." This book, then, examines the way that English Canadian national identity has been formed and the significance, or moral effect, of its nationalism. Its goal is to contribute to a reformation of the national-popular collective will, or a counter-hegemony, through proposing some components of a social and political philosophy that are developed from an immanent critique of the tradition of English Canadian thought.

THE POLITICS OF ENGLISH
CANADIAN IDENTITY

A politics of national identity connects large-scale transformations at the level of states and international power with the *salience* of experiences of selfhood, tradition, language, and place at the most intimate level. From this vantage point, society is understood, not as an objectively existing structure that can be studied apart from social consciousness, but as something that is constituted through the practices of social actors whereby they identify with selected aspects of their social world. One of the key aspects of a given society is thus these practices of identification. This is not to say that social actors are always right about themselves, as it were. The self-understanding of a society may be criticized, but it may not be overlooked or bypassed in defining what the society is. Therefore investigation of the politics of identity must necessarily involve an analysis of *for whom* the question of identity is an issue, *why* the issue arises at the present time, and *the terms* in which it has been cast. For this reason, the forms of expression in which a society externalizes its self-understanding are of particular interest. These may include conventionally "cultural" phenomena such as art forms, but should be understood in a wider, more anthropological sense of culture to include everyday activities "in their characteristic style" (Edmund Husserl), which comprise a "structure of feeling" (Raymond Williams) that is lived as a "form of life" (Ludwig Wittgenstein). Actually, it is not so much a matter of conferring importance on cultural forms as such, as it is of viewing and analysing ordinary practical activities as "forms of expression" whereby a certain style of life is maintained, represented, and altered.

One's social identity is always plural. A person may be, for example, a son or daughter and a parent, as well as a worker, a community member, a member of an ethnic group, a political activist, and so forth. Each one of these identities is "hailed," or selected as salient, in a different context. When a person or a social group defines itself in a certain way, a certain context and set of relationships is implied to be the relevant one. The self-definition of a social group is, in this sense, an expressive phenomenon that indicates the changing cultural form of a society. Social movements are often the vehicles of these changes. Through feminism, for example, "women" as a group have become actors on the social stage. Similarly, there is now a social identity of "environmentalists" that plays a role in defining social problems and issues. Understood in this way, social movements do not merely *represent* existing groups or interests, but *constitute* the social identities in question through the activities and ideas that they circulate. Even in the case of ethnic identity, which normally draws upon a sense of a traditional cultural unity inherited from the past, it is nevertheless the case that a contemporary politics of identity actively recovers and rearticulates the received culture and projects it into the future.

It is in this context that the question of the social identity of English Canada becomes a particularly interesting phenomenon. *How* and *why* we regard ourselves as Canadians are clues to the values and activities that constitute "Canadian-ness," as is *to whom* this issue is relevant (obviously not to all those who are, empirically speaking, Canadians and, at least theoretically, to others who may not be Canadians themselves). But, even more, the ebb and flow of English Canadian nationalism is an indicator of the extent to which Canadians see their Canadian-ness as important. It is not only, or even mainly, an issue of whether we are, in fact, somewhat different from Americans in our way of life and values. This has come to be called, appropriately enough, "sociological nationhood," a term that refers to the descriptive sense in which the way of life in English Canada is different from that in the United States or China. Something more than this is at issue in nationalism. The main point is when and why this difference is seen as something worth preserving, worth defining and extending – why, at some times, we pick out this particular social identity to define ourselves and to articulate our vision of social alternatives. In short, the issue is to what extent the feeling of national identity commands an importance for the social actor overweening other identities which are also, from time to time, salient. One might say that the process of active identification with national identity is the *figure*, or theme, that is articulated on the *ground*, or background context, of the sociological nation. Understood in this way, for example, the historical emphasis on "preservation" in Canadian nationalism is itself very interesting and symptomatic. Both English Canada and Quebec have articulated their goals through an emphasis on preserving themselves (though, of course, against different perceived threats), which is an index of the "conservative" or traditional cast of the Canadian social formation and the tendency to deal with political issues by "muddling through" rather than making them issues of principle in a rationalist fashion. Perhaps this is one reason why our constitutional wrangles have been so agonizing. Such an emphasis on preservation implies a background context in which sociological nationhood is perceived as existing but disappearing or endangered. The issue of nationalism in English Canada is less likely to be argued between those who think that the international power of Canada should be enhanced and those who think not, than between those who believe that our way of life needs to be protected from its probable disappearance and those who consider that its disappearance would not really be a bad thing. The rhetoric of English Canadian nationalism centres on whether the division of the world into nations, and thus into our own way of life versus others, should be seen as a valuable diversity or whether it should be regarded as a dismal affair leading to international conflict. Though the key rhetorical term is "preservation," the key *topos*, or theme, is a contemporary evaluation of the validity of the nation.

The emphasis on national identity in Canada pertains to the postwar period especially. Throughout the capitalist world, a new hegemonic formation came into being that is variously called Keynesianism, the welfare state, Fordism, and so on. This formation has been coming apart in the last decades with the attack on government social spending, globalization of the economy, and the creation of competing free trade zones around the world. One key aspect of this contemporary transformation is the declining influence of the nation-state. Though this change was clearly already in the making in the mid-1970s, we may conveniently and symbolically date the post-war consensus from the end of the Second World War in 1945 to the beginning of the Free Trade Agreement in 1989. Within a relatively stable hegemonic formation such as this, there is a fixing of social actors and of social goals that is sufficient to distinguish it from the large-scale and basic transformations that preceded and have succeeded it. This certainly does not mean that peace and equality reign triumphant, but it does imply that social conflicts are restrained within a hegemonic framework that is, as a whole, rarely open to question. This period was characterized by an "end of ideology" in the sense that the goal of capitalist expansion and stabilization was accepted throughout the society and radical alternatives were associated with the external enemy of communism and the Soviet Union. Labour unions were largely brought into the system through collective bargaining, and the state became a major actor in economic development and in a certain redistribution of wealth. Jane Jenson calls this period "permeable Fordism" to emphasize that, although Canada shared with other North Atlantic capitalist countries the main features of this "mode of regulation," its peculiar characteristic was that "since 1945 the Canadian economy has been permeated by international – or, more exactly, continental – effects. Its fordism was designed domestically but always with an eye to the continental economy."[28] The social actor that came to the fore was the nation-state, which became the leader of the historic bloc. In this period the national pole of identification held sway over other social identities. "The collective identity around which the societal paradigm formed was a national identity, one which stressed the spatial commonality of all residents of a large and dispersed country. It identified the country's natural resources rather than its workers as the source of its greatness."[29] Given this background, we should not be surprised that with the dismantling of the post-war consensus in recent years, new social actors have entered the picture and have come to vie with national identity as significant poles of identification. Growing regionalism, increased power of provincial governments, Quebec separatism, Native land claims, all indicate that the ability of national identity to hold sway over other identifications has significantly weakened. As well, the new forms of identification allied to new social movements, such as feminism, environmentalism, and sexual and minority liberation movements, indicate the possibility that national identity will be a decreasing pole of identification in the future.

We are now situated in a period of transition from the prior consensus of permeable Fordism towards a new hegemonic formation that will come about in a world of globalization and new social movements. In this period the politics of national identity may well go the route of the declining influence of the nation-state. However, it is also a moment in which new questions arise regarding the formation of a nation, in which the possibility of change in the connection of various nations to states is imminent (such as the relation of the Quebec and Aboriginal nations to Canada) and in which a new role for national identity between globalizing forces, on the one hand, and new social movements, on the other, may be possible. As a result of this period of transition, it is not possible for a thinker situated in English-speaking Canada simply to assume a traditional relation to the nation-state, any more than it is possible for a Québécois or an Aboriginal person. In rethinking the nation, one must begin with English Canadian national identity, an identity that has perhaps been notable for its lack of self-assertion as such.

The term "English Canada" is doubly problematic. First of all, it is often rejected out of hand by multicultural advocates on the ground that we are no longer an English society and it can no longer be said that most Canadians are of English extraction. This objection, however, occludes the fact that the key role of English as the language of everyday interaction, commerce, and politics has never been seriously in question, despite the successive waves of non-English-speaking immigrants. As Quebec writers have often pointed out, this aspect of the multicultural issue can polemically serve to deny the specificity of Quebec distinctiveness, which is articulated through a politics aiming to protect the French language. For that reason they have often – wrongly, in my view – regarded the multicultural claims of English Canada as fake.[30] One advantage of accepting the term is thus that it makes clear that the referent of "English" in this context is neither to persons nor their country of origin, but to a common feature of the entire society and, further, to any and all consequences that the language of everyday interaction might be said to have.[31] This point is rather difficult for many in English Canada to accept. Since "heritage" languages have been kept out of the public realm and the cultural difference between English Canada and the United States does not revolve around language (combined with the role of English as the language of commerce and technology internationally), language has been generally regarded as merely a neutral "medium of communication" without cultural significance.[32] The status of English has not been open to question publicly and is therefore not widely regarded as an issue for multiculturalism. As a result, there has been virtually no investigation of the consequences of this banal view of language, and perhaps culture outright, either for speakers of minority languages or for native English speakers.

Moreover, the origin of most, though not all, of our commercial and political institutions in the English tradition tends to be regarded simply as an unavoidable consequence of history, whether inflected with a positive or a negative slant. But after all, even the most multicultural society requires a commonality of institutions, and it risks a dangerous degree of blindness to its own functioning if these institutions are not available to a discourse of public justification. Regarding the English origins of our institutions as just a historical fact without contemporary significance involves cutting off justificatory discourses from historical facts in a destructive fashion. Indeed, it leads to the most fundamental contemporary dilemma with regard to multicultural society: can all social institutions be understood as relative to (multi)cultures and their internal resources of justification? If so, in what sense do we live in "one" society? Are we not in danger of thereby falling into disarray and fragmentation? On one level, this issue is simply a priori, or definitional. It has been pointed out by Peter Winch that unless the members of a society share some common understandings, there is no sense in which they can meaningfully be said to belong to the same society.[33] But it can be the case that these common understandings at the level of everyday practice and institutions do not issue in a common justificatory discourse; or, to put it differently, that there is a schism between the common understandings of everyday life and the fragmented plurality of justificatory discourses. If this were so, one could speak of "one" society that was nevertheless in a crisis of legitimation. There is some reason to believe that this crisis is a dangerous tendency of what one may call "actually existing multiculturalism," but it would be merely a conservative reaction, such as that of Reginald Bibby, to regard this as a necessary consequence of multiculturalism.[34] The task is thus to show how common everyday understandings can coexist beneficially with a plurality of justificatory discourses that is not merely a fragmented plurality. This issue is taken up in chapter 5, where it is argued that the dilemma is not an inevitable result of multiculturalism, indeed, that it stems from a fundamental misunderstanding of what is involved in a multicultural society. It can only be avoided by admitting the origin and glue of our commonness in institutions and history that are tied up with the predominance of the English language. For these reasons centring on the consequences for a multicultural society of the historical influences inherent in the common majority language, I think that the term "English Canada" should be retained.

But there is a second source of problems for the term. English Canada is neither a nation nor a state; "Canada" is. In the English tradition (unlike the French and like the German), "nation" and "state" are virtually identical terms, often compacted into "nation-state," implying that any people who claim enough commonality to regard themselves as a nation should also claim and be accorded independent nationhood.[35] Not only has this view led to a virtually innate incapacity to regard Quebec as a distinct nation, but it has also seriously impeded viewing English Canada itself as a nation, or indeed any kind of a unified identity. The current practice of calling English Canada the "Rest of Canada" or "Canada outside Quebec" underlines this inability. We can talk about provinces, regions, ethnocultures, and so forth, on the one hand, and Canada, on the other. But the entity "English Canada" is nearly impossible to grasp. It tends to disappear downwards into the elements that make it up or upwards into the nation-state. We do not seem to have the necessary concepts to grasp it for itself. This inability is itself constitutive of the current situation to the extent that without a conception of common identity, we are indeed not a nation in the full sense, which requires that national identity be a theme articulated by a social actor. We can perhaps start to make some headway in this matter by beginning from the external context that surrounds English Canada. We are neither French Canadian nor Québécois nor Aboriginal people. English Canada came into existence, and persists, in distinction from these two other groups – as well as, of course, from its historic rejection of the American Revolution. Moreover, today, largely as a result of the self-assertion of the other two groups and occasionally their wanting to talk or negotiate with "us," we are perhaps coming to ask who "we" are. Who we will be in the future will be determined in large part by how we negotiate with these two external groups and whether we are willing to understand their desire to perpetuate their own identities. But this book risks another and, it must be admitted, less-precedented option for English Canada. Instead of discovering ourselves mainly on the rebound from our encounters with others, we may also define ourselves through the coming to self-consciousness of the cultural and political identity of English Canada itself, through our own definition of our national identity. In this way we may at last begin to appreciate the claims and desires of the other two main groups. It may even be good for us. There has been a significant tradition of social and political thought in English Canada that has urged us in this direction of national self-expression, though its impact has never been mainstream. Is it already too late for this option?

THE DISCOURSE OF ENGLISH CANADIAN LEFT-NATIONALISM

The discourse of English Canadian left-nationalism was the key component of the self-expression of English Canada in the period of permeable Fordism from the end of the Second World War to the beginning of the FTA in 1989. In retrospect, it may be regarded as English Canada's self-expression even though its mode of identification, correlative to the historic bloc predominant in the period, was the federal government. In any case, it never made inroads either in Quebec or in Aboriginal politics and could not really be expected to do so. There were two main components to this left-nationalist discourse: an analysis of the historical reasons for the continued dependency that characterized the Canadian economy and an argument for the necessity of cultural autonomy, both intrinsically (as the key aspect of the expression of national identity) and strategically (as a condition for gaining control of the economy). While the political-economic and cultural components of left-nationalism were inseparable within the analysis, its impact on Canadian society (its Liberal domestication, one might say) was such as to propose the assertion of cultural autonomy without fundamentally altering the conditions of economic dependency. The argument for cultural autonomy influenced Canadian cultural institutions and policy, whereas the power to put the economic analysis into practice was never gained. I want to sketch the main contours of left-nationalism and its social effect in order to suggest that the conditions which gave rise to it have now fundamentally altered and that it can be seen as a sign of a historical period which has come to an end.

But first I must explain what I mean by calling left-nationalism a "discourse" rather than an argument, a position, a theory, or a politics – even though it contained all of these. The term "discourse" refers to something much larger: a *space for discussion* and debate in which many (often competing) positions are possible.[36] One might use the term "framework" also, but it has the disadvantage of suggesting that the framework is somehow separate from the individual contributions. Through the term "discourse" I want to suggest a more complex interrelationship between individual left-nationalist analyses, the sum total of debates and discussions, and the evolving "discourse" of left-nationalism itself, for the last is only available to us through the individual contributions and debates themselves. A discourse is structured by what one might call, in a diagrammatic metaphor, "axes" that define a realm of reference points from which arguments can be made. Thus it allows for disagreement and debate even while it structures these disagreements in relation to each other, and it ensures that the different speakers are speaking about "the same thing" even when they disagree. The discourse of left-nationalism thus constructs a space of knowledge in which a plurality of knowledge claims coexist and conflict in determinable relationships. The term "discourse" refers primarily to the organization of this space. I do not think that there is any rule for how many axes a discourse must have, but it seems that at least three are necessary for the discourse to have enough internal space to allow the development of sophisticated arguments, analyses, and histories whose interaction and mutual criticism can articulate a reasonably complex realm of understanding.

The two main axes of left-nationalism were the historical diagnosis of the Canadian economy as "dependent industrialization" as a result of the successive colonial relations of Canada to France, Britain, and the United States developed in the staple theory of Harold Innis and the lament for the failure of Canadian cultural autonomy by George Grant. These two axes constituted left-nationalism as an interdisciplinary intellectual space focused on the topic of Canada in relation to the usual division of academic specialization in the university structure – English, sociology, political science, geography, philosophy, and so forth. The third axis was usually supplied by the individual researcher or writer. Sometimes it was a set of interests formed within one of the academic specializations, such as English literature. An investigation would then focus on the issues raised by the history of Canadian literature in relation to a country that has been, and is, economically dependent in the context of a project of self-assertion of national identity. In this book, the third axis is my own continuing

concern with nineteenth- and twentieth-century European philosophy. Canadian Studies departments at Canadian universities were
constructed by collecting scholars from different disciplines and
bringing them into relation through the addition of these two axes,
which they then had in common. However, it is important to note
that the third axis need not necessarily be a university-based specialization. It might be, for example, the concern of union organizers to
promote the interests of workers, of local librarians or historical societies to develop and disseminate knowledge about their area, of
regions and localities far from federal power to account for their marginalized condition, and so forth. Left-nationalism was an intellectual
discourse with a political orientation that connected academic
inquiry with a wider political project which could involve Canadian
society as a whole. It was a case of intellectual leadership in Gramsci's sense (not solely, but often importantly, university-based) – the
articulation of a world-view with a goal of social transformation that
appealed to a coalition of the currently less powerful groups in Canadian society. This intellectual leadership was not confined to the universities. It also embraced union leaders and researchers, some
politicians (mostly in the New Democratic Party), community activists, and other radicals oriented to various issues. They are all intellectuals in Gramsci's sense: they articulate and propagate the ideas
central to an emerging world-view.

The two main intellectual figures in the left-nationalist discourse
were Harold Innis and George Grant, a fact that explains why they
are key reference points for this book. This starting point expresses
the continuity of this work with the project of left-nationalism and,
even deeper, the tradition of English Canadian social and political
thought. Innis and Grant were continuous reference points for discussions within left-nationalism and also for more polemical debates
with opposing political forces.[37] This does not mean that the works of
Innis and Grant were accepted uncritically within left-nationalism,
but rather that they became axes in relation to which criticism, empirical research, and theoretical development could be situated. Innis's
classic analysis of Canada's staple economy centred on the dependency of a society developed through a colonial relation between peripheral colony and imperial centre. In the well-known conclusion to
The Fur Trade in Canada he wrote: "The economic history of Canada
has been dominated by the discrepancy between the centre and the
margin of western civilization. Energy has been directed toward the
exploitation of staple products and the tendency has been cumula-
tive. The raw material supplied to the mother country stimulated
manufactures of the finished product and also of the products which

were in demand in the colony ... The general tendencies in the industrial areas of western civilization, especially in the United States and
Great Britain, have had a pronounced effect on Canada's export of
staples."[38]

Here were all the basic components of the staple theory of Canadian economic dependency: a centre-periphery colonial relation, an
underdeveloped manufacturing sector in the colony, the significance
of transportation and communication links, and cultural continuity
with Western civilization. Development of Innis's staple theory proceeded in a number of directions. To mention a few: a cleavage between commercial-financial and industrial sectors of the capitalist
class was investigated by R.T. Naylor;[39] Melville Watkins pointed to
the consequences of the high degree of foreign (United States) ownership for the export of resource-generated capital, over-concentration
of resources in the export sector, and the failure to develop renewable
forms of industry, that he called the "staple trap";[40] Wallace Clement
investigated unequal development of regions within Canada by successive waves of staple extraction.[41] The political issue of the relation
between the industrial working class and farmers was a prominent
theme because of its immediate political implications.[42] Even Marxists who contended that the internal class formation of Canada was
more important than foreign ownership and dependency felt obliged
to argue their position as a critique of Innis,[43] but more thorough and
influential was the attempt to reconcile Innis's ground-breaking
empirical account of Canadian economic history with Marxist analysis. The point here is not to catalogue all of these developments and
certainly not to enter into the debates between them; it is rather to
indicate how the staple theory provided an axis for reference,
research, and critique that tied such developments to the overall discourse of left-nationalism and its political project even as Innis's
work was expanded, criticized, and surpassed in many specific
respects.

George Grant's lament for the failure to achieve cultural autonomy
was similarly used as a continuing reference within left-nationalism.
In 1945 he had published a pamphlet that defended Canada's continuing membership in the Commonwealth and the maintenance of
the British connection. It sounded a theme that persisted throughout
his life's work: that the independence of Canada from the United
States presupposed the notion that, even though we share language
and cultural background with that country, some different way of life
was – or ought to be – pursued here. Grant argued, "The meaning
and significance of Canada as a nation is that on the northern half of
this continent a sovereign state has been created, friendly to the

U.S.A., but essentially different."[44] The American empire, he suggested, was based exclusively on the principle of the freedom of the individual. He defined the difference of Canada as based in the British tradition of effecting "a compromise between the two extremes of liberty and order" and a Canadian as "the blending of the best of the ancient civilization of western Europe with its maturity and integrity, with the best of North American life."[45] Here are, in germ, the main political themes of Grant's work: the definition of the United States (at least in the post-1945 period) as an empire, the description of its culture as based exclusively on the liberal doctrine of individual freedom, the defence of the greater European connection in Canada as the result of a non-revolutionary tradition and the heritage of Loyalism, the search for a principle of Canadian difference, and the definition of this difference through a communitarian stress on social order.

These themes remained the political backdrop of Grant's later philosophical development. In 1945 he thought that such a principle of Canadian difference might survive in North America. By the time he published his most famous book, *Lament for a Nation: The Defeat of Canadian Nationalism*, in 1965, he had come to the conclusion that such an option was no longer possible. He defined his lament as "to cry out at the death or at the dying of something loved," which was based on tradition rather than philosophy and whose object was the romanticism of the British dream of Canada.[46] His claim that the possibility (perhaps never a real historical one) of an independent Canada had passed would never waver, though he could never be said to have taken pleasure in this judgment and often made political pronouncements suggesting its reversal. Grant's evocative writing gave expression to the popular feeling and desire for an independent Canadian identity. The communitarian stress on social order became a reference for many socialists as well as Tories and led to the influential argument that there was a continuity between conservative and socialist strains in Canadian society because of their common opposition to liberal individualism.[47]

The appropriation of Grant's work within left-nationalism was always controversial. His own Toryism and Platonism, not to mention the influence of Leo Strauss, also led to more traditionally conservative interpretations. Left-nationalism revoked in one major way the formation of his work. It rejected, in the final analysis, the standpoint of lament. Certainly, a rhetoric of lament has strong overtones in left-nationalism insofar as it uncovers the historic failure of Canadian government to provide the policies that might lead the country from a cycle of dependence towards an independent economic and cultural existence. The emphasis on the "preservation" of our historical cultures has been a significant rhetorical form within which left-nationalism has articulated its prospective world-view in relation to the past. One might say that the main rhetorical form of left-nationalism is a lament for the failure adequately to preserve the past and an argument that such preservation requires a radical reorientation in the future. It is a vision of a Loyalist, Tory past and a socialist future. To call it a rhetorical form is to say that it goes far beyond specific arguments and analyses. It is a thought structure, or a form for the elaboration and presentation of ideas, which is often present even when virtually invisible and which derives more from the discourse of left-nationalism as a whole than from any one component. The influence of Grant on left-nationalism is through his provision of this rhetorical form of lament, as well as many of the specific themes of its vision of cultural autonomy.

However, left-nationalism was bound to reject this standpoint as the final word – as perhaps Grant himself did when faced with pressing political issues.[48] Lament, in the left-nationalist version, was relegated to covering only the story *up until now*. The other half of the story was oriented to the possibility of independence in the future, which was contingent on its most characteristic rhetorical component – as with any engaged political movement – the necessity for decision in the present. The present as endangered and as the locus for radical decision is the primary rhetorical form of left-nationalism. It has this characteristic in common with Marxism, which is the formative-rhetorical basis for the Marxist-nationalist synthesis (as opposed to the thematic basis, which is the analysis of the intersection of class and nation). Thus left-nationalism devalues Grant's rhetoric of lament in order to replace it with a rhetoric of a decisive present. In an influential collection entitled *Canada Ltd.: The Political Economy of Dependency*, Melville Watkins oriented his argument for Canadian socialism around a reassessment (in 1973) of Grant's book. He took issue with Grant's claim that socialism is impossible in Canada's current context and thereby turned the lament into a call for a new socialist and nationalist party.[49] In addition, consider the closing lines of a more recent essay by Mel Hurtig. "In conclusion, there can be no question that George Grant was a prophet. But so far his followers have failed – not because they are in the minority, but because they have used the wrong tactics. It remains to be seen whether or not they can learn from the bitter lessons of 1988. They have one last chance."[50] It is quite a move to interpret a lament as prophecy! Left-nationalism must always position itself one step before the end and point to "one last chance." Thus it cannot really indulge in lament from first to last, as perhaps Grant himself as a living and acting individual could not. The revoking of lament was the condition for his inclusion as an axis of left-nationalist discourse, and it explains the impossibility of entirely capturing his legacy within that discourse.

Within left-nationalist discourse, Harold Innis and George Grant are thus rather more than the names of two major Canadian thinkers. They are the symbols for two of its axes. They are the integrating conditions whereby the interests of specific researchers and activists became incorporated into the discourse by being placed within a common space. Moreover, these two axes, though they deal with economic dependency and the project of cultural autonomy, are not simply different; they bear important relationships to each other. For example, Harold Innis also referred to American imperialism, Loyalism, and Canadian autonomy, even though his work was not mainly about cultural issues.[51] Also, Grant's conception of culture was primarily an anthropological sense of everyday practices and routines and only secondarily that of scholarship and the arts, as reflected in his tendency to use the term "civilization" rather than "culture." In this sense, culture encompasses political economy and is not counterposed to material life. Grant often referred to political events symbolically, in the sense that they were not simply single events but condensed the meaning of larger turning points in the way of life of a people. This was the way he treated the 1963 defeat of John Diefenbaker in *Lament for a Nation*. I certainly do not mean to say that scholarship and the arts are irrelevant, but that they are expressions and understandings of the practical life of a people, not diversions separate from the rigours of practical life. Their significance must be comprehended within a larger concept of culture that illuminates their role in the expression of practical life. In sum, the works of Innis and Grant became almost canonical within left-nationalism – not in a static sense, but as the condition for the elaboration and development of the discourse in a way that held it close to the practical concerns of Canadian society and that articulated a project of its political transformation.

There were thus good reasons to suppose that an integration of Innis's dependency theory and Grant's cultural vision could be made meaningful within left-nationalism. These two axes provided the references whereby specific studies and activities could be integrated into a larger national project. But there was another component too, which relates to the rhetoric of "decision in the present" that marked the appropriation of Grant's lament. The three axes of left-nationalism had to be put together in such a way that its focus on the nation could be connected to the "left" character of the synthesis. This core, which enabled the construction of the discourse, has not yet been explained here. It was a matter about which there was much debate and which marked the difference between competing political tendencies. It concerned the status of the national capitalist class and its relationship to the project of nation building. The most characteristic tendency of left-nationalism was to argue that the Canadian bourgeoisie was throughly compromised by its dependent role. Jim Laxer wrote in *Canada Ltd.*, "Canada's dependency is a function not of geography and technology but of the nature of Canada's capitalist class ... At no stage have native Canadian industrialists who profited from the production and sale of manufactured goods dominated Canadian capitalism ... Dependency has shaped the character of Canadian capitalism and has created a capitalist class that has needed continued dependency for its continued well-being."[52] This straightforward statement was open to considerable discussion and debate. It was argued by Daniel Drache, for example, in an echo of Innis's claim that Canada had moved "from colony to nation to colony," that bourgeois nationalism had been a factor but that now it was a "spent force."[53] The core of the integration of the discourse of left-nationalism was, of course, argued almost incessantly. It was the focus on this issue that defined left-nationalism as such. This is a consequence of a "discourse" that it defines through the intersection of axes a centre of concern which is open to continuous debate. Whatever the nuances of the specific analysis, the political conclusion was that nationalism had ceased to be (or never was) a bourgeois force in Canada and that it could become a factor in the politics of the working class, and perhaps a coalition of all subaltern classes.

This core defines left-nationalism "proper," that is, its clearest and most explicit form. Through this delineation it can be distinguished from two closely related analyses on either side, as it were, of the core. There was a Marxist argument that the Canadian state operated in the interests of a nationalist capitalist class, a class that often had imperialist interests and was thus in principle no different from those of other countries. Nationalism, on this argument, contained no possibility of being connected to the political aspirations of working and subaltern classes. At its extreme this argument rejected the discourse of left-nationalism entirely except insofar as it was oriented to political opposition to the policies of the U.S. government. One characteristic text argued, "Canada is not moving towards colonial status in the American empire; it is moving towards a greater imperial role in the world imperialist system."[54] If critics could depart from the "nationalist" side of the analysis on one hand, they could just as well depart from the "left" side as well. Non-left nationalists such as Mel Hurtig accepted the argument against American ownership and dependency, but posed the question in this way: "Who should be in charge of society – the community or big corporations?"[55] There is a populist note in this appeal to be sure, though its undifferentiated concept of the community leaves a lot unsaid. A considerable overlap with left-nationalism is possible depending on one's interpretation of this point.

The core of left-nationalism was therefore the argument that the capitalist class had no (further) interest in nationalism and that a certain version of popular nationalism could become the political vehicle of the subaltern classes. Radiating from this core were the axes of the discourse. With this definition of the discourse of left-nationalism it is possible to clarify its practical effect on Canadian society. Simply put, the account of economic dependency was thoroughly documented, but did not have significant impact on Canadian society or policy. The Foreign Investment Review Board, possibly the only real institutional consequence to which one could point, was set up by the Liberal Party under nationalist pressure in the 1970s and never had any teeth to repatriate the economy. Rather, it presided over the continued takeover and reorganization of the national economy by international forces. On the other hand, the argument for cultural autonomy had some effect. Perhaps this severing of the left-nationalist discourse was the basis for the later pervasive polarization in English Canadian intellectual life between political economy and cultural approaches to social and political thought. This separation and opposition is by no means necessary, but it becomes unavoidable when political economy is interpreted reductionistically and culture is defined in opposition to economy.[56] The remnants of the left-nationalist synthesis and its social effects are deeper and more widespread in English Canadian intellectual life than is normally appreciated, especially in a time when all of this might appear to be merely ancient history.[57] I will briefly explore two examples of the limited success of the argument for cultural autonomy.

The first example I want to consider is the foundation and growth of the Association for Canadian Studies, mainly within tertiary education (universities and community colleges) but also with some impact on earlier and adult education, public libraries, and publications such as magazines. In 1969 Robin Mathews and James Steele published *The Struggle for Canadian Universities*, a report that documented the high numbers of American professors teaching in Canadian universities and the consequent lack of attention given to Canadian issues and themes. The report was careful to clarify that "there should be a large number of foreign scholars in Canadian universities at all times," and it focused attention on the fact that the overwhelming majority of foreign scholars were from the United States and on the difficulties encountered by qualified Canadians in finding positions.[58] Despite this important clarification, this document and its surrounding circumstances created controversy throughout higher education in Canada, a controversy that went beyond the persons involved (or not having the chance to be involved) in teaching to the content of what was taught. In particular, attention was directed to the minimal Canadian content and preponderance of American world-views, ideologies, and histories, especially in the social sciences and humanities. One result of the controversy was the incorporation of an analysis of the universities into a rapidly developing left-nationalist analysis of Canadian society. As Ian Lumsden, the editor of the influential 1970 volume *Close the 49th Parallel: The Americanization of Canada*, put it, "The reversal of the Americanization of Canada can come about only through the substitution of a new world-view among its people in place of their addiction to the 'American way of life' and their adherence to the values perpetuated by the North American bourgeoisie. These values are diffused through a wide variety of cultural, educational, and social institutions."[59] The ignorance of Canada fostered by Canadian educational institutions was diagnosed as part of a process of cultural domination that accompanied and legitimated Canadian economic dependency on American capitalism and imperialism. While this analysis was hotly debated, defined, and extended within left-nationalist circles, it came to have an influence on the many university people who would not have defined themselves as left-nationalists and on many in the society at large.

In 1972 the Commission on Canadian Studies was formed by the Association of Universities and Colleges of Canada. It produced a report entitled *To Know Ourselves*, which is widely recognized as the intellectual legitimation for the Association for Canadian Studies and for Canadian Studies in educational institutions generally. The Symons Report, as it is generally known, in its chapter on "The Rationale for Canadian Studies," carefully separated the concern for Canadian Studies from nationalism, national unity, and other issues of sovereignty, but it argued that our differences from the United States are important and must be studied in order for us to come to grips with our own problems. The root issue was defined in the following way: "it is impossible to attempt to deal with problems unless our attempts are built on the strongest foundation of self-knowledge; as Northrop Frye has suggested, a citizen's primary duty is 'to try to know what should be changed in his society and what should be preserved' – a responsibility that we cannot begin to discharge until, as citizens, we *know* our country."[60] This was a weaker form of the left-nationalist rationale, purged of references to imperialism and nationalism and legitimated with reference to English Canada's most internationally known scholar, which could be accepted by a much wider public. The Association for Canadian Studies was formed in 1973 and has had a continuing influence on the agenda of Canadian universities, though it has never displaced the traditional academic disciplines or disciplinary-based scholarly organizations from their dominant position. A recent (1996) report on the current state of Canadian Studies, known as the Cameron Report, points out that the relation between Canadian Studies and what it calls the "national unity rationale" is loose: "To teach about Canada's historical experience and its social and economic life is not necessarily to reinforce identification with Canada."[61] The practice and rationale for Canadian studies seems to have watered down considerably its original legitimation to the point where it appears divorced from any political project at all. This increasing divergence from the left-nationalist discourse that presided over its institution is the basis for what Rowland Lorimer has called the bland character of these reports and the "narrow line of development" that Canadian Studies has taken.[62] In the end, it has tended to accomodate itself increasingly to the dictates of established university structure rather than engage in the reconstruction of a national-popular collective will.

My second example is the rich cultural-policy discourse that emerged in Canada with the Massey Commission in the 1950s and continued until the exemption of cultural industries from the Free Trade Agreement (article 2005). The condition for this limited success of left-nationalism was a *separation of culture from political economy* that was not only not a part of its own internal discourse, but was explicitly denied by left-nationalism itself. The cultural-policy discourse that has emerged in Canada is tied to the intervention in culture by the Canadian federal state. It can be called a "discourse" in the same sense as left-nationalism, though it is of a more limited scope. Its justification is the argument that cultural industries are special insofar as they are concerned with the formation of the identities of Canadians and therefore that they need to be regulated in a manner distinct from other industries. The success of this argument has created a federal cultural-policy discourse with institutional, economic, and regulatory dimensions. The separation of culture from political economy should be more accurately formulated as a separation of cultural industries from the political economy as a whole through an argument concerning their specialness based upon the issue of Canadian identity. In other words, political economy is discussed, but only the political economy of cultural industries. This special status is conferred upon these industries by the extraction of the argument for cultural autonomy from the discourse of left-nationalism.

The cultural-policy discourse is structured through three axes[63] that create a "slide" between the terms such that they become, for all practical purposes, equivalent within the discourse. In other words, each term elicits all the connotations and effects of the others, to which it becomes pragmatically equivalent by the structuring of the discourse. The cultural-policy discourse compresses three cultural oppositions, each of which becomes an axis for the discourse: Canada versus the United States, high versus low culture, public versus private ownership. These terms are structured so that the first of each of the pairs becomes practically equivalent to the others, as does the second of each of the pairs. Thus it is suggested that the United States produces low, or popular, culture through private ownership of the media. This is the polemical object that the discourse constructs. Paul Litt has documented the equation of American influence with mass commercial culture in the Massey Report and connected it to the influence of Canada's cultural elite in government circles. It was entirely overlooked that mass culture critique was also largely imported from the U.S. and that American high culture was not regarded as a baleful influence.[64] Thus an equivalence is constructed between Canada, high culture, and government intervention that justifies government regulation of cultural industries in Canada and makes it difficult, though not exactly impossible, to argue against.

This slide between terms affected even the most perspicacious critics. Harold Innis, in his commentary on the Massey Report, concluded by claiming, "We can only survive by taking persistent action at strategic points against American imperialism in all its attractive guises. By attempting constructive efforts to explore the cultural possibilities of various media of communication and to develop them along lines free from commercialism, Canadians might make a contribution to the cultural life of the United States by releasing it from dependence on the sale of tobacco and other commodities."[65] Notice the equation of commercialism with the United States and the slide towards the worst "low" example of tobacco sales, whereas Canada is equated with the enlightening *possibility*, not its low actuality, of constructive efforts free of commercialism. Any argument against this policy of federal government regulation preferred by the discourse will tend to be conflated towards the polemical object. Margaret Prang concluded her study of the origin of public broadcasting in this way, "As in earlier Canadian enterprises there was no commitment to public ownership in principle, but once convinced that the choice was between 'the State or the United States,' most Canadians of the thirties had a ready answer."[66] This attitude accounts for the success of the cultural-policy discourse in Canadian public life until recent times. It seemed essential to protecting (not developing or changing) Canadian identity and thus required no action oriented to redressing the issue of economic dependency, either of Canada on the U.S. or between unequal economic groups within the country. In this way the left-nationalist argument for cultural autonomy become the federal cultural-policy discourse.

This discourse incorporates a three-way *reductionism* from a comprehensive anthropological concept of culture as a "way of life" (Wittgenstein) with "a characteristic style" (Husserl) that incorporates a "structure of feeling" (Williams) utilized in left-nationalist discourse to a more limited domain. Each of these reductions produces a significant *silence* within cultural-policy discourse because of the systematic non-investigation of relevant aspects of Canadian culture to which they lead. First, the concept of culture utilized in the cultural-policy discourse is reduced to industrially produced culture. Thus the significance of the marginalization of autonomous *cultural production in everyday life* by commercially organized processes is left uninvestigated. Second, the concept of *public intervention* in culture is reduced to government regulation, specifically by the federal government. The conflation of widespread public discussion and debate with government regulation leaves uninvestigated the conditions for a well-functioning and democratically organized public sphere. Third, it cannot help but promote a notion of Canadian culture as uniform because of its emphasis on industrial production and federal government regulation.

These three silences can be seen in a significant document from the cultural-policy discourse, *Vital Links: Canadian Cultural Industries*. Of the nine chapters, eight focus on various cultural industries. The rationale is given in the introductory chapter, called "Culture in Canadian Society." It begins by pointing to the "counterpoint" between communication technologies and the desire of a people to "nurture and sustain their historical distinctiveness."[67] Culture is defined first anthropologically as "knowledge, beliefs, art, morals, laws, customs, and all other capabilities and habits acquired by the members of a particular society." Two sentences later it shrinks to "artistic products," and the next paragraph states that "the vigor of a culture [is] determined by the liveliness of the exchange of ideas [etc.]" and that "the principal instruments for the exchange are the cultural industries." Having moved from the most general concept of culture to the cultural industries within four short paragraphs, the document never again returns to the larger concept of culture with which it began. Clearly, any larger discussion of culture is merely a backdrop for, and legitimation of, discussion of government policy towards cultural industries. My point is not that such policy is unnecessary or useless. Rather, it is that the policy discourse is organized through a narrowing and forgetting of the larger concerns that generated the discourse in the first place. This reductionism occurs through the severing of cultural-policy discourse from the argument for cultural autonomy that was part of the left-nationalist discourse as a whole and thus integrated with a political economy of dependency.

These two examples are intended to illustrate the limited success that the left-nationalist discourse has had as the self-expression of English Canada in the period of permeable Fordism. They are, of course, not the only possible ones. Nor is this a comprehensive evaluation of the effect of left-nationalism as a whole. However, they do show the extent to which the project of cultural autonomy has had a certain efficacy as a result of the institutionalization of the project of self-knowledge of national identity. Moreover, they indicate the price of this success – the precise character of its limitation. The project of self-knowledge has been cut off from any national vision addressing issues of economic dependency by being narrowed to a conception of culture as dealing solely with the federal regulation of scholarly, artistic, or media expressions separately from their relation to the popular practices and feelings that constitute the national-popular collective will.[68] As a consequence, the discourse of cultural autonomy has become severed from the analysis of dependency in left-nationalism. It is this focus on dependency that could be the bridge between the legacy of left-nationalism and the other critiques of domination proposed by contemporary social movements. To date, this bridge remains unconstructed. The point thus far is only that its construction is not impossible, but has only come to appear so because of the precise character of the limited impact of left-nationalism on English Canadian society.

A PLURALITY OF DEPENDENCIES

The discourse of left-nationalism was tied to a historical period whose demise can be indicated, though not fully explained, by reference to the new era of continental integration inaugurated by the FTA and NAFTA. There have always been movements for economic and sometimes political union with the United States within Canada, but this time they have come at a moment and achieved a success that has changed the context in which one can speak of English Canadian identity or nationhood. I will sketch the reasons that I believe we should now regard the historical moment of left-nationalism as past. As with Grant's lament, this judgment is made without any enthusiasm on my own part. The reason for my discussion of left-nationalism above is that I do not think that one can proceed forward by entirely rejecting the past. My reading of Innis and Grant is motivated by, informed by, and in dialogue with the left-nationalist discourse. However, it attempts to go forward in another direction that might give a content to English Canadian identity which goes beyond left-nationalist concerns. The attempt to negotiate continuity and discontinuity is characteristic of immanent criticism.

Left-nationalism was a discourse that attempted to reform the national-popular collective will in Canada. It linked together nation and class as an oppositional force in an era in which multinational, or transnational, corporations had become the leading economic force. Transnational corporations, it was argued, were really mainly American corporations extending beyond their borders into a multinational context to dominate the political economy of Canada. This contemporary situation was given historical explanation through an Innisian analysis of the colonial dependency of a staple-producing economy. The staple trap documented by Innis was such an essential part of Canadian history that it had an influence, or perhaps was independently discovered, even among analysts who would be more likely to insist on class factors over national concerns. The Communist Party, under the leadership of Tim Buck, similarly focused on the failure of indigeneous industrialization in Canada as a result of the dependent, resource-extracting character of the capitalist class. Buck referred to "a definite policy on the part of monopoly-capital in Canada and the governments serving its aims ... They are selling our country, as she stands, to the United States; not the whole country, but its resources of industrial raw materials which are absolutely indispensable for the development of large-scale modern manufacturing industries. They are alienating ownership of the sources of those priceless raw materials. And, what is even more criminal, they are alienating them deliberately on terms that block a development of large-scale Canadian industry based on them."[69]

Class analysis of Canadian society required an explanation of the *historic weakness* of the capitalist class, and this was provided by colonial dependence based on staple extraction and failed industrialization. This explanation, however, obscured the new forces that were at work in the global economy, which have since come to fruition in the phenomenon known as globalization. In the interim a significant portion of the Canadian capitalist class initiated, through the

Conservative Party, the process of formal economic integration of a free trade zone in North America through a bilateral agreement with the United States, which has since expanded to include Mexico and will soon expand further to encompass South American countries and potentially all of the Americas. In this context the core argument of left-nationalism that transnational corporations are really American ones has been undermined by several factors: the willingness of "American" transnationals to abandon the United States if it suits their interests, the growth of "Canadian" transnationals that operate outside of Canada, and the decreasing percentage of foreign ownership of the Canadian economy. In other words, globalization refers to a genuinely transnational economic environment dominated by large corporations that are increasingly gaining leverage over nation-states and whose influence cannot therefore be theorized as the influence of one nation-state over another.

Perhaps the simplest way to indicate this change is to compare two assessments by Melville Watkins, a major left-nationalist theorist of economic dependency. The first is from 1969, when he claimed that the "multi-national corporation is simply the extension of the corporation into other countries. Most of the multi-national corporations are, in fact, American-based with Americans as shareholders and top managers, so their foreign activities can be regarded as global extensions of American corporate capitalism."[70] In an edited collection published in 1989, Watkins referred to "the considerable decrease in foreign (meaning mostly American) ownership of the Canadian economy since 1970 and the offsetting emergence of new centres of indigenous corporate power – an occurrence for which the political economy literature on foreign ownership, from myself and Levitt to Naylor and Clement, hardly prepared us. The Canadian capitalist class is now – and perhaps long has been? – more impressive than some of us thought."[71] This reassessment has been echoed by others formerly in the left-nationalist camp. Philip Resnick has argued that "there has been a qualitative change in Canada's position over the past two decades and that, economically at least, Canada has now reached a stage where it must be seen as one of the seven leading capitalist powers in the world."[72] Gary Teeple has stated that "it is perhaps not possible to say when the global economy became a reality as distinct from interrelated national economies, that is, when the 'capitalist world economy' became the 'world capitalist economy,' but certainly by the mid-1970's the end of the interregnum could be seen."[73] The current economic environment consists of the construction of large-scale, perhaps hemispheric, free trade zones dominated by transnational corporations without a national home.

Does this development mean that there has been an end to dependency? Dependency theory was oriented to the dependency of nations and was concerned with the use of the dependent nation-state in the interests of a foreign capitalist class operating through its own nation-state. It was concerned to construct a counter-hegemonic national-popular collective will to use the nation-state to steer domestic industry for the benefit of all citizens. This formulation has been surpassed by the globalization of the economy, in which dependency between nation-states does not play a central role in the analysis. But this does not mean that all forms of dependency have been eliminated, that the Canadian economy is independent of the American one, nor does it reduce the commercial dependency on American markets or cultural domination by U.S. media industries.[74] Further, it does not mean that the Canadian economy as a whole has escaped the staple trap. British Columbia is still exporting raw lumber and importing furniture and other finished wood products. This historic pattern remains pervasive throughout the Canadian economy. Globalization does mean, however, that it is impossible to describe adequately the dynamics of domination in the global economy mainly through the category of the nation-state – or, more exactly, through the nation-state as the main social actor in the interests of nationally based, but internationally operating capital – as does dependency theory. As Resnick has argued, "It was only when American imperialism began to weaken internationally in the 1960's that English Canadian sentiment began to shift, and that anti-imperialism, or simply anti-Americanism, became a potent force."[75] In this sense, left-nationalism can be seen as a transitory phenomenon between the years of full-fledged American hegemony and globalization.

Left-nationalism was the critical counter-current of the era of permeable Fordism oriented to the nation-state as the major social actor, which occurred between the Second World War and the free trade agreements. In this period, an analysis that focused on class required a supplement to explain the weakness of the indigenous capitalist class.[76] This supplement added a different component – national dependency – to the class analysis that was nevertheless different in quality. Alternatively, if one began from the national question – why has Canada not achieved an independent status like other nations? – one was similarly drawn to the key link – the historic weakness of the Canadian capitalist class – that required that the analysis of national dependence be supplemented by a class analysis. In a mirror fashion, the analyses of class and nation were mutually reinforcing. Each on its own was insufficient and required a supplement from the other. This double supplement explains the compelling nature of the left-nationalist criticism in this period. It also explains what is lacking now. The "core of left-nationalism," as it was defined in the previous section, is now lacking. The failure of the capitalist class to perform its nation-building function in Canada now appears, not as a comparative lack that needs explanation, but as characteristic of capitalist classes in general, which – to recover a much earlier formulation – seem to have no national allegiances at all. It is important to emphasize that to claim that the historic moment of left-nationalism has passed is not to argue that the issues to which it pointed have been resolved, only that the linkage which wedded nation to class in a condition of mutual supplementarity no longer obtains.

Dependency theory was mainly concerned to argue against the notion that underdevelopment was original or traditional. André Gunder Frank, probably the best-known dependency theorist internationally, claimed that the peripheral underdeveloped regions were entirely penetrated by the world capitalist system and that it is not feudal survivals that constitute underdevelopment but the dominance in the satellite of a commercial (not industrial) capitalist class linked to the powerful metropolis of the world capitalist system. The system of dependency was thus thorough, multi-levelled, and pervasive. Referring to Latin America, he stated that "just as the colonial and national capital and its export sector become the satellite of the Iberian (and later of other) metropoles of the world economic system, this satellite immediately becomes a colonial and then a national metropolis with respect to the productive sectors and population of the interior."[77] The strength of this analysis is to show, not that contemporary forms of dependency are survivals to be overcome by progress along the prevailing line of development, but that underdevelopment is produced in the contemporary situation by the subordination of local, regional, or national development to the requirements of the world economic system.

However, while it recognizes that the forms of dependency vary from one locale to another, there is nevertheless no place in the analysis to theorize this plurality of forms of dependency. In a critique of Frank, Ernesto Laclau has argued that the concept of the world economic system must be distinguished from that of the "mode of production" in order to understand how different modes of production and dependency in local, regional, and national contexts can be linked to the same world economic system. In other words, with its contemporary focus on the system as a whole, dependency theory fails to capture the specificity of local modes that are subordinated to this system but nevertheless survive. Laclau suggests that Frank (and also Wallerstein) distort "the relative autonomy of mercantile forms from the modes of production which sustain them" and that "the nature of the relationship between metropolis and satellite – to use Frank's terminology – is no less one of dependence, but it operates in each case as a very distinct type of dependence. It seems to me more useful to underline these differences and discontinuities than to attempt to show the continuity and identity of the process, from Hernan Cortes to General Motors."[78] Laclau underlines these differences in the mode of production and dependence by introducing the concept of "articulation" to describe the *linkages between* local, regional, and national sites and their inclusion into the world economic system. Thus, according to him, it is not necessary to deny the differences between sites of dependency in order to assert, following Frank, that they are included in, and reproduced by, the contemporary system.

This argument is important in the English Canadian context for several reasons. First, it clarifies that the end of left-nationalism (as a dependency critique of Canadian society) does not mean the end of dependency as such. Rather, it implies a recognition of the *multiple forms of dependency* that exist in contemporary society and requires that each be analysed in terms of the *specific linkage* that ties it to the system as a whole. Second, it answers a nagging question that Marxist critics often put to Innisian dependency theory, that it implied that Canada is essentially a Third World country with problems of dependency equivalent to those of Latin America, for example.[79] Third, it directs attention to the plurality of new social movements that have arisen to criticize the multiple forms of dependency in a contemporary context. It resists the tendency to want to reduce the plurality of such movements (and their diverse critiques of contemporary society) to an underlying unity that is common both to left-nationalism and Marxism, whether the underlying unity be thought of as that of a dependent nation or as a central, and universal, class. Thus the issue of dependency is not dead, even though the moment of left-nationalism has passed. Dependency has become more diffuse and plural. It is no longer linked only to the nation-state but also to the various new definitions of dependency that are being invented by social movements. The analysis of dependency throughout society must become more extensive, not less. The end of left-nationalism with the end of the era of permeable Fordism means that social identities have become loosened from their arrangement under national identity. The nation does not seem to be able to play the key role assigned to it by dependency theory any longer.

But what if we pose the question from the other way around? Is it possible to imagine any collective will for change in Canada that does not take on a national-popular colouring? In the era of globalization, various social movements have appeared that are attempting to transform different aspects of the society – feminism, the ecology movement, gay rights, community groups, and so forth. They often encounter the power of capital and have to design strategies to limit or divert this power. At this juncture the various institutions of government may provide some means of leverage, means that are rooted in the democratic and social justice traditions of the country through the nation-state as an instrument of social protection – the national identity. It seems that in this context the nation-state is, at least potentially, a hedge against the unrestricted power of transnationals. There is no doubt that this hedge is increasingly difficult to utilize because of the power of transnationals to use the threat of moving abroad to attain concessions. But does this fact justify abandoning the nation as a site for political struggle? While the construction of an alternative national-popular collective will is not limited to the institutions of the nation-state, it does need to address and encompass them. The forms of belonging developed within the nation still have some purchase on the popular passions.

There has been an unfortunate polarization between left-nationalism and analyses rooted in new social movements (often under the heading of postmodernism) in recent years.[80] This book avoids that polarization. It begins from analyses of the work of Innis and Grant in order to maintain a continuity with the left-nationalist discourse. It attempts to define the limitations of these thinkers in a more precise manner, going beyond their utilization by left-nationalism. Through these critiques it defines several new thematic areas and attempts initial theorizations of them. This is the procedure of immanent critique. It begins by accepting the thinkers in question and their definitions of the issues, and proceeds later to critique and extension. A continuity is thus maintained throughout the critical process, and one is forearmed against mere dismissal. Its presupposition is that simply discarding the past will not provide a sufficient foundation for the future, that despite criticism there can be continuity and community. Immanent criticism is the method whereby emergent theory can retain a tie to its history and aim at a relevance to a new formation of the national-popular collective will.

My aim in this chapter was to provide a contextualizing introduction to the formulation of an English Canadian social and political philosophy that follows and to situate it within the evolving project of Canadian Studies, left-nationalism, and social movements. Both Innis and

Grant attempt to theorize what is particular to English Canadian history and identity. After discussing their contributions in the next two chapters, in chapter 5 I address directly the question of English Canadian identity. All concern with English Canadian identity, formulated abstractly, is engaged in maintaining a *border* between us and the United States. I thus take the border as the leading metaphor for this work and suggest that it can also be seen as a border between self and other and between humanity and nature. The argument suggests that the direction of English Canadian social and political philosophy is oriented towards sustaining a border between self and other, in order that what is one's own may be preserved and that the Other may be maintained and respected.[81] The philosophical basis of the book is thus the relationship between the defence of one's own through the concept of particularity that I derive from George Grant and the abjection of the Other that I have encountered though the new social movements, especially the multicultural project of recognizing a plurality of cultural traditions within a single polity and the ecology movement's rethinking of the relation between humanity and nature. There is a remarkable similarity between the "multi" of multiculturalism and the necessity of diversity to ecological stability that orients contemporary philosophy away from unity and towards diversity or plurality.

This ethical formulation is then extended to address directly the issues of multiculturalism and environmentalism in chapters 6 and 7, where I attempt to follow out the implications of this new acceptance of diversity for social and political philosophy. The core of the argument is that respect for the Other can only be established through an ethical practice that maintains a border which refuses to cannibalize the other by the self. I take this to be both a limitation and a completion of the focus on self that is characteristic of English Canadian social and political thought. It is an ethics that tries to think through our historical opposition to "manifest destiny" – a suspicion of homogenizing universality that defends the particularity of one's own and also, I suggest, urges an acceptance of, even desire for, the self's limitation by the Other. This extension of the work of English Canadian social philosophy is incomplete. It does not address all the relevant issues, nor does it push the two I do address through to final philosophical positions – which would revolve around a new formulation of particularity, Otherness, and a human universality that is articulated *through* and not *against* plurality.[82] I claim only to advance the task somewhat and hope to have said something useful. In any case, it is not merely my own invention, but an emergent theory that has been crafted from my meditations on what it means to belong here and those who have most helped to define that condition.

CHAPTER THREE

Harold Innis's Dependency Critique of European Civilization

Post-colonial societies may be divided into two types: those with a long recorded history and civilization prior to their reduction to a colonial status and those that were perceived by Europeans as savage because primarily of the "undeveloped" state of their technology and the lack of a state organization. Within the British empire, India and China fall into the first category and the colonies in Africa, America, and Australia the second. "Uncivilized" societies were perceived as original and unspoiled as well as undeveloped and savage on the model of the archetypical European myth of the Garden of Eden and original sin. The apparently rival accents of the noble savage and the unredeemed natural man derive from this same source. It may still be necessary to emphasize that the perception of this difference was lodged more in European cultural history than in the characteristics of the colonized societies that were selected as emblematic. However, its consequences were extremely significant for the subsequent development of colonialism. This fact is perhaps clearest in the extent of immigration. While previously "civilized" societies were colonized, reorganized, and exploited through a British military-administrative class aligned with an indigenous elite, "savage" societies were subjected to genocide, slavery, and/or removal and confinement. Their populations have been largely displaced by European immigration, which itself cannot be discussed apart from the class and ethnic/national exploitation that motivated it.

In the present post-colonial context, distinct issues arise as a consequence of this difference, which is deeply rooted in the European conception of civilization. In India, for example, it becomes important to place the British episode and its influence on later post-colonial history in the context of a much longer history.[1] With respect to "New World" societies, the post-colonial enterprise takes two different shapes. The first is the struggle of aboriginal peoples for independence and/or influence and the assertion of a traditional heritage that can address contemporary social problems caused by European society and the technological domination of nature. This issue immediately raises fundamental questions about the origin and status of what Europeans have called "civilization." Second, there is the question of the history and fate of the ex-European people who have found themselves on the margins of European power and who are faced with a choice of identifying with it or questioning its foundations on the basis of their historical experience in the New World. In this case, the issues of their identity, their relation to nature and technology, and their relation to aboriginal peoples are enfolded in questioning the concept of "civilization." For a thinking situated at this juncture, it is fundamental to bring to articulation the experiences rooted in the social histories of colonial societies. For if we are anything other than Europeans manqué, a pale reflection of the real stuff, it is to be found in the history of our relations to the environment, to the aboriginal people, and to European colonial power. Of course, this relationship will begin to take different forms and to pluralize the location of the post-colonial, ex-European critic, but it is remarkable, for example, how the question of "identity" is key to discussions in Canada, Latin America, and Australia.[2]

A danger arises at this point that reflection will take the form of a mere "experiential catalogue." Northrop Frye used this term to suggest that Canadian literature tended simply to list experiences as if doing so were adequate to constitute a cultural tradition. He suggested, by contrast, that it is only when experiential contents are formed into a universal mythic pattern that a contribution of more than local interest is attained.[3] The problem, of course, is that such supposedly universal myths – for Frye it is the biblical story – are by no means self-evidently universal, but are themselves rooted in a particular cultural history. The articulation of the identity of English Canadians requires not only experiential content that is new, but that the form of structuring itself be crafted from their cultural history. To this extent Frye is right: unless the new cultural experience transcends a catalogue and becomes a structuring form, we have simply the extension and deeper imperialism of European culture – new grist for the old mill. The necessity to express the experience of Canada "free from all preconceived ideas" was also confronted by Lawren Harris and the Group of Seven. As Harris phrased it, the artists "came together drawn by an irresistible urge to replace this 'foreign-begotten technique,' by a way of painting dictated by Canada itself, to concentrate all their energy on making a Canadian statement in art in Canadian terms."[4]

One might express this relationship in various ways: as the difference between an experiential catalogue and a mythic form (Frye), as the difference between painting Canadian scenes and a "way of painting in Canadian terms" (Harris), or perhaps more prosaically stated, as the difference between content and form. It is fairly easy for a new cultural identity to fix upon the contents of experience that distinguish it from other identities. It is much more difficult for the form of expression itself to be crafted from these same materials. The materials, or experiential contents, must be taken beyond themselves to become the form or structure of experience. This level of form – a manner of expression and not only a content expressed – is not really separate from content, but is rather a raising, or lifting, of experience from its particular towards its universal dimensions. It is the work of art and philosophy to accomplish this lifting. Without it, one simply recycles the mythic and structuring forms crafted from previous identities. Thus art and philosophy rooted in the post-colonial experience face a demand to express creatively their experience in terms that lift that which is expressed beyond its occasional features towards its mythic and universal dimensions. One must craft not only new content but new form. From this demand for an interplay between the experiences rooted in social history and the forms of thought issues the possibility of post-colonial culture by ex-Europeans in English Canada. Without this kind of reflexivity, we fall back to European models at a later date. Our experiences are neither simply contingent nor immediately universal, but concern the possibility of a universalizing articulation from a particular location. Experience must be articulated into theoretical models through metaphor.

Metaphors drawn from social life have allowed a reflexive conception of the formation and role of theory throughout the history of philosophy and the human sciences. Consider the (usually) conservative model of society as an organism, for example, or the liberal theory of society as an aggregate of atoms. Marxism has articulated its conception of theory mainly on the architectural metaphor of base and superstructure, though it has also at times used labour itself as a model in order to clarify the tasks and claims of theory. The basic metaphor in Harold Innis's communication theory of society is transportation, the traversal of space. It is interesting to note that the concept of metaphor is itself a metaphor, elaborated through the notion of "carrying-over," which is the meaning of the Greek word. Metaphor carries over a meaning from one domain to another or, as we often say now, from one level to another. Thus theoretical discourse is itself necessarily elaborated through metaphorical use of experiential materials. Innis's communication theory rediscovers, in his own sense, the root from which the idea of metaphor began in trans-portation. It involves the reflexive doubling inherent in the imbrication of a historical theory and a contemporary diagnostic-therapeutic intention.

The demand for an interplay between experience and forms of thought opens a space where one can discuss Canadian thought and put it into dialogue with a more general post-colonial discourse. Here I am concerned with the contribution of Harold Innis to marking such a space. It suggests that his humanism both makes possible and forecloses a post-colonial social and cultural theory. In the tradition of Innis, communication theory is concerned with the formation of the senses in the perception of the world, the constitution of social relations in institutions, and the labour of conceptualization that orients thought. Communication media are thus thoroughly constitutive of the three dimensions of perception, institutions, and thought, not merely representations of a previously existing world. In this sense, communication theory requires both a historical theory of civilization and a therapeutic diagnosis of its present state. The following critique of Innis intends to push this requirement further to reveal the presuppositions of this notion of civilization itself.

FROM DEPENDENCY ECONOMICS
TO COMMUNICATION THEORY

Harold Innis was initially a political economist who documented the economic dependency of Canada through its reliance on the extraction and export of staple resources. His approach was in the tradition of institutional economics, which has a historical emphasis rather than focusing on synchronic mathematical modelling like conventional economics. The staple theory of economic dependency is an attempt to explain the distinctiveness of Canadian economic development from European development, on one hand, and that of the United States, on the other. Marx's work, for example, primarily sought to explain the transformation from feudalism to capitalism in Europe – from a system based on personal dependence in which the economy is subordinated to political relations of dominance to a capitalist system in which there is private property in both land and labour, as well as all other commodities. Land and labour are the two major exceptions to things that can be exchanged in pre-capitalist economies. While there is money in a feudal system, the capacity of land and labour to produce a surplus are not capitalized. Marx was primarily concerned to explain the development of capitalism as an internal dynamic emerging from feudalism. In the United States, by way of contrast, early economic relations were largely those of independent producers creating a commodity that they sold on the market. This process coexisted with colonial feudal-type relations of dominance and slavery in the South until the dominance of the comodity producers was established in the Civil War. There were of course large differences of scale between the export-oriented "merchants of Boston" and small farmers; nevertheless the widespread predominance of immediate producers who were directly tied to production for exchange goes a long way towards explaining the attenuation of the class struggle in U.S. politics, an issue that was posed in the classic book published by Werner Sombart in 1905 called *Why Is There No Socialism in the United States?* Independent commodity producers provided the basis for relatively widespread democracy and for a certain independence of opinion that was expressed in populism, though the later concentration of capital and consequent crowding out of competition has rendered this democratic component progressively weaker over time. As Marx remarked, the great fact about the United States is that its capitalist development is not based on a prior feudal heritage.

In Canada, up until the time of the development of the staple theory by Harold Innis and others (and, unfortunately, even more recently), there was a tendency to assimilate Canadian economic history to either the European or, perhaps more relevantly, the U.S. model of development because clearly Canada is like the United States in being a New World society without a feudal stage (though the settlement of Quebec might well be considered an exception to that generalization). The basic fact that the staple theory explains is the development of a colony as the exploitation of a successive set of staple resources for export – furs, trees, fish, wheat, and so forth. The central relationship involved is between an imperial centre and a colony at the periphery or margin. This spatial separation implies significant transportation costs both in the export of raw materials going to Britain from Canada and in the import of manufactured goods, and these costs must be reckoned into the prices of the goods when they reach the market. The significance of transportation extends even into the unity of the nation and its relation to the empire since transportation was developed by "public" expenditures and remains under political control because of the impossibility of capitalizing such huge enterprises privately. Moreover, it explains the cultural continuity between the colony and the imperial centre. Import of finished manufactured goods is based upon the demand formed by the export of the way of life at the centre and is reinforced by continued emigration. The process marginalizes the influence of the pre-existing aboriginal cultures on the colony and promotes the continued identification of the settlers with the empire. The staple theory of economic dependency thus theorizes the specific development of a colonial political economy – Canada has been, successively, a colony of France, Britain, and the United States – that is sustained in a pervasive structural tension between the modern industrial character of the imperial centre and the almost unhistorical, primal encounter with wilderness at the periphery.

It was against the background of this dependency theory that Innis later developed his communication theory. When the Second World War broke out, he started giving public lectures and addresses about what society owed to those who fought and also spoke in the same breath about the collapse of civilization as something that had simply happened. Shortly after 1944 he wrote of the university as "an institution which has played the leading role in the flowering of western culture [,] remind[ing] us of the obligation of maintaining traditions concerned with the search for truth for which men have laid down and have been asked to lay down their lives."[5] Innis had fought in the First World War and was injured in France. After recovering in Britain, he came back to Canada to write his MA thesis at McMaster University on "The Returned Soldier." In short, he was a member of that generation of people who came to maturity in and immediately after the First World War, a generation to whom we owe a great deal for the development of critical social thought in the twentieth century. One might mention Wilfred Owen, Erich Maria Remarque, Edmund Husserl, members of the Frankfurt school, and many others in this regard – thinkers and writers for whom the question "What is civilization?" became an unavoidable issue. The First World War was the first time that Europeans, and European colonials, could no longer blame the conflict on benighted savages from other places. They had to face the fact that it was the civilized nations of Europe who had originated the mass destruction. It could no longer be viewed as a conflict between civilization and savagery, and so the question became for that generation: What is civilization, and what is the source of its current failure? When conflict began all over again in the Second World War, this element of Innis's historical formation resurfaced. His works explicitly focused on communication stem from the period after the war up to his early death in 1952. During that time he shifted his inquiry away from political economy and was concerned to undertake some sort of diagnosis of civilization under the aegis of communication.

Aside from the biographical dimension to this shift, there are also internal reasons within his political-economic studies. While some commentary has emphasized the sharp shift in focus from Canadian economics to world history and asserted, rather commonsensically, a break in Innis's work, the main burden of scholarship has been to argue for a deeper conceptual or thematic unity. It has been suggested, for example, by Donald Creighton, Melville Watkins, and Ian Parker that through his analysis of the pulp and paper staple industry, Innis was brought into the study of the newspaper industry.[6] It seems likely that his interest was at first simply in another staple study along the established lines of his previous work, a connection that is indicated by a number of transitional articles on the role of public opinion in economics. But there is a deeper point to be made with regard to his interest in the role of transportation and communication in economic theory. Innis said in his presidential address to the American Economics Association, "The effectiveness with which information can be made available regarding commodities to be exchanged, will depend on the development of media of communication. It would become evident in the emergence of highly organized exchanges."[7] Similarly, W.T. Easterbrook explained that transition "via his study of the effect of prices on the movement of goods ... it is natural for a student of prices to shift attention from the flow of goods to the flow of information."[8] From this point of view, the connection is not merely the investigation of another staple but of the deeper structural dependence of contemporary economic activity on communication and information. Moreover, it derives from Innis's "Smithian," neo-mercantilist stress on exchange rather than, for example, a Marxist focus on production. In any case, while the focus of his interest certainly broadened in the later studies, the continuity of Innis's theoretical development seems clear. In particular, it emphasizes the elements of the later work that focus on the political economy of communication. As David Crowley has pointed out, this is an interpretation that works to the advantage of the theoretical priority of political economy.[9] We may extend this observation to suggest that there is a matter of disciplinary monopoly of knowledge at issue here, which may well function to pull back the interdisciplinary innovation of Innis's later work into an established theoretical framework. The "discipline" of communication did not exist in Canada in his time, though it has now been institutionalized in several universities. Thus the temptation of disciplinary imperialism can now work either way: should it go to the advantage of communication studies, it is necessary to point out that very little work in the established field has anything like the historical breadth, theoretical innovation, and observational wealth of Innis's work on communication.

Thus, while continuity of development is certainly significant, it is still a very large step indeed from staple economics to the grand scope of the later studies of communication as a theory of civilization. An adequate explanation of the relationship between the two parts requires sufficient emphasis on what is new and ground-breaking as well as the location of its emergence within previous studies. Robin Neill has argued that the early studies convinced Innis of the role of values and public opinion in economic development and that the history of communications addressed the origin and institutionalization of these factors.[10] Since the role of values and opinion is not generally the focus of political economy, this argument provides an account of the discontinuity that could mushroom into the altered scope, style, and theme of the later work. Moreover, it has the advantage of linking the shift to Innis's prior involvement in debates concerning the role of values in the social sciences and converges with Crowley's claim that the communication theory should be seen as a corrective to the state of the social sciences in North America.[11]

Each of these interpretations, stressing continuity and accounting for discontinuity respectively, may lay claim to a partial truth. But it would be a mistake to overlook, as both do, the influence of the larger historical situation that was indicated above. The crisis of civilization inaugurated by the First World War resurfaced in the Second in such a manner as to provoke Innis into a diagnosis of its root causes. Certainly, this process involved an extension of theoretical tools developed in earlier work, and no less certainly did it take off from perceived inadequacies in the social sciences. Nevertheless, the turn in his work must be understood as a response to the world-historical crisis of European civilization as it has emerged in the twentieth century. Literally, the world shook and Innis was provoked to look into what had made that world. And the upshot was to see in Canada's crisis the crisis of European civilization – no mean task for a thinker marginal to Europe, though only possible for one implicated in its shaking. Innis's work shifted because he accepted the task, and the gamble, that his location at the margin as a post-colonial intellectual proposed in this crisis.

The key aspect of the distinctiveness of the staple theory is its focus on the role of transportation in a colonial economy. When the impact of the Second World War raised the issue of the earlier conflagration and the current prospects for civilized existence, this focus on transportation was both generalized and transformed into a communication theory of society and civilization. This intellectual situation, after all, hardly has the status of a biographical detail. As James Carey has asserted, until the introduction of the telegraph, communication was coextensive with transportation.[12] Innis's communication theory retains all the features of dependency economics, but generalizes the concept of transmission, or movement through space, into a fundamental constitutive component of the social order. Given the priority of history and time over geography and space throughout modern thought, this emphasis on space is a key component of his originality.[13]

Whereas the staple theory has a clear reference to Canada, the communication theory has no such immediate reference. Nevertheless, it is a theory worked out from the periphery, which argues that it is the undervalued, or unrecognized, media that sustain the balance required by a viable civilization. Media theory is thus a critique of institutions. Moreover, the biases of institutions tend to be invisible to social scientific analysis, since the social science disciplines are built upon, and generally justify, the prior institutional arrangements through incorporating their presuppositions into the basic theoretical propositions. For this reason, media theory is also a critique of the disciplinary organization of thought. The centre systematically misrecognizes the conditions of its own existence, failing to understand that it does not sustain itself except through its relations to the periphery, on which (in a reversal) it is "dependent." The communication theory of Harold Innis is thus a theory and diagnosis of civilization from its periphery – not an outright rejection, but a taking on board of the ideal of civilization in the moment that it becomes apparent that the centre has become the source of a new and intensified savagery. In the light of these themes, which bear considerable resemblance to contemporary post-structuralist and deconstructionist ones, it is important to notice that Innis's defence of time and oral tradition is not merely a re-establishment of key assumptions of European thought – today usually called phono- and logo-centrism. The paradox is this: even when a conventional European "metaphysical" assumption is rediscovered in a colonial context, the context of (re)discovery confers a different meaning – neither as an *assumption* nor as *autonomous*, since its constitution through the periphery has undermined its apparent self-evidence and supposed independence. To use the terms introduced at the beginning of this chapter, the mythic form loses its privilege to structure new experiences and itself becomes open to contestation by emergent forms. In this manner, the Eurocentrism of European culture becomes (at least potentially) simply European, though not merely "wrong," and clears a space for a cultural interchange beyond dominance by the cultural forms of "the West," for the way that a *centrism* works is to organize new experiential contents in its own form. To the extent that an emergent form is articulated, a centrism retreats to being simply another cultural form.

COMMUNICATION THEORY
OF CIVILIZATION

According to Harold Innis, the study of communication is concerned with the question "Why do we attend to the things to which we attend?" understood not only in a psychological, but also in an institutional, historical, and intellectual, sense.[14] Its contribution to critical social theory is thus through the analysis of different forms of attention and their relationship to power and social change. The main thesis of his communication theory is "that civilization has been dominated at different stages by various media of communication such as clay, papyrus, parchment, and paper produced first from rags and then from wood. Each medium has its significance for the type of monopoly of knowledge which will be built and which will destroy the conditions suited to creative thought and be displaced by a new medium with its peculiar type of monopoly of knowledge."[15] The thesis that forms of power are developed from media of communication and, by means of monopolies of knowledge, give rise to characteristic cultural forms of attention is the core that connects Innis's communication theory to his earlier studies of economic dependency. A dependency theory of communication centres on the diagnosis of institutional monopolies.

In *Empire and Communications* Innis introduces his focus on the materiality of media of communication by distinguishing centrifugal and centripetal social forces – forces tending to make a society more integrated over a given area versus those that tend to allow more independent peripheral areas. The concepts of time and space are used to describe the constitutive power of the media of communication in constructing and maintaining society. Initially, it is clear that media which emphasize time are durable, such as clay and especially stone. Media that emphasize space, on the other hand, are light and easy to move over large areas, in particular papyrus and paper. He thus connects the latter media with administration and trade because of their space orientation and the former with permanence and time. These characteristics are connected to aspects of institutions. "Materials that emphasize time favour decentralization and hierarchical types of institutions while those that emphasize space favour centralization and systems of government less hierarchical in character."[16] The centralization-decentralization axis refers to the manner and extent of coordination in space. To say that an organization is decentralized is to argue that there is not much (or only very loose or difficult) coordination between social activities over a given area, implying that there are more dispersed centres of power. Innis's claim is that when there are more dispersed centres of power, the tendency is for each of these to be more hierarchical. The axis of hierarchy, then, refers to the administrative chain of command. To say that an administrative organization is more hierarchical is to state that it is more or less continuous from bottom to top – that there are no equivalent, but dispersed powers. Time-oriented media promote means of social organization that are decentralized, involving more dispersed centres of power, but in each of these centres the administrative hierarchy is more direct from top to the bottom. By contrast, media that emphasize space favour centralization and less hierarchy. Centralization means coordination over a large area. Less hierarchy implies that in some of those administrative ladders, the relations of command overlap. There are equivalent ladders of power in different places, one of which does not necessarily subsume the rest. It is through these terms that Innis investigates what is for him the key subject matter of communication theory – the persistence of a society in the two dimensions of space and time, or the constitution of a historical-geographical social unity. Every society persists in both space and time, of course, but with different degrees of effectiveness depending on the complex of media through which it is articulated.

Let us explore in more detail the notion of medium utilized here. It is evident from Innis's historical discussions that he views pyramids and architecture in general as means of communication, in addition to language and writing. A "medium of communication" is understood in a very wide sense as any kind of a formative and integrating social mechanism. Media of communication, understood in this way, are described as having *intrinsic characteristics*. Most straightforwardly, if one writes on stone, it tends to last; if one writes on paper, it can be easily transported. These characteristics are not given to the medium by its environment, though they are certainly used in a specific way in a given environment. At first blush, it may appear as if the characteristics of media are primarily, or even exclusively, physical. But the distinction between heavy and light media as media oriented towards time or space, even though it is used by Innis, is drastically oversimplified.[17] A more thorough analysis of the structure and argument of *Empire and Communications* can clarify the relation between a medium and its object or content.

After the introductory chapter, the second chapter is on Egypt and the third on Babylonia. In both of these the main object that is at issue is water. But it is not the content "water" that is key to deciding the time or space bias in a medium of communication. In Egypt there was a necessity to predict the annual flooding of the Nile. This concern with time led to calendars and exact methods of reckoning time. In

Babylon the problem was irrigation. There was a lot of water, but it was not in the right place. Irrigation solved this problem of space. Thus the same content, water, in the case of Egypt led to a medium oriented towards an emphasis on time, whereas in Babylon it led towards a focus on space. While water was the content at issue in both cases, the "medium" was different. Thus it is not the object carried, but the manner of carrying; it is not the flooding, but the construction of a manner of overcoming the problem of flooding. The characteristics of a medium of communication cannot be defined through the material characteristics of the object with which it is concerned but only through the manner of dealing with that object. Thus the intrinsic characteristics of a medium may include its durability or portability, but they are not confined to these. The issue is more fundamentally about the *manner of organization* that is constructed. It is not only a material resource and a technology (oriented to dealing with a particular object), but also a social relation constructed coextensively with this technology. A medium of communication is thus both a technology and a social relation.

We should notice that in Innis's historical discussions the social influence of a medium of communication is always analysed in relation to the whole environment in which it operates. It is not an isolated thing but the central factor within a complex environment made up of many media of communication and the objects they carry or reckon with as contents. Its bias has to do with its influence on the whole of this environment. Thus the *intrinsic characteristics* of the medium, which is a certain organization of perception, institutions, and thought, lead in a *given environment* to effects of reorganization of that environment. It is this interplay between a medium's characteristics and the media environment that is the main domain of investigation for comparative media theory. However, the conceptual relation between these two aspects of the influence of a medium of communication is not addressed by Innis and does not emerge clearly from the historical discussions. Other writers concerned with the social influence of media of communication fall into two main camps with regards to this issue. The emphasis on the *media environment* is taken to its logical conclusion by Marshall McLuhan. He claims that there are no intrinsic characteristics to a medium of communication whatsoever, that the characteristics that it has in a given situation depend on its relation to the whole media environment and the given state of translations between media. Thus the "content" of a medium is a previous medium, and if we follow the chain of contents back to its origin, the content of orality is thought and the content of thought is the world.

This is a thoroughly rhetorical concept of the social influence of media insofar as the influence in question originates entirely from outside the medium and there is no intrinsic influence of the medium *as such* at all.[18] The opposite view is taken by Don Ihde in his phenomenological investigations of the intrinsic characteristics of each medium considered as an alteration, or "inclination," of human perception.[19] This view might be characterized as "essentialist" insofar as each medium is investigated as such in isolation from its context, but it is not determinist insofar as the inclination can be resisted even though a certain degree of consciousness is required to do so. Further development of Innis's work in this respect needs to address what might be called the inside-outside relation of a specific medium to the complex media environment. It is in this inside-outside tension that the relation of particular local embodiments to the cultural horizon as a whole would have to be determined.

This lack of clarity results in another fundamental unaddressed confusion in Innis's theory regarding the relation between a technology and a medium of communication. The confusion often leads to the interpretation, by both followers and detractors, that Innis is a technological determinist. I would like briefly to address this issue here because it does not pose a fundamental problem for comparative media theory, even though it does require a development beyond his work. The most common usage of the term suggests that a "medium" of communication should be understood as a technology that is *applied to* communication, that is to say, to the transfer and dissemination of information. Thus print, telegraph, television, and film would be technologies of communication and hence "media." One might also include writing and even speech, though the latter is usually excluded because technologies are generally understood as external mechanical contraptions that are distinct from the capacities of the human body. This common-sense perspective implies a distinction between technologies applied to communication and those employed for other things, such as making shoes, automobiles, or contact lenses. It is based on what is usually known as the transportation model of communication, which is distinguished by the presupposition that what characterizes communication is the movement of meaning across space – the *delivery* as opposed to the *formulation* of meaning. In this model, communication is a secondary process presupposing the prior existence of the origin, destination, and content of the message. The technology of communication is thus understood as the *channel* whereby a message, or sign, is transported in space – as the means of this secondary process of delivery. From this common perspective, a medium of communication is thus a particular category of technologies oriented towards the particular purpose of delivery. It can be placed alongside other comparable categories, such as technologies of transportation, oriented to moving people and goods in space, or technologies of agriculture, oriented to producing food.

This understanding of communication, though still the most common one, can be criticized by suggesting that the secondary process of delivery is based upon a more primary process and that this primary process is itself communication, not something other, which has to do with "making common," "being in contact with," "establishing and maintaining participation," and so forth. In this understanding, communication is the constitutive process of social relations. A medium of communication persists in space and time through the establishment of connection between its constituent elements. This process has two aspects: the construction of a technology with a certain practical goal in mind and the establishment of social relations – social identities constructed through the formation of constituent relations between them. Both Innis and certain Marxist theories of communication, notably that of Raymond Williams, depart from this commonsense secondary concept of communication and regard it as a – or even the – primary process in the constitution of society. One of the unique aspects of Innis's theory is that it still understands communication on the metaphor of transportation even while assigning it a constitutive, rather than a secondary, function. In this way it focuses attention on the spatial relations of a society, relations that are particularly pertinent for a (post-)colonial society, in contrast to colonizing or imperialist societies, which tend to hide their spatial relations under a "centric" historical focus. Samir Amin has theorized such centrism as the assertion of a "nonexistent historical continuity [which] constitutes the core of the Eurocentric dimension of capitalist culture."[20] The spatial focus inherent in a constitutive notion of transportation establishes the relevance of Innis's theory of communication to a post-colonial critique of Eurocentrism.

As a consequence of this shift to a constitutive model, the question of the relation between technology and a medium of communication needs to be posed differently. Media cannot be understood as a certain specific category of technologies, but must be conceptualized as the communicative aspect of technologies themselves. Stated generally, the communicative relations of a technology are those social relationships (including their institutional and symbolic forms) which are brought about by the practical functioning of the technology. They are thereby thoroughly imbued with the specific form of the sociocultural context as a whole. They are ethically and politically, as well as perceptually, institutionally, and cognitively, laden. The technology, then, is the same set of communicative relations looked at from the side of the technical combination – that is, from the side of its *productive capacity*, its ability to accomplish socially defined human goals. Technology and communication are thus two sides of the same organization, with technology indicating a focus on the output or consequences of the organization of human abilities and communication emphasizing the social relations that are required in order to accomplish this output – the construction of social identities in definite relations.

The explosion of technologies and communications in the contemporary world has thus given rise to a politics of identity formation. Raymond Williams has noted this qualitative change in the extended, and increasing, development of communication. "The means of communication as means of social production, and in relation to this the production of new means of communication themselves, have taken on a quite new significance, within the generally extended communicative character of modern societies and between modern societies."[21] From this perspective we can understand the complementary character of the social phenomena described within communication as the "information age" and the technological developments that designate this society as an "advanced" or "developed" one in comparison to those described metonymically as the "Third World"; though I want simply to note the relationship between these developments here without endorsing a specific analysis of them – whether they constitute a "revolution" or anything of that sort. We can suggest on this basis that the categorizations of social totality that were previously conceived as a determinate knowledge of the whole – capitalist, state socialist, feudal, and so forth – should rather be conceived as generalizations of common features of certain technology-identity complexes. These categories are not determining of technological-identity development from the whole to the part, top down, as it were. They are rather terms that summarize internal features of these complexes themselves. However pervasive these common features may be, they coexist with other technology-identity complexes of media of communication that contain the potential for alternative forms of social development.

I have criticized the notion of medium for two unexamined conceptual relations: between the intrinsic or environmental characteristics of a medium and between technology and social relations. These confusions in Innis's conception of a medium are important because it is the conceptual nut from which his whole communication theory is elaborated. However, they do not seem to me intrinsically intractable and are a main area in which his work could be productively extended. Such an extension would build on the most important component of Innis's communication theory of society – that a medium is not a neutral channel, but an active formation of perceptual, institutional, and cognitive dimensions of human experience. As such, it necessarily contains a "bias" that identifies the specific socio-cultural orientations built upon the dominant medium.

MONOPOLIES OF KNOWLEDGE

Innis's communication theory was developed with an eye to both historical and contemporary analysis and is oriented to a twofold task because of its reflexive focus on the forming influence of perception, institutions, and thought on the investigator as well as the society. First of all, it attempts to present a historical theory of civilization that would incorporate and surpass previous theories by showing historical changes as emerging from shifting relations between competing media of communication. Second, Innis's media theory is oriented especially towards the modern industrial world, towards answering the diagnostic question concerning the present state of civilization. This focus eventually also implies the reflexive question Why does a communication theory of civilization arise now? What is it about our own society that motivates us to inquire into communication in a way that has not been done before? Innis suggests that our society has been extremely efficient in media oriented towards space. We have more and more organization over a larger and larger area, which has developed into a world system. What the current society does not do well is organize things in the dimension of time. While there is a very efficient and well-integrated world system, it is extremely sensitive to periodic shocks and dislocations. The emphasis on space is taken by Innis to be characteristic of industrialization, mechanization, and modernity – connecting it to the colonial influence – in contrast to the localizing time orientation of oral tradition. In this critical vein, he stresses that "the importance of the oral tradition in an age when the overpowering influence of mechanized communication makes it difficult even to recognize such a tradition. Indeed, the role of the oral tradition can be studied only through an appraisal of the mechanized tradition for which the material is all too abundant."[22] The emphasis on time, by way of compensation, is a metonymic and synechdochic critique of industrial civilization. Innis claims that orality was a stabilizing influence in civilization in the past, though this fact has not been adequately enough understood.[23] In the present we need to recover and extend orality in order to develop greater stability in time, and this is the healing intention of his theory – to restore balance where it has been disturbed. It is the diagnostic and therapeutic intention originating in the crisis of civilization that motivates the contemporary development of the theory of media of communication.

Innis suggests that writing has a centralizing effect tending to promote bureaucratic organization as a result of its one-sided orientation to space.[24] It is inclined to promote analytic, abstract thought and to isolate the writer and the reader from each other. Scientific thought, for example, whose cumulation of results depends on writing, continually liquidates its past to present an analytic, synchronic, theoretical summary of the current state of knowledge. Innis attempts to rescue and justify oral tradition in the context of a society that has been one-sidedly oriented towards the written. Two major aspects of orality are relevant to its contemporary critical function: the role of memory and the central importance of the concrete situation in the here and now.

Sound is essentially immediate and evanescent. Its immediacy connects it to action. Speech as action, though Innis does not seem to have recognized it, has been fundamental to the rhetorical tradition. To speak to someone is to act and to provoke an immediate reaction in a way that writing does not. Oral society is based upon the notion of speech as action, rather than language as description, and has evolved many strategies for overcoming the tendency of spoken words to be forgotten. Stories, rituals, and so forth are built upon formulas and mnemonics. Poetry has a key function in which the rhythmic metre makes things easier to remember and to put in place. Moreover, there is a high level of redundancy and of formulaic assemblage of preorganized parts. The structure of speech in an oral society thereby tends to be additive rather than analytic. In analytic thought one subordinates the higher category to the lower, an example to the general theory, whereas within orality one tends simply to add on without any clear pattern of subordination or hierarchy. This key role of memory is extremely important in primary orality and exerts a formative influence on the whole of societies in which orality is the only, or major, medium of communication. Oral society is homeostatic because of the continuous incorporation of the past into the present.[25] There is no way for that which has really been forgotten to survive. Consequently, oral society orients much of its energy towards not forgetting, towards continuously re-enacting the past in the present.

Equally important, because speech is action, is the here-and-now situation in which an utterance takes place. Originality or creativity does not reside so much in making up new stories but in the quality of this enactment or performance. The oral mind is oriented towards narrative accounts, stories rather than lists. Consequently, there is no neutrality, but a standpoint with both a descriptive and an evaluative dimension. Orality is participatory and inclusive, not distant. It acts over small spaces and unites people in face-to-face encounters. Being situational rather than abstract, oral tradition is agonistic or rhetorical, rather than epistemological (which is based on a separation of the knower from the known).

Innis documents the unacknowledged importance of the oral tradition in maintaining Western civilization, and he wishes, by acknowledging that importance, to promote greater orality in the present in order to increase time consciousness and thereby to heal the one-sided emphasis of space-oriented bureaucratic society. The therapeutic goal of his communication theory is therefore oriented towards a greater "balance" between the competing biases of writing and orality. "Lack of interest in problems of duration in Western civilization suggests that the bias of paper and printing has persisted in a concern with space."[26] For Innis, the traditional humanist perspective outside competing interests is not possible since the biases inherent in media of communication extend throughout the material and intellectual formation of society. Nevertheless, the attempt at reflexive evaluation is not simply abandoned for interested polemic. Rather, it is to be sought in a balance between the differing biases of a plurality of media of communication. In this spirit, Innis remarks that the power of Plato's dialogues is that they involve an encounter between two media of communication They were written when oral society encountered a new literacy, and it is the double-sidedness rooted in this moment of civilizational transformation that gives persistent relevance to Plato's philosophy.[27]

Innis uses the notion of a "bias" of communication to refer to the specific social inclination inherent in the dominant expressive forms. Every medium of communication has a bias towards either space or time. By "bias" is meant the emphasizing of a certain aspect of experience, the time-oriented aspect or the space-oriented aspect of the medium of communicationin relation to the media environment as a whole. Bias is not a bad or distorting use of a medium; it is unavoidable. An important point of interpretation arises here, which is difficult to resolve definitively since Innis's written work on communication tends to use the concepts (monopoly of knowledge, balance, space, time, bias, medium, and so forth) through which his media theory is articulated in large-scale historical analyses rather than directly explaining or defining what they mean. Thus there is plenty of room for interpretation. These dimensions of space and time can be interpreted in two fundamental ways: first, as a Kantian formal structure that is more or less filled out by media of communication. In this case, the space-time schema would be pre-existent to media, and there would be a distinction between the "real" (i.e., scientifically conceptualized) space-time nexus and the extent to which it is known or experienced within a society. This raises several intractable problems since, while the distinction between these two is necessary from this perspective, the two usages of scientific conceptualization and social experience can never, in principle, be related to each other. The other alternative, which I believe to be truer to Innis's historical discussions, is phenomenological and Marxist. Space and time as they are experienced (in the widest sense) within any society are understood to be constituted through media of communication, and these media are formed and developed through human praxis. Space exists only insofar as it is traversed in some manner, and time exists only through the means of transmission between generations.[28] We can thus say that, for Innis, communication media "set up," or constitute, the limits of what is experienceable, and the manner in which it is experienced, in a social formation. In this case, there is no distinction between "real," or "scientific," space/time and the social experience of space/time. Rather, the scientific scheme is a specific secondary cultural formation whose historico-spatial emergence during the Renaissance in European society has its own conditions of existence in the predominating media of communication.

Innis's communication theory places a key stress on institutions as the constitution of an organization of human society. Institutions are based on a medium of communication that, within the institution, is the most developed and that then monopolizes knowledge through monopolizing access to and use of that medium of communication. While Innis discusses the bias towards space or time, he also refers to a "concern," or a concern with the "problem," of space and time. This is best understood as a figure-ground shift.[29] When a society has been reasonably successful in extending itself in space through utilizing media with a bias towards space, this success then comes to be taken for granted and the explicit concern, or thematization, of the social energy becomes directed towards time. Time becomes the problem that must be addressed on the basis of a presupposed success with space, or vice versa. So the notion of bias is utilized also to articulate a relationship between the presupposed taken-for-granted organization of a society and the specific thematic projects that the society pursues.

Since every medium of communication is biased towards either space or time, it is not possible for a single medium to be complete. If the society was only oriented to space, for example, it would be unstable with respect to time. If a society was only oriented to time, it would have great difficulty in occupying a single area successfully.

The notion of "balance" suggests that a society is most successful when it is based not upon one predominant medium of communication but upon several, especially a combination of several media that orient towards competing biases of space and time. This notion of balance is Innis's reformulation of the idea of disinterestedness in traditional European humanism. Though it is no longer suggested that one can "rise above" the conflicts of social life and judge them from an "unbiased" perspective, it is argued that a balance of biases can allow a viewpoint that, in a sense, neutralizes the biases of media. The balance needed in contemporary society, in contrast to its predominant bureaucratic space-oriented bias of writing, could be provided by a stress on the time orientation of oral tradition.

However, there are two incompatible accounts of oral tradition in Innis. In the first place, orality is understood as time orientation and presented as a balance to the space orientation of writing. This interpretation implies that orality, like any medium of communication, is a selection and coordination of human senses and an institutionalization of this selection that leads to a monopoly of knowledge. Therefore, in this version, orality is just as partial as any other medium of communication, such as writing, video, photography, sign language, architecture, and so forth. In this first sense it is a medium of communication alongside others. Its centrality derives from its capacity to balance the dominant space orientation of contemporary society such that, in this specific situation, it may play a healing role. But there is another account of the conception of orality in Innis. It is also viewed as a fundamental synthesis, a basis coordinating all human senses and incorporating both time and space in a unique manner. As he says in "The Problem of Space," "In oral intercourse the eye, ear, and brain, the senses and the faculties acted together in busy co-operation and rivalry each eliciting, stimulating, and supplementing the other."[30] Orality understood in this manner is an integration of human capacities into a functioning whole from which all other media abstract selections and partial developments of human capacities. In this formulation, it is not merely alongside other media of communication; it is the fundamental basis of all human communication from which other media derive and to which they are secondary.

The contradiction between two modes of understanding orality is embedded in Innis's theory and more particularly in the twofold intention of his media theory of civilization – the intention of giving a historical account of the development of civilization based on media of communication and that of investigating and healing the problems of the present. This relationship between the history of civilization and its present crisis gives rise to the two manners of understanding orality that are densely intertwined in Innis's texts. We should resist any tendency simply to solve the contradiction between these two accounts. A great thinker such as Innis does not simply make logical mistakes; this central contradiction motivates and animates his entire work in a manner that is characteristic of it as an attempt to think through dependency in a neo-colonial and post-colonial context.

REFLEXIVE ASSESSMENT

Reflexive assessment of one's own situation raises profound difficulties. In *Empire and Communications*, Innis states that the "significance of a basic medium to its civilization is difficult to appraise, since the means of appraisal are influenced by the media and indeed the fact of appraisal appears to be peculiar to certain types of media."[31] In other words, if our society is constituted through the biases inherent in media of communication, our social arrangements and therefore our manners of thinking are also constituted by these biases. How can we get a standpoint from which we can appraise or evaluate these biases? Are we not so firmly inside the society as to be incapable of really seeing it? This was a continuing concern of Innis that is characteristic of the orientation towards balance as a reformulation of European humanism in his communication theory. In the opening statement of an essay entitled "Industrialism and Cultural Values," he phrased it this way: "We must all be aware of the extraordinary, perhaps insuperable, difficulty of assessing the quality of a culture of which we are a part or of assessing the quality of a culture of which we are not a part. In using other cultures as mirrors in which we may see our own culture we are affected by the astigma of our own eyesight and the defects of the mirror, with the result that we are apt to see nothing in other cultures but the virtues of our own."[32]

The development of reflexive evaluation also has consequences for Innis's method of analysis and his writing style. His method of analysis is what we might call "micrology." He focuses on characteristic events within a society. He does not begin by characterizing the whole but from specific events, giving us a plurality of glimpses of these specific events to create a montage effect that implies the nature of the whole. This micrological approach is not a causal theory, but rather a method of investigation. It is not the claim that the media of communication determine the form of the society, but rather the suggestion that investigation of the constitutive elements of a society as media of communication shows that the micrological organization prefigures and articulates the macrological structure. This is, therefore, not a technological determinism, but rather a procedure of investigation that leads to a manner of intervention. Innis's writing is both descriptive and prescriptive. He uses, as McLuhan has pointed out, a modernist technique of writing in order to shift from the study of economics to "the total social process" – through a plurality of glimpses and montage to encourage the perception of patterns and thereby an oralist intervention in the system of writing.[33] Because the bias of writing is towards bureaucratic and centralizing influences and the bias of the oral is towards time-oriented intervention based in a synthesis of all of the capacities of a human individual, the idea of Innis's writing is to motivate the reader to intervene in the text in an oralist manner, and then, by micrological extension, perhaps to intervene in society as a whole in a similar manner.

Since every medium of communication has a tendency, or "bias," towards either space or time, an empire involves a coexistence of different media of communication. A society that manages to balance the influence of space-oriented and time-oriented media will be successful in both space and time. It is in the context of this reflexive issue that Innis introduces the concept of empire in the introduction to *Empire and Communications*. "I have attempted to meet these problems [of reflexive assessment] by using the concept of empire as an indication of the efficiency of communication. It will reflect to an important extent the efficiency of particular media of communication and its possibilities in creating conditions favorable to creative thought."[34] Thus the concept of empire refers to the efficiency of the plurality of media of communication existing in a certain society to extend in both space and time. Efficient extension in both space and time constitutes an empire, and such efficiency has to do with the capacity for reflexive evaluation. The term is introduced by Innis to describe a society that is persistent with a substantial degree of efficiency in the dimensions of both space and time; that is, an empire covers a large area and it lasts a long time. The apparent simplicity of the term "efficiency" expresses an apparent value-neutrality that is not tenable within Innis's own theory of bias, and consequently, his communication theory itself incorporates an unacknowledged bias towards empire as the presupposed *telos* of communication. It is pervaded by resentment, in Nietzsche's sense, in that it retains an unacknowledged and unavoidable debt to the object of its critique. In this sense, Innis's dependency theory of communication is unable to imagine any possibility of independence for the ex-colony. For this reason, his critique of colonialism remains a *dependent critique of dependency* in the sense that it does not contain the conceptual tools to imagine the possibility of independence. It remains tied to the imperial assumptions of European humanism.

Innis's reliance on the concept of empire as a key term in his communication theory and his attempt to avoid its normative implications indicate his effort to continue the ethical component of humanist tradition through its twilight. If we ask the question "What is successful communication?" it is doubtful whether "extension" in either space or time, or both, can serve as an adequate measure. There is a bias towards empire implicitly built into this criterion as it operates in Innis's conceptualization of a communication theory of society and civilization.[35] Insofar as extension in space or time is characteristic of a medium of communication, the most successful society will be one that extends in both space and time. An empire extends in both space and time with considerable success. Consequently, Innis's theory suggests that the most successful communication, in both a descriptive and a prescriptive sense, results in empire. Moreover, the most extensive reflexive evaluations can also be expected to emerge from such an imperial situation of balance. The concept of balance through which his therapeutic intention is expressed thus seems replete with conservative political implications, and these cannot be removed from his theory entirely, even though recent ecological critiques of industrial capitalist society suggest that its propensity for instability over time should be incorporated into critical social theory.

The conservative implications of the term "balance" can, however, be overcome if we connect this critique of Innis's unacknowledged bias for empire to the notion of monopolies of knowledge. The relation between developed institutional knowledges and repressed or incipient ones is a main concern in this context. Innis spent great energy to argue that the unacknowedged influence of the oral tradition was essential to whatever remaining stability Western society contains. Undeveloped and incipient forms of knowledge, in contrast to the developed and articulated forms of powerful institutions, can be understood as a figure-ground relationship. The idea of monopolies of knowledge necessarily involves conflict between knowledges, but not normally between equally constituted forms, since the resources commanded by powerful institutions allow their knowledges to be more developed and extensive. Rather, conflict is usually between instituted and emergent knowledges. In other words, the oppression of subaltern knowledges means that they are not articulated to a comparable degree as dominant monopolies are. In addition to – in fact, as a consequence of – the lesser social power they command, the knowledge they wield is less developed. While one need not agree with Gayatri Spivak that the subaltern cannot speak at all, it is nonetheless the case that voicing and articulation are radically problematic for emergent knowledges.[36] This is precisely why they are interesting in contrast to already constituted monopolies of knowledge: they problematize and investigate their own conditions of emergence, rather than hiding these conditions behind an ideology of universal applicability. To this extent, Innis's theory of monopolies of knowledge can come to the aid of a critical social theory oriented to the emergent knowledges proposed by new social movements and can aid in the critique of his own central concept of balance.

CRITIQUE OF PLANETARY CULTURE

I have argued that there are two main contradictions in Harold Innis's work: one between two accounts of orality and the other between the notion of balance and the concept of monopolies of knowledge. These contradictions are symptomatic of the historical juncture in which his communication theory was articulated and which it reflexively seeks to address. The twentieth century may be described as the twilight of humanist civilization. In such a situation we are motivated to recover the fundamental notion of humanism – the unity of the human body as the origin of media of communication and human capacities and creativity. Such a unity can provide the empirical and normative foundation of a critical theory of contemporary society. However, the present tendency of communication is to shatter this unity, to fragment human capacities, and to fracture the conception of the self. In this situation, the unity of the human body becomes very problematic and motivates a historical reflection on the origins of the conflicts of our own time that recovers the unity of the human body which is present in orality. In this sense, the communication theory of Innis is deeply reflexive, since the motive for recovery is rooted in the situation of loss. It is a dependent critique of dependency that attempts to reformulate the imperial assumptions of humanism. For this reason, his notion of orality inscribes a similar figure of thought to George Grant's lament for a nation in the moment of its demise. Lament is the favoured rhetorical trope of English Canadian intellectuals.

Nevertheless, it also may be the case that our present situation and the present fragmenting tendencies of media of communication show that this fundamental humanist notion of bodily integrity is simply no longer viable. It may have been a prejudice of previous media of communication, not a fundamentum for communication media *sui generis*. The moment of recovery, because of its origin in the moment of endangerment, cannot erase the doubt inherent in its origin to embrace a humanist metaphysics of bodily integrity. While it recovers this conception, it is obliged to reconstruct it in the present and therefore cannot simply rely on it as established. This reflexive situation leads to a contradiction between orality as the fundamentum to all media and orality as a balance to other media that is rooted in the contemporary situation for radical reflection in which humanism is fading but is needed in order to see what is emerging – a situation of twilight, not of definitive end or beginning.

The contemporary situation of the twilight of humanism has a further consequence for understanding the concepts of space and time as they are utilized by Innis. He criticizes the quantitative notion of time but not that of space. He contrasts time to mechanization and industrialization, thereby allowing the concept of space to stand, through the assumption of quantified space, for industrialism per se. Innis pointed out in "A Plea for Time," for example, that there are two ways of misunderstanding history.[37] We may misunderstand it as antiquarianism, as that which is simply finished, or on the other hand as that which remains and continues, implying that we understand people of the past as if they were just like us in the present. In both cases, we misunderstand history, which is change in continuity and continuity in change. Innis has done a great deal to resurrect the notion of history from this dilemma of reduction backward to the past or forward to the present. We may term it, to utilize a Husserlian terminology, a critique of the mathematical substruction of experienced time. However, there is no comparable critique of the mathematical substruction of lived space.

As time can be misunderstood as a linear progression that poses the apparent choice between discontinuity and continuity, so space can be misunderstood as simple location in a mathematical grid in which the opposition of here to there eradicates continuity in difference, or traversal. While in his concrete descriptions Innis uses the notion of space always as traversed space – that is, space that has been unified and differentiated through media of communication – he simultaneously conceptualizes space as already necessarily quantified. It is only on the basis of this quantified conception of space that the contrast between space and time can stand as emblematic of the problems of mechanization and industrialization as a whole. Thus the contradiction in the conception of oral tradition enters the conception of space as well.

Edmund Husserl, in his critique of modernity, argued that such misunderstandings are a result of substituting an intellectual framework of mathematical concepts for the lived experience of space and time.[38] Science may well be aided by such a procedure, but we ought not to confuse what is precisely the result of a procedure with our ordinary experience of the world. For this reason, Husserl argues that contemporary criticism must return to the living body underneath mathematical substructions, whether they be substructions of space or time. His analysis thus suggests that the fundamental contradiction from which the crisis of humanism emerges is between mathematical scientific substruction, on the one hand, and the living body, on the other – or between system and life-world. The critique that is required, in this case, focuses on the relation between mathematical-formal substructions and lived experience in both spatial and temporal dimensions, rather than the counterposing of time to space. From this perspective, Innis's descriptions capture the inscription of experience through the spatial and temporal components of media quite well, but there is a failure at the level of conceptualization that grounds the therapeutic and critical side of his theory.

The abstraction of various capacities from the unity of the living body has allowed them to be developed in a way that would not have been possible if their integration in orality had never been sundered. This development of separated capacities in the present time is allowing for a new coordination of the senses in the culture external to the individual body. Marshall McLuhan called this phenomenon the "global village." The sociocultural coordination of abstracted and developed capacities is replacing the original coordination of capacities in the human body. We may define planetary culture as this emergent coordination of developed media of communication outside the human body. It is a systematic connection that originated from abstraction from the lived body, but now completes and reverses itself to construct a new synthetic body. Whereas the body used to be the ground for all the figures of the abstracted human capacities, now the synthesis of abstracted and developed capacities is creating a new media environment, a new planetary culture, which is the ground upon which the human body appears as a figure. This situation is not just another change within the continuum of history, but a change that brings this development between the human body and the abstraction of its capacities to some sort of conclusion or closure. It is this situation that can be called the twilight of humanism.

Innis points us to this critical situation of the present, but in a manner that differs from the Eurocentric version that is common to both Husserl and McLuhan. Despite the critique of Innis's conceptualization presented above, his counterposing of space and time, industrialization and orality, gives a marginal, post-colonial twist to the critique of modernity. For him, it is not just a story of abstraction fracturing and synthetic recombination. The story must also include the fact that the abstraction fracturing begins from a specific location, which thereby gains power over other locations (becomes a centre). Consequently, the planetary recombination, while it is a "whole," is a centred whole that skews all phenomena in the global context towards a Eurocentric bias. It is to the post-colonial recuperation and extension of the critique of modernity that Innis makes his most profound contribution. The tension in his work is exemplary of a pervasive tension in our historical-geographical configuration and cannot be simply resolved. In the present context, the tension between orality as fundamental and orality as alongside other media condenses the issue of whether the imperial domination of space can be surpassed or only limited.

By linking orality with time orientation, Innis developed a critique of the mathematical substruction of time and was turned away from a similar critique of the mathematical substruction of space. In order to understand the contemporary tension between the unity of the living human body and the development of the capacities abstracted from this unity, we require a critique of space as well as time. The therapeutic intention of communication theory cannot be properly fulfilled through the notion of balance. It is better served by a metaphor of excavation, of digging down to the fundamental unity from which communicative capacities have been abstracted and at the same time a doubt that this excavation is uncovering a fundamental unity – a suspicion that perhaps that this unity only appears as such through a historical bias that is in the process of disappearing. This reflexive situation articulates a sense of loss, of lament, for the passing of something loved. In this respect Innis shares the rhetoric of lament made explicit by George Grant. Whether it be orality or an impossible nation, what is loved is close, local, and requires a turn against the universalizing and homogenizing dynamics of civilization and thought. This recovery of the particular is most characteristic of Canadian thought. In Innis it succeeds only in a minor key, as a holding action against a dynamic that it cannot criticize fundamentally enough. He reverses empire, but cannot imagine an exit from it. Is it now possible to develop further this reflexive paradox to recover not only what was loved but the lost possibilities of the past? Can the imagination of local autonomy, the lost dream of the New World, be recovered? To do so we need not only a critique of empire but also the thought of the self-sustaining local. How can we justify communications of restricted scope? The fact that these are questions and not assertions indicates that they are characteristic of a conjuncture in which they are not (yet) resolvable. It is the great merit of Innis to have taken social science to the critique of colonialism. It allows us to probe the possibility of a post-colonial exit from Europe. Not to traverse, but to inhabit, our own space. Here.

CHAPTER FOUR

George Grant's Critique of Technological Civilization

North America was inaugurated in the meeting of seventeenth-century Europe with the wilderness. The age of progress, particularly those dominated classes that had most to gain from progress, found itself reinforced by a natural environment that could only be tamed by hard work and an iron will. The aim of technological conquest of nature, deep-rooted in Western history and thought, could proceed in the New World without the impediment of mythical, religious, or philosophic views that kept that restrained it and gave it limits. Now that the candle of European progress has passed to America, its social consequences have become apparent: technological conquest of nature requires massive social institutions and control of the population through behavioural techniques. The relief from scarcity has issued in a world of consumer goods that makes each individual dependent on the whole system of production. Particular concerns, traditions, and histories must be subjugated to the universal claim of the conquest of nature incarnated in the social and economic apparatus. The claim to a particular vision of the good society in Canada fades before the entrenched power of those who place the so-called imperatives of technology beyond question.

The United States has become the leader of English-speaking people and represents the ideals of freedom, equality, and progress. The "melting pot" demanded that all previous allegiances be jettisoned for the American dream, that any remaining particularities would be relegated to private choice without significance in the public realm. Thus the political ideal became the universal and homogeneous state, which includes everyone and guarantees equality through public uniformity combined with private preference. Political options fade to administrative priorities and consumer choices. In English Canada there has been a continuous vacillation about this apex of modern

political ideals. A conservative hope – that one need not throw away
the traditions, histories, and particularities of the past – was woven
into the social and intellectual fabric. Despite the overwhelming concessions to social uniformity and centralized administration presided
over by continentalists who shared the main assumptions of American liberalism, some forces in English Canada have kept alive this
hope, which requires a critique of the dominant tendency of modern
politics. In the rejection of the melting pot for the notion of "two
founding peoples" and in the policies of multiculturalism, the significance of particular traditions for public life gained some recognition.
Regional diversity has not yet succumbed to the federalist view of
Canada. Nevertheless, these threads in the fabric of Canadian society
have not been strong enough to withstand the homogenizing influence of advancing technology. Our failure to think through the claims
of "particularity" is evident in the exclusion of indigenous people as
founders, the trivialization of ethnicity, and our inability politically to
represent regionalism. Against the mainstream, these threads have
been articulated in Canadian intellectual life by questioning the dominant assumption of the modern world: the creation of a free and
equal society through the technological conquest of nature. Recognition of the value of particularity has largely depended upon the conservative influence of the English dominant class since the time of the
United Empire Loyalists. This conservative critique of modernity that
inheres in the social formation of English Canada was brought to its
highest philosophical articulation by George Grant. As a result of the
recent institutionalization of continental free trade by the dominant
classes, the conservative hope embodied in Canada has become
increasingly mute. We can begin an assessment of its contemporary
relevance through a reconsideration of Grant's diagnosis of the trans-
planting of the European technological will to America.

THE TECHNOLOGICAL REGIME

George Grant claimed that the technological empire relegates what he
terms "one's own," or particularity, to being merely a means for the
continuance of the system as a whole.[1] One's nation, one's ethnicity,
and at the most basic level, one's own body are robbed of uniqueness
and treated as uniform means for standardized productive and
administrative tasks. The observation that technology requires pre-
dictability and social homogenization is extended by Grant to the
consequence that all uniqueness is regarded as irrelevant. The term
"one's own" is an excellent English rendering of Heidegger's concept
Eigentlich, which is conventionally translated as "authenticity." One

can see in Grant's use of this term his appropriation of Heideggerian philosophy as a questioning of the entire tradition of Western political philosophy. The private realm (*idion*), which was understood in classical philosophy as merely a *prerequisite* for universal political life, has been *submerged* by modern technology. It thus needs to be rediscovered and reformulated in a radical manner not necessary previously. From Aristotle to Hegel, though in different forms, a private realm such as the household or family was taken to be prior to, and an essential prerequisite for, the political realm. Politics was the arena of discussion about the ends and means of the just and free society. In order to go out into the realm of debate in which one must argue and defend one's thoughts and actions before others, humans were taken to require a prior realm that sustained their need for food, shelter, comfort, and intimacy. From this private foundation prior to argument and persuasion, citizens could enter the common, public realm. Grant contended that the contemporary undermining of one's own by technology is more fundamental than political suppression or tyranny. Technology has undermined the independence of the indispensable *prerequisites* for political life. Through the bringing of private life into the productive and administrative exigencies of technological society, the formation of individual character has been entirely ceded to the imperatives of the technological conquest of nature.

The modern technological state involves an empire that undermines both sides of the traditional distinction between private and public, family and politics, and replaces them with a centralized and ubiquitous administrative apparatus. In order to understand and criticize this development, Grant followed Leo Strauss in characterizing the technological empire as the universal and homogeneous state, which is a critical reformulation of the claim to a free and equal society characteristic of the liberal core of modern political philosophy. Technology is universal in the sense that everyone is included in the economic and political world system that it engenders. It is homogeneous in the sense of standardizing culture in the various parts of the world system. Technology triumphs by breaking down particular traditions. "The end towards which the modern project was directed was the universal and homogeneous state – the worldwide society of free and equal men in which all but a few idiots would be open to the knowledge of science and philosophy and therefore increasingly ruled by it. As all men would be open to the dictates of reason, and these dictates would lead them to agreement about what was good, there would be no conflict, and thus communal life could be ordered by administration."[2]

The pervasiveness of liberal ideology leads to an underestimation and misunderstanding of the project of the conquest of nature through technology upon which liberalism depends. Only by over-coming natural scarcity and inequality can the ideas of freedom and equality be realized. But this technological conquest has conse-quences that are characterized more fundamentally, in Grant's view, as universality and homogeneity. Because of the superficial under-standing of technology in liberalism, we are blind to the endemic vio-lence produced in the most modern societies. Such violence is generally regarded as due to peripheral and removable causes rather than as a consequence of the uprooting of traditions by technology. Standardization of culture by technology requires that all that is one's own be pressed into the service of empire. One's own country, ethnic-ity, work, or body is regarded as merely a means for the maintenance and extension of the system as a whole. In such a situation, love for one's own is indispensable for a vision of the good. Only by loving particular things can we gain an idea of a universal good that is not merely a sacrifice of what is one's own on the altar of technological progress. While the traditional task of philosophy was to justify the universal over particular attachments, in the present condition the task of justification is reversed. Philosophy must justify particularity in order to recover the relation to one's own from which one can pass over to a love of what is universally good for all humans. This does not mean a rejection of universality, but rather a recovery of the par-ticularity, or love of one's own, without which the justification of uni-versality becomes the dry standardization and homogenization required by the technological empire.

The term "universal and homogeneous state" was introduced by Alexandre Kojeve during his debate with Leo Strauss in order to illustrate his Hegelian account of the realization of philosophy in his-tory.[3] Kojeve claimed that Alexander's ancient empire was the first universal state in the sense that it included everyone on the basis of their common human essence rather than on geographic or ethnic particularity as in the Greek *polis*. However, this concept of the hu-man essence was based on the Greek conception of reason and there-fore presumed that natural differences in reasoning ability justified the social division into masters and slaves (and, ultimately, between a few philosophers and the many others). Only with Christian revela-tion is the concept of equality introduced insofar as each one can con-vert to Christianity and become equal in the eyes of God. Conversion is a human act that negates natural differences and consequently the Greek master-slave distinction. Initially, universality and equality were displaced to a heavenly reconciliation – a heaven beyond human society – but in the modern world this egalitarian tendency was secularized by the French and American revolutions and Hegelian philosophy and made a goal of human social organization. Thus the immanent development of civilization based on Greek and Christian roots is towards a universal and homogeneous state embodying reason and negating natural differences.

Strauss accepted Kojeve's designation of the modern state, but argued that it must necessarily be a tyranny. To elucidate tyranny he wrote a close commentary on Xenophon's *Hiero*. There are three basic reasons offered in this argument that the modern state must be tyrannical. First, since the Hegelian claim is to establish mutual recognition of all citizens as self-determining subjects, the chief of state is no more qualified than the others. As Grant encapsulates it, "Those others then have a very good reason for dissatisfaction: a state which treats equal men unequally is not just."[4] Though this criticism applies to Hegel, it might well be taken as a motive for Marx's further development of modern political theory, which claims that mutual recognition is only possible on the basis of radical democratization of all spheres of life, including the industrial and administrative apparatus required by the conquest of nature. It is a fundamental question for modern political theory whether this development is really possible or is merely a product of a utopian imagination. In his comments on Herbert Marcuse and the New Left, Grant claims that it is not a viable political option.[5] This judgment confirms his earlier argument in *Lament for a Nation* that the only option after 1940 for an independent Canada was some combination of nationalism and socialism, but that no such combination was possible.[6]

The second reason offered by Strauss is that, though Hegel sees work and war in the conquering of non-human and human nature as essentially human and as the means for establishing the modern state, the realized state will not require either activity since their completion is a condition for universality and homogeneity. Thus citizens are deprived of the essentially human activities. They come to resemble Nietzsche's "last men," who only shrug and blink. These two criticisms are internal to the Hegelian view of the state in the sense that they utilize its own criteria of evaluation. Strauss's third point goes to the heart of the matter since it proceeds from an assumption rooted in classical philosophy that criticizes the Hegelian criteria of universality and homogeneity. Rejecting the modern doctrine of the popularization of science and philosophy, he followed Greek philosophy in claiming that the division between the few who pursue wisdom and the many who do not cannot be obliterated. Therefore, since the modern state must suppress all thought that does not conform to the dogma of universality and homogeneity, true philosophy and science will be suppressed. This conflict between the few and the many, which is coeval with philosophy, is resolved on the side of the many in the modern state, which claims to be the incarnation of philosophical wisdom. Thus modern tyranny will issue in the eradication of philosophy, not in its realization as Hegel claimed – a realization that, in any case, Strauss deems impossible.

For Grant, the debate between Kojeve and Strauss had the significance of illustrating that the basic division between modern and ancient political philosophy is the acceptance or rejection of the technological conquest of nature. It allowed him to redefine, in sympathy with Strauss, the modern political project of a free and equal society as a universal and homogeneous tyannical state that dominates particularity, extends itself into an empire, and deals violently with other societies and nature. "Liberal doctrine does not prepare us for this violence because of its identification of technology with evolution, and the identification of evolution with movement of the race to higher and higher morality. Such a doctrine could not understand that an expanding technological society is going to be an imperialist society even when it is run by governments who talk and sometimes act the language of welfare both domestically and internationally."[7] In his most widely read book, *Lament for a Nation*, Grant utilized this analysis of modern politics to show the inevitability of Canada's defeat as an independent nation. Canada is a viable political entity only if the conservative hope of publicly recognizing particularities can be kept alive in the face of modern tyranny. But while he accorded an extremely high estimation to Leo Strauss's work both in his discussion of this debate and elsewhere, his utilization of the analysis of tyranny proposed by Strauss is really quite restricted. With respect to the *main* point of Strauss's claim of the universal validity of Socratic political philosophy Grant does not agree. Strauss's argument suggests that classical Greek philosophy posed in a prior and theoretically adequate manner the question of the relation of humans to nature and consequently rejected with good reasons, prior to its historical development, the modern project of the conquest of nature. On the related point in which Strauss takes Greek and Christian morality to be essentially similar in their opposition to modernity, Grant again disagrees and points to the studies of Weber, Troeltsch, and especially M.B. Foster, which emphasize the influence of Christianity in forming modernity. There is also a third point, which is a consequence of Grant's appropriation of Heidegger's term "one's own" as a critique of the tradition of political philosophy. As a consequence, it is misleading to think that the empire of modern technology could be satisfactorily elucidated with reference to an ancient text as Strauss's commentary on Xenophon's *Hiero* implies. Thus Grant's position, in contrast to that of Strauss, leads him to maintain that there is a "truth" brought forth by modern technology that is not encompassed by Plato.[8]

Canada's political identity is threatened by the proximity of the American empire. Moreover, we are ourselves implicated in the un-limited drive to technology that characterizes the New World. It is our destiny to be forced to understand the United States. What is at issue is not only our own political survival but the conservative hope upon which Canada is predicated: public representation of particular differ-ences. Failure to realize this hope will ensure further violent uprooting of traditions and the utilization of our own by faceless institutions.

DEVELOPMENT OF THE ANALYSIS OF TECHNOLOGY

Grant's major works can be read as successive attempts to come to grips with the phenomenon of technology, especially as it affects moral and political life. Increasingly, as his understanding of the phe-nomenon of technology gains scope and explanatory power, technol-ogy is taken to be in contradiction with the biblical-Platonic roots of justice that constitute the philosophical heritage of the West and that still survive, to an extent, in contemporary political institutions. This section documents the development of Grant's understanding of technology through his major works.

In *Philosophy in the Mass Age* (originally published in 1959) Grant de-lineated two characteristics that define our culture: scientific-technical domination of nature and the dominance of some humans (large-scale capitalists) over others. The dominance of capitalists is not, however, a personal dominance in which they can pursue their own goals, but a carrying out of the necessities of the system as a whole. The domina-tion of humans has such advanced techniques at its disposal that the individual, even if in the elite, is subjected to the apparatus as a whole. In this situation, "we ask what it is that man has created in this new society. And as we try to see what we are, there arises an ultimate question about human nature and destiny. And such questions are what philosophy is. What I mean by philosophy arising out of such a situation is that so totally new is our situation in history, that we are driven to try and redefine the meaning of human history itself – the meaning of our own lives and of all lives in general."[9] The search for a moral philosophy adequate to this new situation meets a major obsta-cle in the fact that reason itself has come to be seen in technological terms as an instrument, a tool for subjective purposes. Reason used in this technological manner tends to reinforce the bent of contemporary society and cannot judge it – which is what is required of moral philosophy. Thus emerge two tightly knit themes that pervade the whole of George Grant's work: How can one escape in thought the dominance of instrumentality in contemporary society? and, What are the fundamental principles of moral-political philosophy? Given the pervasiveness of industrial-technical culture, it may seem that these questions are not susceptible to affirmative answers. However, in *Philosophy in the Mass Age*, he points to two factors which indicate that the seemingly closed circle can be broken: conquest of scarcity and the breakdown of traditional meaning systems.[10] At this time in Grant's understanding of technology, he was looking for an internal critique of the technological system. Both of these factors are effects of industrial society that motivate a renewal of moral philosophy from within technological society. Thus they justify a certain acceptance of the validity of modern technology, while at the same time they assert that its achievements must be held up to moral scrutiny.

Grant concludes by stating that "in these essays the central question of modern moral philosophy has been posed: How can we think a conception of law which does not deny the truth of our freedom or the truth of progress?"[11] His response to this question in *Philosophy in the Mass Age* involves a vacillation that the argument of the book fails to resolve. On one hand, Grant is drawn to the tradition of German Idealism and the attempt by Kant and Hegel (and Marx) to reconcile freedom of the spirit with the domination of nature. On the other hand, he leans towards an older tradition of the biblical-Platonic concept of justice, which, although it is not explicitly named or discussed in this work, constitutes its moving principle. It can be seen in his claim that "the spirit knowing itself as free cannot rest in natural joy" and in his pointing to the "revolts of a perverted nature which have so characterized the twentieth century."[12] In his search for a moral philosophy that can accept the truth of technology and yet contain the conquest of human and non-human nature, Grant uncovered the centrality of the concept of limit. Nevertheless, at this point the limitation of human action was thought simultaneously within two incompatible traditions – Greek and German, ancient and modern, heteronomous and autonomous. There is another way of putting this vacillation: freedom and justice are held together as two poles of criticism of modern society, though the manner in which they might be held together is not investigated.

The predominance of the strain of German Idealism at this period in Grant's search for a moral limit to technology can be illustrated by the essay "An Ethic of Community," which he wrote for the volume *A Social Purpose for Canada* (1961), a collection of essays by leading left-wing intellectuals who hoped to influence the nascent New Democratic Party. Here Grant contrasted the diversity of talents and hierarchy of abilities necessary to an advanced industrial society, on the one hand, with a conception of the equality of moral persons, on the other. "Equality should be the central principle of society since all persons, whatever their condition, must freely choose to live by what is right or wrong. This act of choosing is the ultimate human act is open to all. In this sense all persons are equal, and differences of talent are of petty significance."[13] Grant relied on the Kantian distinction between means and ends to maintain that moral personality is not a limited good but an unconditional one and that society must recognize each member as a freely choosing moral being. From this basis he argued for substantive economic equality and noted that the belief in equality relies on religious faith in God. The "ethic of community" is essentially a Christian socialist ethic rooted in a Kantian conception of moral autonomy.

Kant distinguished between technical, pragmatic, and moral imperatives of action. Technical rules of skill are innumerable insofar as action is necessary to bring about a practical purpose. In technical imperatives the rationality or goodness of the end is not questionable, but only the means to attain the end. Imperatives of skill are hypothetical since they prescribe what rules must be followed *if* a certain end is adopted, but do not question whether the end is or should be adopted. The end does not come under scrutiny in hypothetical imperatives. Counsels of prudence are pragmatic; they are means to the end of happiness. This end can be presumed actually to exist in all individuals. However, actions of this type are also hypothetical since they are still means, and the actions are not good in themselves but only relatively so to the end of happiness. Kant further subdivided prudence into worldly wisdom and private wisdom. The first consists of skill in influencing others to one's own ends, the second in combining one's own ends to lasting advantage. He noted that, without private wisdom, worldly wisdom is more accurately called cleverness and astuteness but not prudence. This observation indicates that prudence consists in combining ends in pursuit of happiness and that an unordered collection of ends, however clearly pursued, does not tend to produce happiness. In contrast to Aristotle, Kant argued that the attempt to harmonize ends within the self to achieve happiness suffers from our ignorance. "If it were only as easy to find a determinate concept of happiness, the imperatives of prudence would agree entirely with those of skill and would be equally analytic. For here as there it could alike be said 'Who wills the end, wills also (necessarily, if he accords with reason), the sole means which are in his power.' "[14]

Consequently, our ideas of happiness often conflict with themselves and pose the problem of achieving a unified and harmonious concept. Nevertheless, if it were possible to describe the content of happiness, it would also be possible to describe all means towards it as technical. Since omniscience would be required to decide with certainty about happiness, our decision can only rely on empirical counsels and not on determinate principles. The unification of diverse ends that happiness demands is left to experience and deemed incapable of rational judgment. The distinction between technical and pragmatic imperatives appropriates Aristotle's dichotomy of *techne* and *praxis*, with one important qualification. Like Aristotle's account of *techne*, Kant's discussion of hypothetical imperatives attempts to show that an adequate moral law cannot be a means to an end but only an end in itself. However, he rejects Aristotle's notion of a determination by nature. In other words, Kant's recognition of the active nature of knowledge requires a rejection of deriving a moral law from cosmological intuition of the order of nature, such as was characteristic of Greek philosophy.

Kant's third imperative of action is a moral one and is termed "categorical" since it does not depend on a prior hypothetical "if" that is outside rational discourse. Consequently, the categorical imperative is universal since it applies in every case whatever one chooses to adopt as ends. Moreover, since there is no determining condition – such as the prior choice of an end for a hypothetical imperative – the conformity of the maxim to the law or of the principle of action to the condition of universality is all that is conveyed in the categorical imperative. Kant states it in this way: "Act only on that Maxim through which you can at the same time will that it should become a universal law." If one grants that a rational being exists as an end and not merely as a means, then an alternative and equivalent formulation can be given: "Act in such a way that you always treat humanity, whether in your own person or in the person of any other, never simply as a means, but always at the same time as an end."[15]

Kant's categorical imperative is an attempt to formulate a universally binding moral law for the sphere of interhuman action independent of any determinate concept of happiness. In so doing he opposes his ethic of autonomy to Aristotle's heteronomous or worldly ethic of happiness. Kant attempted to forestall the universalization of technical ends by finding in the sphere of human interaction a moral law that elevates human selfhood to an end in itself. The moral will is determined only by the condition of universality and not by any worldly content. This notion of enlightenment proposes an anthropocentric solution whereby the world of use objects and technical

means is ultimately for the fulfilment of interhuman life, which is
ruled by the moral law. Such a humanistic ethics begins from a distinction between technical, limited, hypothetical ends and ethical
action, which is an end in itself and resides solely in the interhuman,
social sphere. This distinction is equivalent to the claim that technical
action is ethically neutral or, in another formulation, that technology
cannot come to influence, or determine, the content of ethical action.
At this point in his thinking Grant's philosophy is essentially a development of the Christian social-gospel tradition stemming from John
Watson, who began its alliance with German Idealism in Canada.

Grant's attraction to and later disillusionment with the CCF–NDP
indicates a political issue underlying much Canadian thought. As a
popular movement critical of capitalist society, the Co-operative
Commonwealth Federation and its successor, the New Democratic
Party, attracted generations of Canadian intellectuals for many of the
same reasons that Marxism and the Communist Party drew their
European counterparts: the productive and destructive power of capitalist technology became increasingly apparent in the twentieth century, especially in periods of economic crisis. Many of the best
thinkers withdrew their allegiance from constituted authority and
approached working-class and popular movements that held out the
hope of an egalitarian, free, and stable society. In Canada the CCF–
NDP proved itself incapable of articulating a socialist vision that
could transcend the compromises and evasions of liberalism. Grant
left the NDP in 1963 when it failed to support the Conservatives over
the Bomarc issue – the rejection of American nuclear weapons on
Canadian soil. His assessment was that the socialist option was not a
real possibility, as expressed in his rejection of a socialist-nationalist
synthesis in *Lament for a Nation* and his later critique of Herbert Marcuse in *Technology and Empire*. This conjuncture has left critical thinkers without an anchor in the public world, with the consequence that,
as Grant has pointed out, one is forced to choose between thinking
through the problems radically or curtailing one's criticism in an
attempt at political relevance. English Canada has thus been left
a legacy of timid thought, which has allowed public responsibilities
to undermine radical questioning. Grant's choice, which retains a
respect for politics, nevertheless becomes increasingly divorced from
action, and for this very reason it is the most significant source of
philosophical questioning that we possess. In contrast, disillusionment with communism in Europe was not based on the failure to
transcend liberalism but rather on the barbarities of Stalinism. Consequently, there was a motive to discover the philosophic dimensions of
Marxism that fuelled such thinkers as Sartre, Merleau-Ponty, Adorno,

and Marcuse. This focus is not meant to disparage such thinkers as Charles Cochrane, Innis, C.B. Macpherson, and Grant, who have made substantial contributions. Rather, it is to emphasize that they have done so largely in isolation, without the support of a tradition of dissident intellectuals. It is not only the anti-intellectualism of a pioneer society but also the political failure to articulate a socialist vision that has hampered public reflection in this country.

In the 1966 introduction to a reissue of *Philosophy in the Mass Age*, Grant acknowledged the influence of Jacques Ellul and Leo Strauss in his turn from Hegel to Plato for the highest vision of human excellence. While the influence of Hegel on the work is indeed pervasive, this characterization is oversimplified by hindsight. In his discussion of natural law Grant had noted that Hegel attempted to reconcile the two views whose divergence he maintained: man as maker of historical events versus man as discoverer of an order to which he is subject.[16] While he did not explicitly criticize Hegel's attempted reconciliation, in Grant's view the divergence remained, as expressed in his reference to "natural joy." This allusion amounts to a rejection of the Hegelian notion of *Aufhebung* (preservation and transcendence), which is the philosophic core on which the entire Hegelian system rests. Thus, in Grant's view, the quarrel between the ancients and the moderns over the goodness of the technological domination of nature is not resolved by Hegel and remains a live choice. With this move Grant separated himself from a central tradition in Canadian philosophy, which has been attracted to Hegel in the attempt to reconcile Christian morality with the conquest of nature. John Watson is the grandfather of this tradition, which has influenced the Protestant churches more than academic philosophy. Thus Grant sidestepped the "Hegel renaissance" that blooms in Western philosophy every twenty years or so and laid the basis for his later turn from Hegel to Plato. He attributed this shift in his thinking to a greater understanding of the phenomenon of technology, such that he was no longer held by the "progressive faith." "I am much less optimistic about the effects that a society dominated by technology has on the individuals which comprise it. I no longer believe that technology is simply a matter of means which men can use well or badly. As an end in itself, it inhibits the pursuit of other ends in the society it controls."[17] Thus in *Lament for a Nation* (1965), which was written at approximately the same time as the 1966 introduction to *Philosophy in the Mass Age*, Grant documented the necessary defeat of Canadian nationalism and the possibility of an independent politics by the universal and homogeneous American empire, which most completely incarnates modern technological society.

His next book, *Technology and Empire* (1969), was a collection of essays written between 1963 and 1969 and exhibits a growing appreciation, and eventually critique, of Ellul's conception of "technique." In a 1966 review of his *The Technological Society*, Grant credits him with describing "the character of technique in our society, how it has become both geographically and qualitatively universal, how it is self-augmenting and autonomous."[18] Technique cannot be reckoned a neutral tool for good or ill because it has overcome the belief that things are good or bad independent of human choice. In other words, the extension of conquest from non-human to human nature, which Grant was concerned to keep within limits based on a Kantian ethics in *Philosophy in the Mass Age*, is now taken to be a necessary consequence of the society based on technique. This conception of "technique" is utilized to criticize contemporary institutions such as the unversity, the church, and the American empire. It might well be argued that Ellul's claim for the autonomy of technique is grounded only by sociological description rather than theoretical clarity. However, the influence of Nietzsche, which provides this clarity, is already emerging in *Technology and Empire*. It comes to the fore in the 1969 Massey Lectures *Time as History*. In the essay "In Defence of North America," it is stated that "the belief in the mastering knowledge of human and non-human beings arose together with the very way we conceive our humanity as an Archimedean freedom outside nature, so that we can creatively will to shape the world to our values."[19] Technology is thus analysed as the entire historical-theoretical process whereby the self as creative freedom dominates the world as objective stuff, including ourselves as part of the world. Grant points out in his preface that a critique of Ellul is implied throughout this essay. This critique is essentially that the advance of technology was, and probably still is, itself taken as a moral ideal by those who propagate it, thus answering the observation that the ascendence of technique over humans is a mysterious process without human motive, as described by Ellul. Technology is the means for overcoming our subjection to nature and realizing ourselves as creative freedom. This freedom has been taken to be a positive moral good. It may well be the most significant ethic of the modern world.

In *Time as History* Grant probed the significance of the conception of the self as creative freedom through an encounter with Nietzsche. The notion of the world as "indifferent stuff" open to manipulation has been formed by expelling moral order from nature and lodging it in the human subject. The essential characteristic of subjectivity then is this "positing of values," which is necessary to human life but is without objective foundation. Technology in its most fundamental origin is the splitting of experience into inner and outer dimensions, a relation between subject and object that tears value from fact and thereby removes any foundation for values in nature or the order of the world. It is rooted in the Western conception of the "will," which comes to fruition in Nietzsche's work. It is an act of the will that allows the ego to represent the world to itself. "The coming together of willing and reasoning lies essentially in the method which has made possible the successes of modern science. The world is a field of objects which can be known in their working through the 'creative' acts of reasoning and experimenting by the thinking subject who stands over them. This brings together willing and reasoning, because the very act of the thinking-ego standing over the world, and representing it to himself as objects, is a stance of the will."[20] With his acceptance of the Nietzschean analysis of "will" as the origination of the distinction between facts and values such that given facts (nature) can be dominated by creative positing of values, Grant came to view the whole project of modern political philosophy as engendering a tyranny in which there can be no rational basis for limiting the manipulation of the given state of the world (non-human and human nature). The universal and homogeneous state is a combination of reason and will – reason as unifying natural diversity and will in conquering nature. This modern state is a tyranny because its reliance on the conquest of nature eliminates the possibility of a moral limit to creative willing. One way of putting this view is that the Kantian distinction between equal moral persons on the one hand and a hierarchy of abilities on the other is not a sufficient foundation for limiting technology. The Kantian distinction of freedom from necessity is based on the autonomy and universality of the person from all heteronomous, natural, and particular contents. But if the essence of human subjectivity is creative willing, as Grant now understands it to be, why should the positing of values recognize an inherent value in other subjects, especially if they do not will creatively or forcefully? Put in another way: how can the creative freedom of subjectivity be reconciled with moral law? This question poses again the quarrel between the ancients and the moderns. At this point Grant has come to realize that the quarrel cannot be mediated and has come to side with the ancients in rejecting modernity root and branch.

This theme is pursued in more detail in *English-Speaking Justice* (1974). Through his encounter with Nietzsche, Grant came to regard the Kantian teaching of moral *autonomy* on which he had earlier relied to criticize technology as itself an expression of the technological will and thereby as incapable of limiting it.[21] The two alternatives – modern and ancient, Hegelian and Platonic – for moral limitation of the conquest of nature envisioned in *Philosophy in the Mass Age* are at this point in Grant's theoretical development narrowed to one. What he there called "natural joy" was extended into an appreciation of the Platonic conception of justice as rooted in the nature of things, as *recognized* and not made by humans and thereby providing a moral basis for limiting the scope of human action. The idea of freedom is merely an expression of technology. Only "justice" is a critique of it. In an essay entitled "Revolution and Tradition" (1971), Grant concluded with reference to the insight of Nietzsche that technical mastery of the earth and the historical sense are at bottom identical. The primacy of "will" means both that there is no natural order which sustains and limits human action and that, consequently, morality is an expression of historically changing conventional configurations. Here, as always in his discussions of Nietzsche, Grant withdrew from the implications of Nietzsche's thought, regarding it as a symptom of the modern condition, not as a truth brought forth by it.[22] Nevertheless the alternative – human action as limited and defined by a moral order independent of our willing – is rendered unthinkable by the furthest reaches of modern thought.

In the light of the last eighty-five years, however, Nietzsche's question may not be the essential one. The essential question may not be: who deserve to be the masters of the earth; but rather, is it good that the race ever came to consider that mastery was its chief function? I do not know which of these two questions is essential, because I do not know whether the second could be properly posed as an authentic question. How could one have clarity about this? The very fabric of modern civilization has been based on affirmations which exclude that question as a question, and therefore even to raise it is to think about how those affirmations were incarnated in what was said about reason, love, suffering, knowledge, etc. What is an object, what a subject? How can we, who are western men, think about western thought outside the thinking which makes us western men? The very circle is the root cause of why we must say that in this era there is no alternative to being in darkness. But it is that being in darkness from which comes forth the determination to be outside that circle?[23]

One must attend clearly to the formulation at this point: this is a darkness for clarity, for questioning, in short, for philosophy in the modern world.

Darkness is produced in thinking the consequences of modern thought alongside the idea of the good as given to humanity, which has been overcome. Justice cannot be *thought* in the modern age, but Grant remarks that it has been revealed and can be *believed*. As early as his article "Philosophy" for the Massey Commission (1951), Grant had maintained, "Reason not guided by faith cannot but find itself in the position of destroying everything and establishing nothing."[24] The figure of Christ, though not often appealed to in philosophical contexts by Grant, was for him central to remembering justice as given to humans in Platonic fashion. Without such a remembrance of justice the modern age could not be characterized as darkness. Yet it must be recalled that Grant regarded Christianity as a source for modernity, not, like Strauss, as one with Greek philosophy as a critique of technology. Modernity's commitment to the domination of nature was an expression of Christian charity according to Grant. For this reason, despite his deepening philosophical critique of modernity, it was difficult for him to abandon the notion that some "truth" about human life had been brought forth by it. This tension in his thinking led to an increasing tendency to counterpose thought and belief, in order to manifest the legitimacy of belief in the face of the darkness into which thought has fallen.

It is Grant's stance between ancient and modern that brings forth the speech about darkness and requires the distinction between reason and faith. In *English-Speaking Justice* his continuing question of the relationship between technology and liberalism becomes the centre of inquiry. "The first task of thought in our era is to think what that technology is: to think it in its determining power over our politics and sexuality, our music and education."[25] Grant poses the question of whether the determining power of modern technology is overcoming the foundations of English contractual liberalism within which it emerged. Having accepted Nietzsche's uncovering of the will as the origination of technology such that conquest of nature must extend to humans, he turns to Heidegger's development of Nietzsche's thought as the clearest expression of the essence of modern technology.[26] He begins by accepting the term "technology," which indicates the interpenetration of the arts and sciences in the modern era that was not present in Greek philosophy – all modern knowing is a making. In an essay for the Royal Society of Canada in 1974 this acceptance was explained. "I used to think that the French and German distinction between the words 'technique' and 'technology' kept something that was lost in the English use of the single word 'technology.' It maintained the distinction between the particular means of making (technique) and the studies from which it came (technology). I have now changed my mind because the single word 'technology' brings out that the very horizons of making have been transformed by the discoveries of modern science."[27] In Grant's works of the 1970s Heidegger's account of technology both implicitly and explicitly provided the foundation for his questioning about justice. Technology came to be regarded as "the endeavour which summons forth everything (both human and non-human) to give its reasons, and through the summoning forth of those reasons turns the world into potential raw material at the disposal of our 'creative' wills."[28] This "summoning forth" is the fundamental orientation that treats the given world as a resource for posited goals. The "extension" of the conquest of nature to humans is captured in this formulation of technology as an intrinsic aspect of the attitude that takes the given at its disposal. The most visible form of this attitude is the massive social organizations required for productive enterprises to transform nature's resources. Grant's acceptance of Heidegger's account of the technological domination of nature finally explains why it cannot be separated from the social domination that it engenders. It was a formulation of this relationship that he had been seeking through the development of his analysis of technology.

In the use of computers the social consequences of summoning forth are clearly apparent. "It is clear that the 'ways' that the computer can be used for storing 'information' can only be ways that increase the tempo of the homogenizing process in society. Abstracting facts so that they may be stored as 'information' is achieved by classification, and it is the very nature of any classifying to homogenize what may be heterogeneous. Where classification rules, identities and differences can only appear in its terms. The capabilities of any computer do not allow it to be used neutrally towards the facts of heterogeneity. Moreover, classification by large institutions through investment-heavy machines is obviously not carried out because of the pure desire to know but because of convenience of organization."[29] The development of technology proceeds through the intertwining of knowing and making that has removed the horizons within which these were traditionally limited. Creative will facing disposable resources proceeds without limit, rendering the conception of justice (which requires a limitation of human actions by an intuition of the order of what is) increasingly anachronistic. Thus Grant diagnoses our contemporary condition as a "civilizational contradiction" between the driving force of modern technology and the biblical-Platonic conception of justice as "what we are fitted for." In short form: Heidegger or Plato?

For the last centuries a civilisational contradiction has moved our Western lives. Our greatest intellectual endeavour – the new co-penetration of "logos" and "techne" – affirmed at its heart that in understanding anything we know it as ruled by necessity and chance. This affirmation entailed the elimination of the ancient notion of good from the understanding of anything. At the same time, our day-to-day organization was in the main directed by a conception of justice formulated in relation to the ancient science, in which the notion of good was essential to the understanding of what is. This civilisational contradiction arose from the attempt of the articulate to hold together what was given them in modern science with a content of justice which had been developed out of an older account of what is.[30]

Technology was thus finally defined as a "summoning forth" that necessarily creates a difference between the summoning and what is summoned, between creative willing and disposing over resources. Thus technological humanity is continually provoked to be self-transcending in order not to be reduced to a resource. There is a split within the personality that determines the dynamism of technological man. Grant's political point might be put this way: since we are not all capable of self-transcendence (or to the same degree), the split within the personality will become a division within society into masters and human resources. Thus technology undermines the liberal value of equality; it suggests that each individual may not have a "due." Heidegger's late work designates the contemporary situation as the epoch of technology. In this epoch the world presents itself as resources to be utilized for purposes and goals. As Grant has demonstrated, there seems to be no limit to viewing things and humans as resources to be manipulated. This manipulation is made possible by a view of the world that takes all manifested things as objects standing over against the subject such that they can be disposed of by the will. The mathematical science of nature that originated in the Renaissance is the cardinal example of a mode of knowledge which intrinsically lends itself to technological applications. Heidegger calls this representation of the world "enframing" (*Gestell*) – the interaction of knowing as calculation and doing as technique that underlies technology. While Grant utilizes Heidegger's analysis of technology to characterize the contemporary situation, he cannot accept the destruction of metaphysics that this implies since it would undermine the Platonic conception of justice.

The question of technology is often posed as: How can we bring technology under control? However, "bringing under control" is an attitude inherent in technology. Formulations by which we seek more control over events fail to see that they merely extend technology. Similarly, if we say "technology must serve human purposes," we fail to see the "serving human purposes" is characteristic of technology. We may want to enforce our favoured goals over others, but such enforcement itself derives from a technological view of the human will. Enframing appears to exalt the human subject insofar as it is set over against the world of disposable resources. But humans are themselves brought under control and taken as resources. One of the most frightening aspects of Canadian politics, as of most industrial nations, is that this notion of "human resources" has entered into the political vocabulary without any consideration of its implications. The apparent exaltation of the subject by technology is a danger since it blocks the realization that even in the epoch of technology the world reveals itself. As Heidegger phrases this issue, "Enframing does not simply endanger man in his relationship to himself and to everything that is. As a destining, it banishes man into that kind of revealing which is an ordering. Where this ordering holds sway, it drives out every other possibility of revealing ... Where Enframing holds sway, regulating and securing of the standing-reserve mark all revealing. They no longer even let their own fundamental characteristic appear, namely, this revealing as such."[31] The danger of technology is that it conceals its own essence – the world revealing itself as resource. If such a thought can be put simply, it means this: even when we summon forth resources, the world is being *revealed* to us, though this revealing is obscured by the project of control. Summoning forth is not itself summoned forth by a subject. The epoch of technology brings forth this representational subject-object relationship, but the epoch is inaugurated by a new disclosure of the world.

Heidegger places "summoning forth" as the last stage of the revealing of Being in Western metaphysics. It has shown us a possibility that reveals ourselves and the world, albeit a dangerous possibility that conceals itself behind the apparently omnipotent subject. By viewing technology as the truth of our time, Heidegger directs attention to the first phase of metaphysics, which set the stage for various epochal transformations culminating in technology. Plato is the source of metaphysical thinking in which the earlier notion of truth as unhiddenness is replaced by truth as presence. Truth becomes a correspondence between subject and object that is verified in the moment of presence when they fit together. "In this change of the essence of truth a shift of the place of truth takes place at the same time. As unhiddenness truth is still a basic feature of beings themselves. But as correctness of 'looking' truth becomes the label of the human attitude towards beings."[32] As Grant has noted, the fundamental orientation behind the subject-object representation of technology is a divorce between inner and outer experience such that truth becomes their co-presence in Plato and in the last stage of metaphysics becomes a subject disposing over objects.[33] Thus the epoch of technology was instituted by the Greek concept of reason.

Within metaphysics the principle of identity reigns as the unity of all beings, which becomes evident in philosophical intuition. Through identity, philosophy establishes metaphysical knowledge. Knowledge of Being governs human action and the right places of all things. Metaphysical knowledge depends on identity; however, the principle of identity functions both as primal and ultimate. Indeed, metaphysics *is* the identity of these two. "The problem here is obviously not a union of two independent disciplines of metaphysics, but the unity of *what is* in question, and in thought, in ontologic and theologic: beings as such in the universal and primal *at one with* beings as such in the highest and ultimate. The unity of this One is of such a kind that the ultimate in its own way accounts for the primal, and the primal in its own way accounts for the ultimate."[34] The unity of ultimate and primal, God and origin, defines metaphysics. Truth as presence unifies onto-theology (primal and ultimate) through the intuition of the whole – the *presence* of metaphysical identity. Thus it reconciles the nature of things with God: what *is* with what *ought* to be. Plato's conception of justice depends on this metaphysical foundation. In order for each individual to be given his "due" (his place in the whole), the relations of particular/universal and ultimate/primal must be transparent. This is guaranteed by the "ideas" in Plato that give each thing as it really *is*, while the highest idea unifies the ideas in the Good. As it is put in the *Republic*, "the objects of knowledge not only receive from the presence of the good their being known, but their very existence and essence is derived to them from it, though the good itself is not essence but still transcends essence in dignity and surpassing power."[35]

Even to begin to characterize technology as the last stage of metaphysics requires that we have begun to step beyond metaphysics, that we no longer live within the identity of ultimate and primal. In Nietzsche this stage is called the "death of God" and the experience of the "void." In our post-metaphysical age, characterizing technology as enframing requires rethinking identity as the foundation of metaphysics and escaping subject-object representation. George Grant begins this task by thinking the particular, one's own, as more than an instance of the universal. However, since he clearly sees that Heidegger's account of technology requires abandoning the metaphysical foundation of Plato's concept of justice, he stops here and formulates a *civilizational contradiction* – which is the furthest reach of Grant's thought. Unwilling to let go of justice and metaphysics, he pulls back from the consequences of the modern world. His questioning reaches a precipice. He totters on the edge looking into the abyss that technology opens, clinging to the ancient and now precarious pathway opened by Plato. In thinking technology with Grant we are taken from the appreciation of our own fate in English Canada to the contradiction in Western civilization. With this contradiction, he faces a precipice that allow him to name the vertigo of justice in our world.

If we look at the succession of Grant's major writings, we can see a development from the early *Philosophy in the Mass Age*, in which technology as "industrial society" is perceived as having internal contradictions (based on German Idealism), to *English-Speaking Justice*, where technology as "summoning for disposal" (based on Heidegger) creates a modern society from whole cloth in which even apparent criticisms strengthen the technological orientation. In this development we observe an increasing abandonment of any *modern* moral-political philosophy as adequate to criticizing the instrumentalization of human and non-human nature. The evaluation of Kantian morality has shifted from one possibility for the idea of "limit" in the moral law to being merely an expression of technology. Plato, on the other hand, has emerged from an implicit reference in the notion of "natural joy" to become the ontological foundation for the concept of justice. References to the Christian God and to Christ become increasingly central insofar as the Platonic concept of justice cannot be rationally thought as adequate (in the light of what modernity has taught us about reason) and must be believed on the account of revelation in the Gospels. In Grant's most recent work he still claims that one cannot simply reject modern technology since it has brought forth essential new human possiblities. Nevertheless, neither can technology simply be accepted because of the threat it poses to justice as individuality and equality. As it develops, George Grant's work formulates increasingly carefully, and explores increasingly widely, a civilizational contradiction that forces us to rethink the founding prerequisites of the concept of civilization in the West.

HUMANISM AND THE CIVILIZATIONAL CONTRADICTION

Political philosophy centres on the connection of knowledge and human affairs, which has been variously characterized as theory and practice, contemplation and education, insight and action, and so forth. The interpenetration of knowing and doing in modern technology occludes the ground of political philosophy by reducing politics to administration and knowledge to a pragmatic know-how. In this situation, public reflection requires a thoroughgoing critique of technology that centres not so much on its obvious effects as on the human orientation which is its root. Escaping the technological empire requires, in the first place, understanding how deeply we are each caught up in it. Then it demands a fundamental reorientation by refusing to sacrifice one's own on the altar of system maintenance. George Grant locates the roots of the contemporary technological empire in European civilization. At the same time, he is acutely attuned to the New World situation, which removed philosophical and theological restraints on the doctrine of progress. In thinking technology, we are forced to reflection on the fundamental assumptions of Canada and the New World, and thus the situation of our thought requires rethinking civilization itself. Grant defines this contemporary situation in this way: "Our present is like being lost in the wilderness, when every pine and rock and bay appears to us as both known and unknown, and therefore as uncertain pointers on the way back to human habitation."[36] But in the New World there is a clue to this loss of justice in technological society that comes from Europe – defence of one's own, particularity, in Canada – which is both motive and theme in rethinking civilization. But why, we may ask, must the way to civilization be *back*? Only if civilization is irrevocably European. The primal encounter of ex-Europeans in the New World – scarcity and the will to overcome it – has led to the apogee of technological conquest. From the periphery of Western civilization, a new accounting with fear of the wilderness can lead us to question, *through* our own, the universal claims of civilized life. The New World stirs with a possibility that in the wilderness can be found new sources of civilization. In opening ourselves to experiencing the wild, we also experience civilization as a *project*, not merely as a received possession. The wager of Canadian philosophy is thinking civilization from its periphery.

Questioning in the wilderness led George Grant to formulate the civilizational contradiction that our institutions embody – justice or technology? There is a vacillation in his final philosophical formulation in that he affirms that technology and liberalism are based in the same concept of reason and also that technology undermines liberal ethics. "Our contractual liberalism is not independent of the assumptions of technology in any way that allows it to be the means of transcending those technologies. Our situation is rather that the assumptions underlying contractual liberalism and underlying technology both come from the same matrix of modern thought, from which can arise no reason why the justice of liberty is due to all human beings, irrespective of convenience."[37] This vacillation does not result from a lack of clarity, but is rather a historical dilemma – Grant is expressing the deep historical interpenetration of technology and liberalism such that they have often been taken to be identical alongside the burden of his own work, that they have become divided. Insofar as liberalism means equality, freedom of movement, and the value of each individual person as well as contract and the conquest of nature, it is undermined by contemporary technology. Liberalism is based in freedom, but the historical assumption that this means equality and participation is no longer viable. If individuality and equality are to be saved, it will no longer be by a liberal doctrine, but by a philosophical exploration of Grant's defence of particularity.

Grant argues that the continuing attachment of liberals to the non-contractual aspects of liberal ethics is due to remnants of older religious and philosophical traditions that have been historically synthesized with liberalism. Especially in the New World, Protestantism is paramount among these.[38] However, with modern technology, market liberalism becomes severed from, and comes to dominate, its premodern non-contractual ethic such that the ideas of equality and that each individual has intrinsic worth become increasingly untenable. Consequently, the vacillation in Grant's analysis concerns the extent to which this liberal ethic can be extricated from the assumptions that tie it to modern technology after the historical synthesis of capitalism and Protestantism. In this sense, it is a historical dilemma rather than a mere intellectual uncertainty.

Underlying this historical dilemma of liberalism and technology is the larger issue of the relationship of non-contractual liberal ethics to the older humanist tradition of Western ethics. Only by clarifying this relationship can the ethical question posed by modern technology be adequately posed. In Grant's work the key to the relationship is in his changing evaluation of the Kantian ethics of autonomy. From being central to his early critique of industrialism, it came to be viewed as merely an expression of technological will. The concept of autonomy presupposes a decisive rift between nature and freedom that is coextensive with the technological transformation of nature. Commenting on Kant, Grant writes that "we not only transcend nature in our technological ability to correct its deficiencies, but also in our moral willing which is the statement that they ought to be corrected. The human species depends for its progress not on God or nature but on its own freedom, and the direction of that progress is determined by the fact that we can rationally give ourselves our own moral laws."[39] From this point of view, Kant is the precursor of Nietzsche; the break with an ontological foundation for humanist ethics ultimately ends in the arbitrariness of subjectively posited "values" that are the reflex of the technological domination of nature.[40]

This dilemma is deeply rooted in Grant's analysis: technology is an *expression* of humanism, but it has come to *sever the presupposition* of humanistic ethics. Alternatively put, the origin of modern technology has been located in the connection of power and good, but humanism is taken to consist in the claim that technology is ethically neutral. In this dilemma we do not encounter merely verbal contortions. Rather, it stems from the extreme difficulty of attempting to think the implications of our present age characterized by technology. On the one hand, in automated production, biological experimentation, computerization, and, perhaps most clearly of all, nuclear energy, a threat is widely and correctly perceived to the humanist principles that are the proudest products of Western civilization. Grant's work expresses this contradiction clearly. On the other hand, as has been argued above, the current development of technology requires a thorough rethinking of the presuppositions of humanist ethics, and Grant's work cannot help us here since he simply takes over the Platonic conception of justice as adequate even though he knows that it is not, both because it prefigures modern technology and because it cannot be thought, but only believed, in the technological world. The dilemma described here raises a fundamental issue concerning the interrelationship of technology and ethics: any ethics that begins from a distinction between a means and an end-in-itself will be inadequate to judge technology because technology itself is developed from precisely this distinction. While Grant recognized that liberalism is an expression of technology, he did not press this "backward" to the humanistic foundations on which the fate of present-day liberalism depends as did Heidegger. He wanted to have Heidegger's critique of technology without the critique of Western metaphysics upon which it depends.

Thus one may conclude, following Heidegger, that the metaphysics which projects modern scientific technology co-projects humanistic ethics. The conception of the subject as creative will disposing over a world of objects simultaneously projects an ethic based on this concept of subjectivity. Plato's notion of justice was an early form of this subjectivist ethic and cannot be used to criticize modern technology. As Heidegger has explained, "every humanism is either founded in a metaphysics or converted into the basis for a metaphysics. Every determination of the essence of man that presupposes the interpretation of beings without asking the question of the truth of Being, be it wittingly or not, is metaphysical. Therefore, and precisely in view of the way in which the essence of man is determined, the characteristic of all metaphysics shows itself in the fact that it is 'humanistic.'"[41] The attempt to recover and defend "liberal" ethics in the face of modern technology requires, Grant claims, that it be rooted in a pre-modern humanist ethic. As was demonstrated above, this is the contemporary root of his defence of a Platonic-Christian concept of justice that he called "natural joy" as early as *Philosophy in the Mass Age*. However, while this view of liberalism explains its contradictory role with respect to modern technology, it serves only to deepen, not to remove, the historical dilemma. This dilemma results from standing at the end of metaphysics, the long historical development from which both technology and humanism emerged. Grant's "civilizational contradiction" remains: humanism requires a conception of justice rooted in the whole of what is; technology reveals our unlimited capacity to alter the whole. Against Grant but with Heidegger, I claim here that humanist ethics (as a whole and not only in its modern form) and technology emerge from the same fold, that modern science cannot be opposed to Greek virtue in a manner adequate to criticize technology. Thus Grant's civilizational contradiction can be interpreted as being situated between the inception and end of humanist metaphysics. This "between" is an interpretation of the contradictory nature of the contemporary situation that can be called the twilight of humanism. Humanism is over because of the ubiquity of the framework that disposes over Being as resources. It is continually rediscovered as the creative will of the subject who disposes. Grant does not formulate this twilight; he lives it as an experienced contradiction – which is why its expression in his philosophy takes us to the centre of the contemporary condition. Nevertheless, it is not only that the Heideggerian explication of technology undermines the Platonic concept of justice. It is also the case that Plato's metaphysics of justice opened the way for technology. In this sense, Grant's contradiction does not allow a deep enough formulation of the extent to which they belong to the same civilization. Unlike Strauss, he does not claim that the issue was definitively posed by Plato, yet at the same time he does not sufficiently clarify the "truth" that modern technology has brought forth, which makes such a return impossible.

The epoch of technology reveals all Being as resource for making. Knowledge occurs within a horizon that orients it towards future action. In atomic physics this relation is palpable. Thus the ethical principles that might guide human action are divorced from any ground in the nature of things and come to be seen simply as "values" that are chosen, or willed, by individuals. Technology is the age of nihilism. George Grant turned to Heidegger to illuminate the epoch of technology while he simultaneously affirmed the Platonic concept of justice as eternally true, even though he was well aware that the Heideggerian destruction of metaphysics removes the ground from the *Republic*. Unwilling to let go of either position, he pointed to a civilizational contradiction that underlies the contemporary situation –

we are beyond metaphysics but cannot do without it. Grant's philosophy illuminates, but does not remove, this contradiction. By formulating civilization's contradiction in thought, he was forced to find a basis for belief in justice outside of philosophy, which we might provisionally define as "unaided reason." At crucial moments, upon which turn the very possibility of philosophy, Grant appeals to the Christian Gospels – though the unity of technology and justice cannot be *thought*, it can be *believed*. The ontological argument is a matter of faith; here can be glimpsed the unity of Being and Good. Faith allows Grant's philosophy to abide the contradiction that his thought diagnoses. But if one is not held by faith – even more, if one takes seriously the origin of modern technology in Christianity – one cannot be satisfied with a thought that terminates in contradiction.

FROM HUMANISM TO ECOLOGICAL ETHICS

In George Grant's earlier work he based his ethics on the modern attempt by German Idealism to reconcile human freedom with the Good. In the later work he shifted to a Platonic conception of justice that rejected freedom as the origin of technology and asserted the supremacy of the Good. It is as if he travelled the path of Western philosophy in reverse, seeking the origin and justification of an ethics that could criticize modern technology adequately. Finally, he remained held by Plato, but unable to give a philosophical defence for his belief or to define the truth brought forth by technology. This truth, which becomes thinkable with the full unfolding of the epoch of technology, clarifies a common thread between modern and ancient ethics that allows them to be defined together: the error of a humanist definition of ethics as interhuman action separate from technology. The conception of technology as simply a "means" to "ends" defined by humans implies that the human realm of ethical ends is non-technological. This is humanism. The separation itself derives from the same root that allows the emergence of technology. Thus the separation of technology from ethics that characterizes technology is inadequate to comprehend the threat that it poses in our time. Humanist ethics is an expression of technology and cannot ground its critique. An ethics that responds adequately to the epoch of technology would thus need to address the interpenetration of technology and ethics and, even more fundamentally, the separation of the creatively willing subject that summons forth the world as resources.

Grant's thought can be called "humanist" insofar as it is circumscribed by the attempt to find an ethics outside technology that might limit technological power. The civilizational contradiction that he comes to define through this attempt is by no means merely eccentric, but is emblematic of the crisis of humanist-technological civilization itself in the epoch of its planetary dominance. We have seen in the previous chapter that a similar contradiction animates the thought of Harold Innis insofar as he attempted to recover the unity of the human body as the ground of communication precisely at the moment that its disappearance seemed inevitable. The contradiction in Innis's analysis of orality matches Grant's such that it is possible to regard this basic figure of thought as characteristic of English Canadian social and political thought in its meditation on the meaning of civilization from the periphery.

English Canadian social and political thought has centred on the problems engendered by modern industrial-technological society from the peripheral standpoint of a society whose own industrialization has been arrested, dependent, and incomplete. Thus its critique of industrial-technological society has not been internal, has not focused on specific problems in order to encourage future progress, but has pressed towards a global critique of the form of society as a whole. In this way it has tended to be articulated through a close relationship between a *critical component* oriented to the diagnosis of contemporary society and a component of *moral reason* oriented to the justification of the critical standpoint.[42] Innis defined this form of society as bureaucratic, based on writing, and space-dominating and thus sought to recover locality through the dimension of time. Grant defined the form of society as the universality and homogeneity attendant upon technology and thus endeavoured to recover one's own particularity through the Platonic concept of justice. In both thinkers there is a characteristic turning away from the universal orientation of contemporary civilization – by defining it in terms that reveal its actually deficient universality – back towards the local and particular, which is the provenance of every movement outward to universality. It is a regressive form of thought towards what is prior in the logical sense. It devolves inward rather than moving outward. It is in search of its own foundation rather than moving confidently towards explaining the world. English Canadian thought has centred on questioning *what it means to belong here*. This local and experiential emphasis is the basis for my own attempt in this book to bring this tradition together with phenomenological philosophy. It is not an arbitrary juxtaposition, but is based in the common attempt to recover what is nearest in the here-now, what is normally passed over in the rush to generalize, what are the prior experiential preconditions for human universality.

But I have criticized both Innis and Grant. Innis, it was suggested, overlooked the mathematization of time as well as space and therefore thought that he could criticize industrial-bureaucratic society by counterposing time to space. This approach had the positive aspect of focusing attention on space, an emphasis which derives from the dependency of a (post-)colonial society, but which contains the danger of reducing the "spatiality" of embodied localities to impersonal, mathematized space. Innis's insight can be better preserved through the distinction of place from space that contemporary ecological thinkers have proposed. Place refers to the qualitative, embodied experience filled with meaningful things, whereas space denotes the empty, quantitative, and homogeneous space criticized by Innis.[43] This differentiation would have the additional advantage of recalling that time can also be reduced to quantitative, empty time as opposed to the full, meaningful temporality of evolving cultural traditions.

Grant, I have suggested above, brings this civilizational contradiction to clarity, though he maintains it and is prevented from seeking a way out of or beyond it by ceding the ethical ground of his critique to religious belief rather than philosophy. The diagnosis of technology has been traced back to the divorce of inner from outer experience that separates ethics from Being and locates it in "values" chosen by humans. The origin of the contemporary problem of technology is in the assertion of human will over against natural Being, which is deep-rooted in Western culture and comes to its clearest expression in Nietzsche.[44] Thus, it is implied, only an ontology of participation, in which the human world is limited and defined by its place within what is as a Whole, could root values in Being and fundamentally dislodge nihilism.[45] Such an imbrication of humanity and Being would require a rethinking of Western civilization from the viewpoint not only of philosophy – as Grant, following Heidegger, accepts – but also of religion. Both Greek and Hebrew sources of Western civilization are characterized by the separation of human thought from the Order of Being, by the transcendence of God over the world. As H. and H.A. Frankfort have explained in *Before Philosophy,* "with infinite *moral* courage the Hebrews worshipped an absolute God and accepted as the correlate of their faith the sacrifice of an harmonious existence. In transcending the Near Eastern myths of an immanent godhead, they created ... the new myth of the will of God. It remained for the Greeks, with their particular *intellectual* courage, to discover a form of speculative thought in which myth was entirely overcome."[46]

Overcoming technology thus implies an ontology of participation and an immanent concept of the sacred. For this reason Lynn White Jr suggested in his classic essay "The Historical Roots of Our Ecologic Crisis" that "by destroying pagan animism, Christianity made it possible to exploit nature in a mood of indifference to the feelings of natural objects" and that "modern technology is at least partly to be explained as an Occidental, voluntarist realization of the Christian dogma of man's transcendence of, and rightful mastery over, nature."[47] Grant was well aware of the historical role of Western Christianity in the development of modern science and the domination of nature by technology, and he consequently sought a conception of Christianity removed from the occidental glorification of the will.[48] The point here is that the civilizational contradiction of which he speaks encompasses religion as well as philosophy. Furthermore, moving beyond this contradiction implies an ontology of participation and an immanent concept of the sacred.[49] These same issues are raised by the ecological problems of our time that are rooted in modern technology. For this reason, Grant's concern with the social consequences of technology can be expanded to include also the natural and ecological consequences.

Innis and Grant can be called humanists insofar as they both sought the basis of their critique of industrial-technological society in a conception of moral reason that was outside, and impervious to, the phenomenon they criticized. Insofar as they both identified the object of their critique – industrial-technological society – with modern society as such, their stance was anti-modernist and, it may even be said, incorporated an archaic dimension. Thus their position might be more completely characterized as involving a polarity between humanism and archaism.[50] This position makes it impossible to pose the issue of what technology or mode of communication might be used by a new form of society promoted by their critique. An ethical society, following Grant, is implied to be entirely non-technological, even though this is impossible for a human society. A local, time-bound, oral society, following Innis, is assumed to be entirely non-spatial, which is similarly impossible. Actually, this point can be phrased more precisely: Innis and Grant do not acknowledge these implications only because they do not consider that industrial-technological society can ever really be surpassed. This position is the basis for what I term in chapter 7 their "strategy of containment" of industrial society. Thus their own perspective is recognized to be partial, even polemical, in the sense that it is incapable of articulating the concepts needed for a practical overcoming of the criticized society. It is a form of criticism that accepts the inevitability of the form of society that it criticizes. The critical standpoint is articulated through concepts that are untenable to sustain any alternative social form. In this sense the moral reason proposed by English Canadian social and political thought has itself been dependent. It has not been capable of imagining an alternative, self-sustaining form of society.

The rethinking of civilization that characterizes English Canadian social and political thought can thus be pressed further than it has been taken in the work of Harold Innis and George Grant. The critiques of their work that I have elaborated suggest a philosophy in which an orientation to place and to local cultural traditions is the basis for a conception of moral reason which does not separate inner from outer experience and which thus elaborates an immanent concept of the sacred through the participation of human life in Being. This philosophical teleology is indeed anti-modern and, at least in part, archaic. It does not necessarily imply, however, a root-and-branch rejection of the differentiating and democratic components of modernity as does Heidegger's philosophy, which contains a romanticization of pre-modern life that implies a regression.[51] The work of Innis and Grant is characterized by a *polarity* in which one term is anti-modern and archaic. The other pole is a humanist ethics. I am suggesting that this polarity be thought through in the direction of a post-industrial ecological ethics based on an ontology of participation – a tall order, one which this book cannot fulfil in its entirety. I have chosen the themes of multiculturalism and ecology to follow up in later chapters of the book because they respond to precisely the contemporary issues in English Canadian society that are most pertinent to this philosophical orientation. I argue that this philosophy represents the teleology of English Canadian thought, and while I attempt to follow it up in some important aspects, I am under no illusion that this current attempt fulfils the teleology that it describes.

CHAPTER FIVE

Maintaining the Border

Philosophy, like any other intellectual discipline, can be converted into a tradition that becomes a received acquisition, but it does not begin as received tradition nor as a specific discipline among others. The beginning of philosophy is in a decisive act whereby the situation of the thinker is interrogated as a way of understanding the human condition. While a received tradition incorporates this situation as a centre that is presupposed within it – a centre that defines both the content and the form of inquiry – the decisive act that initiates radical inquiry can count on no precedent. One cannot suppose that the exigencies of one's own situation have already been brought into the tradition of thought, nor that the received divisions and boundaries of thought are adequate to one's task. In this way, the attempt to philosophize from a marginal situation necessarily encounters the question of the beginning of philosophy itself. While one cannot ignore tradition, neither can one rely upon it. One is forced to risk a decisive act that institutes, brings into being, a philosophy. A tradition is founded on this act, not the reverse, and in this sense philosophy belongs in the wilderness.

A MARGINAL PHILOSOPHY?

Canadian identity has been a matter for self-preservation and its definition a problem for self-reflection since Confederation. Bringing this identity to philosophical articulation requires that "one's own," as Grant called it, be regarded as sufficiently significant to motivate and sustain philosophical inquiry. It requires a wager that one's experience is not really marginal to understanding the human condition, or at least need not be so. In the Latin American context this process of the beginning of philosophy has been described by Arturo Andres Roig in a manner similar to Grant's emphasis on "our own": "it is necessary to place ourselves for *ourselves* as valuable."[1] This decision and act is the prior condition for the development of an English Canadian philosophy. It cannot be justified externally, but only by its fruit, and it is instituted by the decisive act that forms a mode of questioning and situates it within a social and historical horizon.

One cannot be insistent about the existence of Canada as an independent nation without giving some content to the distinctiveness of Canadian identity. Doing so immediately leads into a paradox that must be dissolved before the question of identity can be adequately posed. If one is looking for something to preserve and develop, then one must stress one's uniqueness. It would seem that this distinctiveness must be unique in the sense of not occurring anywhere else or being important to the formation of the identity of any other people. Distinctiveness seems to require that one's own be located only in elements that are not shared with any other humans. The search for self-identity thus seems to be shunted towards uniqueness, non-general elements, parochiality – which consequently leaves the search open to the often-encountered criticism that it deals only with what is non-essential and of merely local interest. The Mexican philosopher Leopoldo Zea explained the same issue in this way: "problems like the ones Latin American philosophy raises about its identity seem to be only parochial, that is regional, and because of that limited to a relative point of view proper to a concrete man, and thus, alien to what is truly universal."[2] But, of course, this explanation runs against the basic motive that leads one to the necessity to define a marginal identity in the first place: one feels that one's English Canadian-ness, or Latin American-ness, is an essential part of what it means to be human. One seems to be faced with a choice between defending one's own in a merely parochial fashion and ceasing to be concerned with it in the name of the universal.

If one is caught in this paradox, it may be better to take an interest in one's own merely because it is one's own, apart from any more universal significance it might have. Leslie Armour has elaborated a defence of the study of Canadian philosophers *even if they are bad philosophers* because "they cast a good deal of light on our plight and on our adventures."[3] This seems to be also the approach of Northrop Frye insofar as he suggested that Canadian literature tended to take the form of a mere "experiential catalogue," as if this were adequate to constitute a work of art or a cultural tradition. He claimed, by contrast, that it is only when experiential contents are formed into a universal mythic pattern that a contribution of more than local interest is attained – when experience becomes not only content but form.

For Frye this is because Canadians are latecomers to Western civilization and the universal mythic form, at least for the West, is the Bible.[4] Nonetheless, he devoted considerable time to the study of Canadian literature, as has Armour to Canadian philosophy, even though it was based upon this parochial justification. Such a parochial interest in one's own is valid, even healthy, but it is not sufficient for any contribution of note to literature or philosophy, which requires that experience become more than parochial by straining towards the universal and that content overcome itself towards the shaping of mythic form. The task, then, as stated for painting by Lawren Harris and carried out in the work of the Group of Seven, is "to make it possible for [artists] to see and paint the Canadian scene in its own terms and in their own way."[5]

Such are the pervasive and profound effects of dependency that we seem to be forced to choose between taking an interest in ourselves and in human universality.[6] Dissolving the paradox between local parochiality and foreign universality demands another approach to the question of distinctiveness. Any defence of distinctiveness requires a division between inside and outside. The most straightforward, but naive, way to approach the division is to suppose that what is inside is not outside and what is outside is not inside. Thus the paradox emerges: if something is unique to Canada, then it must exist nowhere else on the planet; if something is not unique, then its existence in Canada seems to be of no importance for the national identity. Obviously, this approach will marginalize any definition of Canadian identity to parochialism. The paradox can be dissolved, however, if we pose the issue of inside versus outside in another way, if what is inside is separated from the outside, not by a unique content, but by a *distinctive relation between contents*. Similarly, the outside is different from the inside because its contents are related such as to constitute, as a whole, a different arrangement or pattern. While some elements may be different on either side of the division, it is not these elements that define the difference between inside and outside. It is defined through pattern rather than content.

National identity thus does not *require* original contents, though there may well be some. It is significant that the theme of "limited identities" as constitutive of Canadian history, first proposed by J.M.S. Careless, suggested that such limited contents achieve a certain unity by "the articulation of regional patterns in one transcontinental state." Such unity was distinguished from the homogenizing unity that he called "unification or consolidation," but it does not imply the decomposition of the nation into a mere sum of parts.[7] National identity requires an investigation into the patterning of contents as they are arranged into a mythic form that implies neither a homogeneity of the contents themselves nor an absence of a certain kind of unity. In nations where this pattern has not become pervasive and solidified into an independent national tradition, there is dependency, and thus the question of national identity is posed as a social and political issue. The role of intellectuals at this point is to give form, and therefore universality, to the experiential content of the national-popular. When this process remains incomplete, we may speak of forming and universalizing as a project of leadership in articulating a world-view. While we may criticize the false forms and universals that marginalize our experience, we do not yet have a new universal to confront them with. Our procedure must then be immanent critique, and our theory is still emergent.

In place of the paradox between local parochiality and foreign universality, we may then discover an interest in the distinctiveness of our arrangement of contents. Even when something is imported, it takes on a different use, is applied to different issues, and is crafted in a different manner. For the question of national identity this difference becomes more interesting than origin. As Zea has said, "Even in imitation, there was creation and re-creation. The philosophizing adopted took thus another sense which, compared to the models, resulted in 'bad copies of the originals' but were original with respect to the problems they tried to solve."[8] This notion of the originality of a marginal and dependent formation expressed by Zea parallels Innis's idea that the innovations in civilization tend to come from the periphery. He referred to the "significance of the geographic factor in language – technology tends to have impact first in frontier areas and to push inward to break up conservative factors."[9] The new context of application does not simply repeat the old and may even be the condition for innovation within the old. Formulated universally, undoing dependency requires shifting significance from origin to the new context of application, from provenance to destination.[10] Even many of those whose rationale for their interest in their own did not surpass parochialism focused on the new context of application sufficently for their practice of interpretation to surpass it – certainly such was the case with Northrop Frye and Leslie Armour – even though the next step towards the articulation of universality and mythic form was not made.

It is legitimate for us, and for any people, to be interested in ourselves purely and simply because we are ourselves. But this legitimate self-interest threatens to become an unhealthy and resentful narcissism if its justification is confined to parochiality. Thus, while a straightforward and, in the literal sense, naive interest in oneself may well be praiseworthy and is certainly unobjectionable, the *intellectual justification* of such interest must surpass self-absorption. It must address the universalizing dimension that is inherent in the intellectual enterprise as such. As Leopoldo Zea put it in the context of the development of philosophy in Mexico, "concern for the concrete does not lead toward provincialism. To the contrary, the concrete is considered as an ineluctable point of departure for passing to the universal."[11] Clearly, the project of questioning English Canadian identity cannot be to defend one's own at the cost of situating all human universality elsewhere. Any defence of our own must therefore include at least a suggestion that it is not merely our own in an exclusive sense. George Grant defined the issue of a particularity that does not remain mired in mere particularism, or parochiality, in this way: "In human life there must always be place for love of the good and love of one's own. Love of the good is man's highest end, but it is of the nature of things that we come to know and to love what is good by first meeting it in that which is our own – this particular body, this family, these friends, this woman, this part of the world, this set of traditions, this country, this civilization. At the simplest level of one's own body, it is clear that one has to love it yet pass beyond concentration on it."[12] But this "passing beyond" can be thought of in two ways: either within the terms of the paradox explained above, which implies that the particular must be left behind and one must cease to be concerned with one's own; or through a dissolving of the paradox, in a new apprehension of the intrinsic worth in particularity, which must not be sacrificed in passing beyond to universality. This second possibility directs us to the rethinking of the relations between particular and universal in a post-colonial context, which Grant's work initiated and which carries forward philosophically Harold Innis's focus on the social dimensions of dependency. Such rethinking goes beyond, without revoking, the defence of one's own.

Therefore artistic and scholarly defences of an interest in what is one's own demand a universalizing philosophical justification that is rooted in a meditation on the human condition as such. This demand for philosophical justification necessitates a critique of attempts to define the lineages of human universality from an exclusive location – a critique of Eurocentrism that, in the end, implies the critique of any *centrism* which attempts to monopolize the principles through which a discourse of human universality might be articulated. Eurocentrism does not consist simply in being concerned with something European. A concern with any particular contents, at least on the face of it, is legitimate. The issue is with regard to the principles, or mythic form, that are used to understand any specific content. Thus the classic accounts of European industrialization in Marx or Weber, for example, do not raise the question of Eurocentrism. However, when this account is considered "standard" or "normal" and is thus used to discuss other experiences of industrialization in America, Africa, or Asia as "arrested," "abnormal," or "incomplete," then a Eurocentric standard of measure is being invoked. A "centrism" pertains to the standards of measure – the form or explanatory model – not the subject, or content, being explained. In this sense Gianni Vattimo has asserted that "the idea of a world history is revealed as what it has in fact always been, namely a reduction of the train of human events from a single perspective which is in each case a function of domination, whether class-based or colonial, etc."[13] Zea argues that for this reason the discovery of America created a "restlessness for the philosophers of history in Europe who were looking for an interpretation of universal history that would have its centre in Europe. Here began that which today we call Eurocentrism."[14]

A centrism consists in the subsumption of diverse experiences and contents under an explanatory scheme that is *presupposed as universal although it incorporates elements that arose in a particular history.* A return to concrete and diverse experiences thus does not negate universality, but opens the possibility that a genuine universality might emerge through the displacement of centrisms. Such a new and genuine universality cannot be attained in traditional fashion by ignoring one's location – which leads precisely to the false postulation of one's standpoint as straightforwardly universal that underlies a centrism – but only by embracing one's own and opening it to thought. All thought is derived from and articulates a provenance. As Andres Roig has phrased it, "the 'placing ourselves to ourselves as valuable' is completed from a determinate horizon of comprehension, certainly conditioned socially and epochally. The 'we' has in this way its history and meaning."[15] This epochal conditioning must be itself interrogated by the thought that articulates it. Thus, while philosophy certainly articulates a social and epochal location, it is not simply confined to this location (which would reduce philosophy to being merely an ideology), but reflexively turns to clarify its own instituting decisive act, which originally opened the location to articulation. Reflexively, philosophy opens its own location towards its universal meaning. It must always heave close to its own particularity, but becomes philosophy precisely to the extent that it universalizes. The concept of philosophy that animates this project must obviously be distinguished from that of an academic specialty addressing issues defined within professional journals and associations, which is predominant in the university nowadays. It stems, unlike academic specialities, from a decisive act. Philosophy is rather concerned to articulate the issues inherent in the social history and identity of a people and to press questioning about these issues, which is always already abroad in the society, to the deepest level possible where it addresses the relation of the destiny of this people to the human condition as such. Philosophy begins in the decisive act to take seriously one's own as a locus of questioning about human universality, not in the history of previous philosophers.

I will suggest below that English Canadian identity has been predicated upon a need to maintain the border between one's own and the Other. Its most distinctive philosophical theme is thus the explication of this notion of the *border*. Previously, English Canadian thought has turned inward towards the "own." I argue below that it also implies a turn towards the perception of the Other as the ground of ethics. This capitalized Other refers, by philosophical convention, to an Other that cannot be encompassed within the framework of the self.[16] It is not an "alter ego," another self, but an Other to the self – which therefore poses a radical question for the constitution of the self and its ethical responsibility. A border, after all, cannot be one without separating and yet relating two distinct sides. In the epoch of permeable Fordism between 1946 and 1989 English Canadian philosophy was turned "inward" towards its national identity. Today, in the era of globalization and new social movements, it needs to turn "outward" towards an ethical responsibility to the Other that similarly sustains the border. Whereas it was concerned to preserve its own, it must now prepare for its own abjection. This explains the continuity with the present project, allied to the new social movements, with the surpassed project of left-nationalism. They meet at the border.

ENGLISH CANADIAN IDENTITY

Before proceeding to my elaboration of the philosophical theme of the border, which I argue is the core of the issue of English Canadian identity, in accordance with the procedure of immanent critique I must devote some discussion to previous attempts to define this identity. Again, a preliminary problem blocks our way. The question of English Canadian identity has rarely been posed directly. It represents rather a space that has tended to be evacuated either "upward" to refer to Canada or "downward" to refer to the internal differences within English Canada. In fact, the works of Innis and Grant referred to Canada and not specifically to English Canada. Why engage in this apparent restriction of interest to a part of the country?

From the point of view of political history, the main reason for confining a current interest in national identity to English Canada is the self-assertion of the First Nations and Quebec during recent years. Both of these groups have raised issues about their inclusion in Canada and have put forward the possibility of secession, to the point where it is not clear whether Canada, at least as presently constituted, can incorporate the sense of belonging that they experience. Both groups have asserted the right, even if not the intention, to separate. They experience a conflict between a sense of belonging to their own nations and one of belonging to Canada. A choice may be necessary, and the latter mode may turn out to be weaker. My point is neither to predict the future nor to suggest what other groups should do. It is rather to state a contemporary fact about nation(s) in Canada: the nation-state can no longer be assumed to be the main locus of nationality as it was in the era of permeable Fordism. Unless one wishes, as I certainly do not, to suggest that such groups should be held in Canada by coercion (either overt or covert), it is necessary to accept that what the country will be in the future is open to discussion and negotiation between the relevant groups. There are at least three such groups: First Nations, Quebec, and English Canada. The last, however, has not referred to itself as a nation. In calling itself as Canada, it has elided the key question of its relation to the others and especially the history of violence whereby the Canadian state, as all other states, was constructed (see appendix 2). A genuine debate about the future of the Canadian nation-state cannot occur if one group claims to monopolize the term "Canada" without discussion. For this reason, we must recognize our distinctiveness as English Canadians – that is, those Canadians who inhabit the part of the country where English is the ordinary language of public interaction.

Representatives of these other groups have often needed to characterize us in order to speak about their relation to us. Chief George Watts has pointed to the belief "that somehow acquiring wealth and pushing down on other people to acquire that wealth is all right because you have the chance of being the wealthiest."[17] Daniel Latouche has claimed that the "1982 Constitution was not a conspiracy but an act of state-making and nation-building" for English Canada.[18] Pierre Fournier has observed that in English Canada, "There is an implicit rejection of the possibility that reconciling multiple identities can be a factor for cohesion rather than division."[19] It is common to react to such definitions by outright rejection, claiming, "I'm not like that!" But this is a matter of collective "national" identity, which cannot be reduced to personal identity. All of these comments contain some truth, but they are built on an assessment of the identity of

English Canada as seen from outside. This fact is clear, for example, when Latouche and Dufour refer to multiculturalism in English Canada as "radical chic" and a "cosmetic facade."[20] It is true enough that the issue of multiculturalism has often been used in English Canada to deny the difference of the claims of Quebec, as if there could not be a French-speaking multiculturalism. But these comments take that aspect of the identity of English Canada that is most relevant to the concerns of Quebec and use it to characterize the whole. I think that there is more to it than that, but if we are dissatisfied with these assessments, we have to begin to assert our own. The context of the contemporary assertion of other national identities within Canada is thus one main reason for confining one's definition of identity to English Canada. If we are to negotiate with these groups over the future of the country, we must inquire into who we are as a part of this negotiation and leave the question of what we share and might become a common identity pending until the negotiation itself.

There is another side to the issue as well. The existence of English Canada has been predicated on distinguishing ourselves from Americans. To the extent that we have done so directly through "Canada," it has been, in part, in bad faith because the inclusion of Quebec within the federal state guaranteed a difference from the United States that was none of our making. Quebec writers have often taunted us about this fact, and they have a point.[21] However, it is also because the federal state has been the locus of public enterprise and government interventions for social protection from the effects of the capitalist economy, which have become a source of identification for English Canadians. Free trade and identification with Ottawa have been polar opposites in English Canada. It is ironic that our self-assertion in the face of the threat of incorporation into the United States has tied us to a federal government that does not express our national identity but also incorporates other elements. It is thus understandable that these other elements, such as Quebec, can become symbolic of this identification through a process of displacement. However, such an unselfconscious identification will no longer do. Without some clarity as to why and where we are recognizing our national identity, its preservation through transformation is unlikely.

In sum, for reasons of both political history and contemporary self-expression, it is necessary to focus on English Canada as the relevant locus of identification. Doing so requires a distinction of nation from state that is difficult (though not impossible) for the English-speaking political tradition and the recognition of the possibility, at least in theory, of a multinational state. This would have the consequence that it would thereafter be much easier to regard the First Nations and

Quebec as nations, such that a dialogue about the prospects for a multinational state of Canada might begin. Thus I agree with Philip Resnick's statement that "we need to distinguish nationality from citizenship and our identity as English-speaking Canadians from our membership in a larger political framework that includes Québécois and aboriginal peoples."[22] We must come at last to address the question of the social identity of English Canada. In what follows, I will not review these definitions in a sequential and comprehensive manner, but in a thematic way that is more useful for the critical and philosophical orientation of this work. In this sense, there are two main abiding themes throughout the history of definitions of English Canada: political continuity articulated through the public intervention of the federal state and a sense of break, of difference, elucidated through relationship to the land, nature, environment.

These two themes are the temporal and spatial dimensions of English Canadian identity. Unlike most New World nations, English Canada has never had a revolution, which is a main reason why it has a weak national mythology. The temporal dimension of the nation suggests continuity and gradual pragmatic evolution, unlike the focus on temporal break and new foundation in the republican tradition, for example. Thus it has tended to articulate its difference from Europe through a relation to the geography of the new land. In revolutionary traditions, time suggests discontinuity and thus difference from Europe. Space, geography, land, may then be perceived in a European way as a storehouse of resources without this continuity becoming threatening to identity. In the English Canadian case, by way of contrast, geography becomes important for identity where history has failed to provide it.

Let me summarize, first, the theme of the land. Before Confederation, Canada First nationalism emphasized the characteristics of Canada as a northern nation and derived the individualistic, hardworking, and freedom-loving virtues of northern peoples from their relation to a harsh environment. This crude environmental determinism led to a racist downgrading of other peoples.[23] The theme of the environment has persisted since, though not always in a determinist fashion. Cole Harris has documented the continuing appeal of the demanding northern environment as a source of identification, in opposition to the American myth of nature as a garden, and has argued for the notion of wilderness preservation as an environmental ethic that can be derived from this history.[24] Margaret Atwood has suggested the theme of survival against "menace, not from an enemy set over against you but from everything surrounding you" as the unifying national symbol.[25] Northrop Frye has claimed that the abiding theme in English Canadian literature is not the establishment of identity as such but the question "Where is here?" which Robert Kroetsch sees as leading to a predominance of characters who have no name.[26] And in a recent shift of attention, Melville Watkins and Arthur Kroker have claimed that technology, as the means of ensuring survival by subduing the environment, is the key to English Canada and its intellectual tradition.[27] The notion of the land and its dangers, its subjugation, and the anonymity of humans against the presentness of place runs throughout the history and literature of English Canada. On the whole, it is not so much a geographical determinism as a continuing meditation on place, experienced often as a dangerous, identity-undermining threat that requires the winning of an always tentative security through the imposition of human will in technology. As Grant argued, this encounter with an environment experienced as hostile was the foundation for the Protestant belief that taming nature was not only a necessity but a moral task.[28]

The environmental theme is closely related to the focus on political continuity, government intervention, and the federal state. Harold Innis has documented the relation between staple extraction and the construction of a transportation infrastructure by government enterprise.[29] George Grant has made the same point through the connection between United Empire Loyalism and the conservative collective tradition of the federal state.[30] The unity of the tradition of social and political thought in English Canada emerges from the linking of these two themes through an extractive economic relation to the environment and a political relation to the activist federal state.

The non-revolutionary and collectivist orientation of English Canadian identity has been a source of continued reflection and debate. Beginning in Loyalism, this tradition gained considerable influence through the Protestant churches in the nineteenth century. It was philosophically represented by John Watson, whose interpretation of German Idealism was the basis for an influential conception of social justice overriding individual rights and self-interested economic activity.[31] The main reason why George Grant's Lament for a Nation became a constant reference point in later discussions was his argument that the conservative continuation of the Loyalist tradition had come upon its historical limit and that consequently, "After 1940, nationalism had to go hand in hand with some measure of socialism."[32] In Grant's view, such a socialist alternative was impossible and, because of its sharing of progressivist, pro-technology assumptions with liberalism, undesirable.[33] Many later commentators would take issue with him on this point. As I argued in chapter 2, Grant's position was an essential foundation for the discourse of left-nationalism that came later. Thus the stage was set for the argument that the collectivism of Canadian socialism was in historical continuity with Loyalism because of their combined opposition to the individualism, progressivism, and revolutionism of American liberalism. Gad Horowitz argued in this manner that "the tory and socialist minds have *some* crucial assumptions, orientations, and values in common, so that *from a certain angle* they may appear not as enemies but as two different expressions of the same basic ideological outlook."[34] It is not too much to say that the social identity of English Canada, at least since the Diefenbaker defeat described by George Grant, has revolved around the definition of this "certain angle."

The notion of English Canada as undergoing a transition between a Tory past and a socialist future was elaborated in the discourse of left-nationalism. Herschel Hardin referred to the "public enterprise culture" based on "a fundamental principle, of the unAmerican transactional mode of redistribution, as opposed to the American transactional mode of the market exchange."[35] English Canada was, on this analysis, already incipiently anti-capitalist and needed to be pushed further in the same direction to become socialist. Robin Mathews criticized this version as telling only half the story. He claimed that Hardin, because of the inaction of Liberals and Conservatives, had chosen "to simplify the Canadian dialectic until the individualistic, free enterprise side was merely an aberration in Canada, a fantasy that only applied because of our colonial-minded readiness to accept outside descriptions of our country that did not in reality obtain."[36] In contrast, Mathews's version was a more realistic and descriptive story of an English Canada whose history and politics was defined through a dialectic between collectivist, public-enterprise culture and an individualist, free-enterprise culture shared with the United States. The individualist strain is thus not only external, but has its representatives within English Canada. Philip Resnick criticized Hardin in a different manner, saying that he "elevates the crown corporation tradition into a mythology," noting that such state enterprise is "characteristic of all capitalist societies *except* the United States," and suggesting that only those working for the state could be susceptible to such nonsense.[37]

What Resnick fails to understand in this critique is the consequence of English Canada's traditional preoccupation with distinguishing itself from the United States. That country is not just any axis of comparison in English Canada; it is the axis that has been historically essential to our claims of distinctiveness. In this context, a feature of English Canadian society that it shares with many other societies around the world could still become a pole of identification. And, perhaps even more odd, English Canadian society could construct its identity through a government, public-enterprise culture *in opposition to* an individualist culture that it stigmatized as "American" even while, as Mathews showed, that culture also had solid roots in English Canada. As I have argued, it is not parochial distinctiveness that is important here, but a distinctive *pattern* of contents. In the main context of English Canadian identity, which is that of making a distinction from the U.S., a content widely shared with other countries can nevertheless be a synechdochic condensation of English Canadian identity. This fact might be even clearer nowadays in a period of cutbacks of federal and provincial social services. Opposition to such cutbacks comes, of course, from self-interest – as well it might – but it also comes from a sense that what is distinctive about our society is being undermined, that our claim to being a kinder, more inclusive society than the United States is diminishing. From the perspective outlined in this book, it is a grave error to dismiss such historically based sources of identification on merely empirical grounds of the comparison of isolated contents. Identification neither covers the whole of the contents of national experience, nor evaluates them as equally important, and may even stigmatize as "external" that which also exists inside. Identification with a nation – or any other social identity, for that matter – is an *active process* of selection of salient contents and their articulation by an actor. To reject the importance of national identification with some of the "socialist" contents, such as medicare, brought about by the welfare state is not only poor politics in a pragmatic sense, but it fails to understand that an alternative formation of the national-popular must build upon such identifications rooted in prior acts of the collective will. From this point of view, Mathews's argument can be made even more strongly than he made it. If national identity consists in a dialectic between collectivist and individualist notions, the widespread desire not to become American is a domestic force against English Canadian liberal individualism also (at least in some situations). The fact that one does not *identify* equally with all aspects of one's social condition is politically important. The selected features of one's social condition that become symbolic of identity have a strength far beyond their empirical significance in the formation of a historic bloc.

The extent of identification with public-enterprise culture among left-nationalists was so strong that, ironically, it was George Grant who reminded them that it is necessary to distinguish "American liberal ideology from what is true about political liberty for all sane people."[38] Another reminder is needed as a corrective to Mathews and to left-nationalism in general. Free-enterprise liberalism is not just one strain among others in English Canada. It is the dominating hegemonic framework within which other world-views have operated. Public-enterprise culture is a mitigating reaction to the capitalist world-view, not a tendency of equal strength. However, it is a mitigating formation that has become an important point of identification for English Canadians – one whose day is not yet done, I would bet. In recent years, free-enterprise liberalism has gained increasing strength as against collectivism. The 1982 constitution, the Free Trade Agreement, and the North American Free Trade Agreement have combined to push English Canada increasingly towards the "American" pole of its identity. Some Quebec writers, such as Dufour and Latouche, define us through this pole alone when they regard the 1982 constitution as defining us or accuse us of an irrational fear of becoming Americans.[39] Such fear certainly exists, but its existence should not impede recognition that it is based in the desire to defend a tradition of collective rights, a tradition that, of course, has always been more sympathetic to the collective rights of Quebec than free-enterprise liberalism. It is this factor that is at issue in Americanization, as Pierre Fournier has appreciated.[40]

There is no doubt that the interpretation of English Canada through a tradition of collective rights is in serious disarray in the public realm today. The context of this tradition as a mitigating formation within a capitalist world-view has increasingly rendered it marginal. While the present work retains a connection to this tradition and consequently uses it as a point of departure, it is more fundamentally an immanent critique oriented to formulating an emergent social and political philosophy for English Canada. This standpoint is necessary because the changing context has marginalized the national identification that defined this tradition and rendered it unlikely to be realized in its present form. Moreover, new social issues have come to light in the new social movements that also are based on claims for collective rights. My goal here is not to address each of these issues and movements one by one, but rather to push through to a philosophical formulation that can be useful in the new context.

THE BEGINNING OF PHILOSOPHY

The idea of English Canadian philosophy – indeed, of any national philosophy – is fraught with dangerous paradoxes. The first one I addressed above: philosophy is supposed to deal with the universal, with the human condition as such, rather than the contingencies of time or place. Thus an emphasis on the social and historical situation of philosophical thought tends to reduce it to an experiential catalogue of contents, rather than the articulation of experience in its breadth, depth, coherence or tension, and implications that creates a mythic artistic form or philosophical universality. Through the notion of a national identity as a distinctive pattern of contents, rather than distinctive contents, I attempted to dissolve the false opposition between parochial locality and a foreign, absent universality and to demonstrate the sense in which English Canadian philosophy can be open to influences from outside without losing a concern with its distinctiveness.

There is also a second danger, which I will deal with here. While it is easy enough to say whether a certain philosophical work or idea appeared in English Canada, it is impossible to say that it is characteristically English Canadian without developing the idea of English Canadian philosophy. In other words, the definition is self-referential. Clearly, there is the threat of a vicious circle here. It is tempting to deny "English Canadian-ness" to any philosophical contribution that does not fit into one's idea of what it should be. It should be noted, however, that this danger is not unique to the definition of a national identity. It is implicit in the definition of any social identity that some are defined outside it and that the boundary of this definition will be controversial. This danger indicates a deeper paradox in the very idea of English Canadian philosophy – indeed, of English Canadian culture generally – insofar as it claims to be more than a local oddity. It has two parts, and it is important to recognize their reciprocally confirming character. The first is simply envy: we have never been at the top. English Canadian culture is permeated with resentment of those who are at the centre and consists, in many secret ways, of strategies of self-promotion. The second is more subtle and may be called "the purity of origins." Since we have never been in charge, we do not have to take responsibility for the way things are. One imagines that Canadians *just are* more peaceable, less greedy, more concerned with justice, and so on – simply and naturally better than Americans. The first part of the danger concerns climbing the ladder in the existing structure of dominance. The second part is a reversal of this dominance and contains a more hidden danger. If all the evil is at the centre of power, then all is innocence and grace at the periphery. "If you can't beat 'em, join 'em" on one side and "We wouldn't do that!" on the other. English Canadian culture oscillates between these two parts of the danger, which block questioning by confining it within a repetition of its relations to the empire. That is, dependent English Canadian culture exists through a discourse that repeats its own impossibility of being more than marginal. The attempt made here to define the ground of English Canadian philosophy must thus be other and deeper: a critique of dependence and marginalization and thus a risk of independence, but one that will not posit itself as an imagined or future centre. An English Canadian philosophy, in order to think through the legacy of dependence, can recycle neither marginalization nor centrism. It must therefore be very careful in articulating its own *beginning* and *procedure*. Indeed, this focus might well be one of its most characteristic features. It does not so much spin out worlds, but look down to meditate on its own frst step.

The *procedure* may be called deconstruction – running the further danger that what is attempted here may be simply subordinated by critics as a "case," or "example," of an already existing philosophy.[41] A main characteristic of deconstruction is that it begins by revaluing the marginalized side of a dualistic relation. Then, in a second move, it proceeds by developing new concepts that attempt to displace the dualism, to render it questionable and insufficient. The extent to which this procedure may terminate in the elaboration of a self-sufficient philosophy must be left in abeyance. Deconstruction is a procedure for those underway, more than for those who have already arrived at conclusions. While beginning from the second side of the relation of dominance, the present argument must avoid the dangers of both envy and the purity of origins. Neither by copying the discourses of others (accepting dependency) nor even by revaluing what is said but devalued within a discourse (criticizing dependency, polemically opposing the centre – the first deconstructive step), but only by excavating that which is repressed by the relations of dominance themselves (recognizing that dependency requires a centre, criticizing the centre-periphery relation itself – the second deconstructive step) can we glimpse the new possibility. The preliminary reversal of the relation of dominance must finally invite an exit from it. Only by articulating this still-unsaid invitation can the wilderness become civilizing.

An adequate response to the two dangers in the idea of English Canadian philosophy can take its bearings from our understanding of the danger in English Canadian culture: that we remain trapped in a cycle of dependency, often even in the moment that we criticize it (again, the first step). Our task is to voice the possibility that our own can shed light on human universality (the second step), and here the central issue is that of the completion of philosophy. If the truly universal philosophy, or at least its methods and outline, has been discovered, then the various paths by which this truth was reached diminish in comparison with the result. The fact that Plato was a Greek, for example, is significant only if it would help one comprehend the universal reach of philosophy, which is unlikely if it is indeed truly universal. If, by contrast, one sees the present situation still in search of the genuinely universal, then the recognition of the manifold paths by which the universal may be approached will be an important reference for the plurality that a genuine universal must encompass. This recognition can be buttressed with the quite classical claim that philosophy is not knowledge, or science, but the love of wisdom. Were the searching and desiring characteristic of love to be superseded by certainty and possession, philosophy would come to an end, as Hegel claimed that it had.[42] This is all the more urgent to the extent that one regards previous claims to the universal as the elevation of specific cultural configurations to a supposedly universal status. If existing claims to universality are insufficient, they have succeeded only by hiding their actually partial character, as with Eurocentrism or indeed any centrism. To the extent that truth is not yet discovered, we may be suspicious that the bogus universal claims of the past were in league with political power. Some doubt, some questioning that cannot be certain the teachers have all the answers, is therefore essential to opening up the terrain of English Canadian philosophy. Like English Canada itself, it is an uncompleted task whose completion has now become all the more difficult. One worries that the Owl of Minerva's feet have become stuck to the branch through inactivity and that its encrusted wings will no longer bear flight. We are stuck at the question of how to begin.

If the *procedure* may be called deconstruction, the *beginning* of English Canadian philosophy cannot be so easily named or described. It was remarked above that there is the possibility of a vicious circle that denies English Canadian-ness to any philosophy of which it does not approve. Resolving this issue of the circle of interpretation and of its potential viciousness takes us to the core idea of English Canadian philosophy. In the first place, we need to recognize the validity of a circle of interpretation in the extension of a philosophical tradition. In this first step, it can be argued that this hermeneutic circle can be saved from viciousness. But in the second place, the absence of origin in the experience of wilderness implies that English Canadian philosophy cannot remain within, or rely on, the hermeneutic circle of interpretation that founds a tradition. Consequently, we need to distinguish two senses of incompleteness: first, a limited, initial sense, which English Canadian philosophy shares with any philosophical tradition; second, an unlimited, radical sense of incompleteness. It is this latter sense that is most characteristic of the ground of English Canadian philosophy and its difficulty in beginning.

English Canadian philosophy cannot be defined in total innocence of what has been done in English Canada under the name of philosophy. However, neither can this precedent become sufficiently normative to exclude the possibility that there are characteristics of English Canadian social and historical life that have not been brought to philosophical articulation. The interweaving of experience and its thoughtful exploration is thus crucial to English Canadian philosophy. In consequence, it cannot be assumed that the best philosophical articulation of experience is confined to those who have commanded the institutional and linguistic resources to define their activity as philosophy.[43] For this reason, English Canadian philosophy must be interdisciplinary and must begin with the historical-geographical formation of English Canadian identity rather than with "philosophy" understood as an officially sanctioned activity within the current academic division of labour. Philosophy in the sense propounded here sheds its recent cloak as a special technique of analysis and also its older one as an esoteric tradition of knowledge, and draws on other cultural resources to become the articulation of the experience of a people in its deepest dimensions and widest implications. Thus philosophy must begin from an exploration of the contours of English Canadian experience in its social, political, and economic dimensions in order to discover and develop the metaphors that can give it both theme and shape. This circle of interpretation is the development of English Canadian philosophy. It is prevented from becoming vicious by being in dialogue with previous English Canadian philosophers, other cultural expressions, and all those to whom the articulation of English Canadian identity is of importance. Publicness of reflection saves the continuing dialogue from viciousness, though it cannot guarantee that any single contribution will not be superficial or irrelevant or will contribute to the masking of English Canadian experience by subsuming it under imported models. In short, the tradition is constructed through a hermeneutic circle of interpretation that folds together socio-historical experience, artistic and cultural expressions, and the tradition of English Canadian philosophy.

English Canadian philosophy in this hermeneutic sense thus requires a doubt about the completion of philosophy inherent in every attempt to replace questioning with systematic knowledge. It is something to be done in public reflection, a bringing of the unsaid into language, that plumbs initially anonymous experience by forging metaphors that give shape to further reflection. Its incompletion is challenging but not radical. It occurs within a circle of interpretation that relates present contributions to the beginning of English Canadian philosophy. Thus, like any tradition, it engenders a dialogue of present and past that presses the tradition forward into the future.

In order to describe the radical sense of incompletion that inhers in English Canadian philosophy, we must distinguish the functioning of the circle of interpretation in European metaphysics from its impossibility in the wilderness; that is, we must enter a discourse on the nature of philosophy itself. Despite my use, following Grant, of Heidegger's conception of the closure of metaphysics, I do not accept the equation of philosophy and metaphysics proposed by Heidegger, which, among other consequences, would render impossible the task of developing an English Canadian philosophy. He attempts to move beyond philosophy to a poetizing conception of thought that would be undistinguishable from myth.[44] While philosophy certainly incorporates a poetic component as a result of its necessity to forge metaphorically a form of thought from the contents of socio-historical experience, I nonetheless resist the notion of the end of philosophy as a distinct manner of thought that this conception implies. I am trying to recover the possibility of philosophy through a reflection on the historical-geographical formation of English Canadian identity. All this depends, of course, on the prior question of what is philosophy.

Philosophy begins when a culture is separated from its origin. The holding together of a culture with its origin in unreflective, narrative unity is myth, which is a fusing of internal experience and external world order such that the world is made a home. Philosophy thus begins with homelessness, and in moving from a particular home towards a universal belonging, it makes a new discursive home in the world at large. It struggles to close internal and external through reason, though when this closure is taken as accomplished, we have not philosophy proper but metaphysics. Heidegger defines metaphysics as the conception of the mutual implication of origin and goal, which is established through the giving of reasons. "The unity of this One is of such a kind that the ultimate in its own way accounts for the primal, and the primal in its own way accounts for the ultimate."[45] The striving for this metaphysical closure that is philosophy nevertheless ends philosophy if the striving is satisfied. Philosophy is thus always on the way. Metaphysics is its dream of arrival, of recovery of mythical home solely through unaided reason.

Metaphysics establishes its closure through the connection of two origins: the temporal origin, always partial and particular – though leading towards the universal because of the giving of reasons – and the present origin, the originality of the present moment. As Edmund Husserl said in *The Origin of Geometry*, "if the originally self-evident production, as the pure fulfillment of its intention, is what is renewed (recollected), there necessarily occurs, accompanying the active recollection of what is past, an activity of concurrent actual production, and there arises thereby, in original 'coincidence,' the self-evidence of identity: what has now been realized in original fashion is the same as what was previously self-evident."[46] There are thus two origins: one from the past and another in the present. It is the matching of these two origins, the perception of them as the Same, that connects present experience to temporal origin in an unbroken unity that can project a future destiny of the completion of giving reasons, a mutual implication of origin and goal. It unites mythic origin and experiential origin in a metaphysical recovery of home through reasoning. The civilizing moment is this matching of dual origins, their fusing into one, which establishes a continuity of interpretation as a dialectic of continuous universalization that unfolds out from a particular origin. The circle is the metaphor for this fusing: simultaneously completion, repetition, and confirmation of experience. Husserl's account of the fusing of the two origins in the self-evidence of knowledge made possible Heidegger's account of metaphysics; it is its phenomenological kernel. The closure of metaphysics is thus not a complete termination of philosophy. It is rather a question of how one conceives the relation of present experience to primal origin. This relation must be continually re-established and redefined. It requires the continuous practice of interpretation. In this limited hermeneutic sense, philosophy always remains incomplete. Nevertheless, from the viewpoint of a radical, limitless incompletion, this circle of interpretation occurs within a metaphysical closure.

In the epoch of technology the attempt to reconnect inner and outer experience that characterizes philosophy has faltered. Technology, as the extreme division, reveals the presupposition of metaphysics as the mutual implication of origin and goal and opens a new appreciation of myth. Grant, following Heidegger, has traced the sundering of experience to a loss of the encompassing belonging expressed in mythical narratives. The alternative to technology would seem to be myth, and indeed we see many holding to some story in flight from the terrors of modernity. But unless we are to abandon all rational thought, we must recognize that these stories have been shown to be merely particular. There are many myths; which is why holding to one in these times can only be accomplished with extreme fanaticism. Grant is too well aware of the truth brought forward by technology to countenance such dangerous fervour, but he leaves us with a civilizational contradiction that requires a turn to faith and thus destroys the difference between myth and philosophy. Within this faith one cannot fully think the *truth* of technology, which removes the ground from justice. If we are truly convinced that not only the modern world but philosophy itself has shown that there are many myths and that within them we live in darkness, overcoming technology means learning to philosophize in the wilderness. This would be the radical sense of the beginning of English Canadian philosophy. It cannot rely on a hermeneutic circle of interpretation, but must confront its own beginning in a decisive act – the drawing of a border in the wilderness.

A BORDER IN THE WILDERNESS

The separation of inner and outer experience that opens the possibility of both philosophy and metaphysics is based in Europe on primal memories of autochthony. Both the Greeks and the Hebrews belonged in a certain place where there remained a memory prior to separation between self and world. The experience that allows metaphysics is a dislodging from resting at home in the world. The memory of belonging (which survives dislodging) gives rise to the metaphysical attempt to close inner and outer and reinstate belonging in truth by fusing recollection of the origin with the present origin. In the New World no such original memory prior to separation underlies Western dynamism. The longing to belong that characterizes much European thought and action is displaced in the wilderness. With the death of God, the European attempt to hold primal and ultimate together falters. The nostalgia for a belonging of self at home with its world that seems to be constitutive of philosophy is replaced by homelessness.

In English Canada our primal is the wilderness. Wilderness does not need us to be formulated as a project. Goal or project, ultimate, the highest – all of these are civilized. Between wilderness and civilization the identity of primal and ultimate that defined metaphysics is impossible. Europe's faltering could then be our chance. Throughout most of our history and throughout most of our thought, we have been dominated by fear of the wilderness, driving into the technological dynamo without Europe's restraint. But another possibility lurks behind the trees, scuttles unhampered across the Great Lakes and endless open prairie, is whispered by the Coastal Range: that the wild might be, or become, our own. Loss of belonging and goal, floundering where all conventions and institutions are without force, one sometimes discovers from unexpected quarters a human gesture that accepts all the wild. There is a deep ambivalence in the English Canadian psyche. Fear of the wilderness, scarcity, leads us to despoil and take without thought of yesterday or tomorrow, but at the same time produces a staggering awe that looks back to the native people and ahead to a civilization that does not imagine itself omnipotent. These two views – which tear at each other in our society and coexist within most minds – are based in the same experience: The wild does not need us – not the muskeg; not the internal chaos, which eliminates individuality as surely. Awe of unlimited and purposeless wilderness leads us to use it like a paper cup; and also to pause, take in the snow-blind, and create limits and goals without denying the wild – to draw a border, a limit.

Separation from origin is itself original for New World societies. Our primal experience is wilderness. Thus the metaphysical fusing of inner and outer cannot occur. Civilizing cannot be a completion, an "again," or an expansion of this origin into wider dimensions. Rather, it must confront radically and repeatedly the question of the beginning of philosophy. If there is a civilizing moment here, it is in the drawing of a line, a border that separates here from there, that lets there appear an Other, a mismatch, a difference. In relation to this difference we are not fused with origin, but drawn out towards the Other. Origin is plural if it is traced back elsewhere; origin is wilderness here. Present experience is related to these origins, but is nonidentical with them. English Canadian philosophy may then turn to interpret metaphysics as the European myth. It must begin in this radical incompletion itself, this struggling on. From this vantage point, the circle of interpretation, it must be admitted, is always vicious since it depends on a past origin that it cannot question but must accept as a primal fact. The task of English Canadian philosophy is, within this radical homelessness, to construct a civilizing moment through the limitation invented by drawing a border.

The encounter with wilderness is characteristic of the ex-European experience of the New World. Plurality of emigrations means that the "other" is now inside. There is no national origin that can give unity to a people and define its destiny. Europeans encountered a place where they did not belong, where the technologies that had been developed to dominate nature came up against an ongoing vastness. Taming the wilderness was not only a necessity, but became a moral project. There is also a psychic side to wilderness in the snow-blind and the bushwhacked. The absence of belonging, of origin, unleashed a wildness, a madness, an intuition of the arbitrariness of all organizations and goals. Multiple and without origin, civilization in the New World must be onward. It can consist of no origin that might be recaptured which might define its destiny. The civilizing purpose is always built on an underlying madness that either it must reckon with or into which it will continually fall back.

The clue to English Canada is: What is this border? In dividing two nations, it prompts us to ask, Can there be a New World society different from the headlong American race through the domination of nature to homogeneity, universality, and the reduction of desires to their satisfaction by commodities? And in this question are hidden others. What is this "I" that confronts an "Other"? What is this wilderness that is never fully subjugated by humanity? How can one speak a language that departs from the assumptions of modernity and progress? These four relations are compressed in the metaphor of the border: between nations, between self and Other, between humanity and nature, and between the said and the unsaid. Canada is this making of a border separating us from the United States, combined with the encounter with wilderness that is characteristic of the New World as such. Here is the wager that defines the possibility of English Canadian philosophy: Thinking civilization from its periphery, not as a way back but on and around. This exploration of English Canadian philosophy begins through a meditation on the border that allows our existence in North America. Can we find a civilizing moment in this primal encounter with lack of ground, wilderness? English Canadian philosophy must face the source of the cultural polarity between archaism and modernity by exploring the possibilities of our unique invention of the border in the wilderness, by questioning the border. Can we found a civilizing project in the wilderness that is not simply a garrison, an outpost of a civilization whose centre is back in Europe?

This, then, is our clue: the task of articulating English Canadian philosophy can begin from the four relations of the in-between that we have discovered in the metaphor of the border. The European tradition – and philosophy, after all, is a central component of that cultural unity we call "Europe" or "the West" – defined the first side of each separation as primary and independent and the second side as lesser and dependent. We may call this discourse of a hierarchy of Being based upon binary oppositions "metaphysics." Canada has always been a colony: France, Britain, the United States, each of these defining itself in its own terms, with an independent history and tradition, could see in our particular conditions only contingent and marginal local divergences from the principles of the centre. But what is an empire without colonies? The wager of English Canadian philosophy is a questioning that begins from the second side, the periphery: the dependent nation, the other from which one defines the self, the wilderness with and against which humanity tests itself, the unsaid that is at the origin of language. Questioning the border from the second, dependent, Other side in order to prepare an exit from metaphysical hierarchy opens philosophy to the radically incomplete task of articulating English Canadian experience. Metaphysics stumbles to an end, having lost direction in the muskeg. There is no hermeneutic circle of interpretation here, but only a vast dispersion in which we hesitatingly draw a border. Four relations are gathered in the border: U.S./Canada, self/Other, human/nature, and said/

unsaid. European philosophy began from the first side. English Canadian philosophy begins from, but will not end with, a reversal.

In order to clarify the metaphor of the border, I will distinguish it from the dominant metaphor of the United States, the frontier. A tension between outward and back inhers in the various forms that New World societies have taken. In the United States, as Frederick Jackson Turner put it, "the frontier is the outer edge of the wave – the meeting point of savagery and civilization." This headlong rush into the wilderness, a perpetual hurtling outward, is characteristic of American history and culture. It sees in this outward rush "a new field of opportunity, a gate of escape from the bondage of the past; and freshness, and confidence, and scorn of older society, impatience of its restraints and its ideas, and indifference to its lessons, have accompanied the frontier."[47] Thus American classical pragmatist philosophy can be interpreted, as it is by Michael Weinstein, as a defence of the city as against the deteriorating effects of wilderness, even though the wilderness is necessary for a distancing perspective on the conventions of the city.[48] The outward rush is without limit and thus claims all of America for itself. The United States names itself "America" since its outward rush is not self-limiting but would extend as far as the natural limit of the continent. The frontier thus continues itself in the Monroe Doctrine, in which Americans claim the right to interference in all the affairs of the continent.

Moreover, this limitless outward rush into the wilderness does not really embrace the wilderness itself. Since the wilderness does not sustain humans in its present form, the outward rush has also meant a domination of the wilderness, a taming, a turning it back into "Europe," that is, civilization. What is new thus escapes articulation since the cultural means of expression itself draws experience back into inherited European forms. Often this process leads to the rejection of intellectual articulation as such – a hatred of culture, because it is this drawing back. Life at the frontier consists in escaping civilized constraints in the very moment that one recreates them. The American identity is at bottom fragile in that it is constituted by this hurtling out, is completely with itself only in headlong rush, which eliminates the conditions under which it can occur. With the passing of the frontier – despite attempts to revive it, such as Kennedy's "Last Frontier" of space – this precarious identity requires something else that it can rush into and subdue, if only in imagination. Communism has repeatedly played this role; the frontier ends in the necessity of an enemy. The reliance on the negation of an other for self-identity is not limited to the United States. It probably exists in all cultures. The Canadian version is Frye's garrison mentality. But while the former annihilates the other in order to reassure the self, the latter circumscribes the self – invents a border – to protect itself from the other. These are imperial and dominated versions respectively. In the outward rush into the wilderness that characterizes the frontier, there remains the "European" opposition between civilization and wilderness: wilderness is turned into civilization without limit; what is new, the living of the frontier, escapes articulation and falls into the silence of violence.

Canadian social history was never articulated around a frontier in this manner.[49] The government was there first; human order was almost always present, though not reducing the threats of nature or the encounter with wildness. Violence was largely monopolized by the state and did not seem to contain a liberation. Northrop Frye coined the term "garrison mentality" to refer to the beleaguered sense of small communities threatened by wilderness and other communities outside, asserting themselves through an undifferentiated, unquestioned morality within.[50] The garrison exists in the wilderness and constructs a border behind which it can retreat to attain order, identity, and self-protection. There is a timidity here, a retreat from wilderness into a frightened normality. The border draws a line and distinguishes human order from that of the wilderness outside, but it is not a frontier in the sense of a receding line of confrontation between civilization and savagery.

In the United States, development was largely by independent commodity producers who continually pushed back the limit of the frontier, while in Canada settlement was by communities, often ethnic ones, in a colonial relationship with empire. The encounter with wilderness retained a colonial dependency on European civilization, thereby creating a tension between undeveloped production at the periphery and highly developed consumption as a result of the imperial connection. Centre-periphery relationship creates a society in deep polarity between modern, historical, civilizing tendencies and a primal, archaic, and unhistorical encounter with wilderness. Wilderness is not experienced as something to be transformed into civilization, but as a limit to the civilizing project, both an external limit – an outside – and a limit of depth. Civilization is not a natural growth, a continuous progression from nature. It is ungrounded, an imposition. Small wonder that we often retreat from this experience into the protective surface accomodation of the garrison. English Canadian thought has revolved around this polarity between civilization and the wilderness. These tendencies are prevalent in English Canadian popular culture also, though in this case the argument for balance, rather than provoking a deep questioning of the fundamental polarity, tends to issue in timidity, a search for compromises. The brittle and embattled mentality of the garrison underlies the famous English Canadian horror of extremes. Popular consciousness continuously recycles this interplay between accomodating surface and depth polarities.

Centre-periphery relationship thus reveals wilderness as a limit to civilization in two senses – an external limit, an outside, and a limit of depth, groundlessness. Now we must ask, Can one take the wilderness inside, transform it, and make civilizing the encounter with groundlessness, the lack of origin? Doing so means acceptance of a kind of abandonment, abjection. Wilderness reveals civilization on its European model to be a limited project. Can we discover in the border a conception of civilization that is not in opposition to wilderness? The tradition of collective rights in English Canada has been articulated through a linkage between an environmental ethic based on an experience of the land, on one hand, and a tradition of social justice based on the federal state, on the other. At this basic level, my own contribution can be said to belong to the same tradition. However, there is a considerable departure with regard to the emergent theory itself that I advocate. By stepping back from the tradition to the constitutive experiences that are presupposed within it, the possibility of a new philosophical articulation of these constitutive experiences presents itself that involves a critique of the English Canadian tradition of social and political thought represented by Harold Innis and George Grant, and thus also the left-nationalist discourse that relied upon them.

The notion of cultural continuity with European civilization that is central to Innis and Grant is suspended, or mitigated, in this emergent theory. English Canada is certainly in origin a settler society predicated on the importation of European culture and the marginalization of Aboriginal cultures by immigration. But more recently this immigration has become more extensive and includes Asia, Latin America, and virually all other parts of the world. There is now a plurality of settler cultures. English Canada is no longer simply English, or even European, and this fact requires that we think through what a multicultural society may mean in a much more radical fashion than was necessary previously. This task is taken up in the next chapter.

The concept of civilization became problematic in Europe during the First World War, when the "civilized" countries were rent by an unprecedentedly destructive conflict, but its problematic character in the New World is of a different origin. Civilization was understood in distinction to two related concepts: "savages" and "wilderness." Calling Aboriginal people savages was a central way in which settler society tried to rob them of their humanity, their land, and their culture – with great effect but, thankfully, without complete success. Regarding Aboriginal people as savages could be justified in several ways by Europeans. Superiority in technology or, better put, superior technological domination of nature was one factor. Another was that civilization was, for all practical purposes, equated with Christianity. As we have seen in the chapter on Grant, these are not really two separate factors because the development of the technological domination of nature was possible through a conception of will that also implies the separation of "values" from nature. Calling the land a wilderness was an expression of the ex-European attitude to a land strange to them, which was not their origin, and often a way of justifying the "development" of the land along capitalist industrial lines connected to the European model. The term "civilization" is therefore a key concept to be thoroughly investigated and criticized in thinking through a new turning for English Canadian philosophy. We may surmise that such an emergent theory will require a concept of civilization that does not oppose it to savagery and wilderness, but rather develops an ontology of participation in which the human world is limited and defined by its place within what is as a Whole and root values in Being.

There are several interrelated ways in which the concept of civilization is reworked in the argument in the following chapters. I mention them here only for clarity since doing so cannot substitute for the elaboration itself. First, the assumption that civilization implies a European basis is criticized through the development of a philosophy of multiculturalism. Second, the association of civilization with industrial development is dropped. Throughout the work of Innis and left-nationalism, development was taken to be synonymous with manufacturing.[51] The model of industrial capitalism taken from a certain phase of Europe's history prevailed. The environmental ethic that was embodied in industrial development was of a wilderness which was so vast that it was not necessary to think about the exhaustion of resources, of a practice of extraction in a commercial framework (i.e., for sale and not for direct use), and a correlated sense of awe at the vastness that made staple extraction possible – a concept of wilderness as sublime, rather than nature as beautiful, since the sublime refers to an experience that overflows the capacity to capture it in a concept. As Innis pointed out, "violent swings are set in motion according to the prediction of unpredictableness. In the main these swings are the result of the intensified application of the machine industry at a mature stage of technique to vast virgin natural resources."[52] This environmental ethic of staple extraction must now be criticized and elaborated in the direction of sustainable development. Grant's work is more useful here insofar as it incorporated the critique of European technological development elaborated by

Heidegger. Rethinking the notion of civilization requires a comparable rethinking of wilderness. The assumption that nature is simply a storehouse of resources to be used for human purposes must be replaced with an ecological ethic based upon an ontology of participation in Being. Moreover, the notion that civilization and wilderness are in an antithetical relationship must be revoked. It was supposed that wilderness must be conquered and replaced by civilization. Rethinking the wilderness through the notion of the wild suggests that this culture-nature opposition is not adequate and that a new environmental ethic must embrace the wilderness without renouncing civilization. The two succeeding chapters on the political ideal of multiculturalism and an ecological ethic follow out these critical points with regard to English Canadian social and political thought.

English Canada may be defined through this metaphor of the New World encounter with wilderness combined with the invention of a border separating us from the United States – a border in the wilderness. Maintaining the border is the beginning of a new civilizing project that does not reject the wilderness, but embraces the abjection of the self that the wilderness proposes. This fundamental invention underlies two main abiding themes throughout the history of definitions of English Canada: political continuity articulated through the public intervention of the federal state and a sense of break, of difference, articulated through relationship to the land, nature, environment. The present situation requires a step back from this history in order to articulate the invention behind the history that has never come to adequate self-expression. This invention can become the metaphorical basis of an emergent theory, a mythic form that can shape the contents of English Canadian identity. By drawing a border between self and Other, the Other is allowed to show difference. This showing of the Other reveals the particularity of the self. Philosophical reflection on particularity is the defence of one's own as the necessary vehicle towards the universal, a process that involves a step back from the relation between contingency and universality to the *conditions under which* a specific being might apprehend a universal good. As Heidegger says, "if it is not a question of something more original, the question arises of what the difference and relation is between the concepts named. They do not represent a gradation, but rather stages on a way back which is opened and leads preliminarily into Appropriation."[53] This regressive step back is made necessary by the absence of authoritative origin. It is the decisive act that opens up the possibility of English Canadian philosophy. Radical incompletion throws us back again and again to wonder how to begin. Here the question is how to articulate, or the limits of articulation itself. This is the last aspect of the border – the emergence of speech from the great well of the unsaid.

The encounter with the primal, unhistorical, is an annihilation of temporal relations into the purely spatial extension of a thick present. Neither before nor after, but splayed out in endless dispersal, this spatial extension is simultaneously thoroughly civilized and thoroughly wild.[54] It is an ungrounded project whose success does not transform its origin. Understood in this way, the border does not separate two distinct spaces, but describes a tension between wilderness and civilization that cannot be erased. Philosophy, in its origin, imagined temporarily leaving the world of convention in order to encounter the cosmos, the world-order, in silent awe. Its task was to translate this silent origin of order into human affairs. But in the forging of English Canadian philosophy, the outside is not silence, but a continuous babble. The wildness is not silence, but an unbroken outpouring of sound. Absence, not of sensing, but of meaning – the Other side of the border a madness of unguided sound. Thus even stronger is the pull back towards convention. Civilization is a kind of madness, wilderness a kind of order, though not a human one.[55] The fusing of internal experience with externality that philosophy once sought to establish is already and always accomplished here, but it does not find an order that can make the world a home. Rather, internal wildness matches the outside; internal order is revealed as existing in wilderness, not as fundamental, as cosmos, but as built on no foundation. Homelessness, as radical incompletion, seems incapable of being overcome.

Between the anonymous murmur of convention and the disintegrated babble of the wild, the border emerges as the place of a civilizing moment, of a switching that cannot eradicate wilderness but is situated at the site where wilderness transforms into civilization, where order and limitation emerge. The border is the site of many descriptions, many speeches. It is not these speeches themselves, but the place where they compete. This place, or site, is thus also a wild babble. As one struggles to describe this site, one reaches beyond the babble of plural speeches towards a universal place whose silence situates them all, that allows a naming which is the origin of language. This naming of place at the origin of language is the construction of silence, between murmur and babble, that situates the plurality of speeches in a unique gesture. Silent unique gesture builds place. From here a civilizing continuous with wilderness emerges. Thus commences the relation of civilization and wilderness, the dual limit of civilization in wilderness, and the perpetual possibility of civilization – not as identity, but as acceptance of Otherness. It is this civilizing experience with the wilderness that is the possibility for English Canadian philosophy through the drawing of a border.

Description of the site continually falls back into just another speech and becomes lost in the babble. There is an ineradicable tension between the discovery of site, the place of this naming, and the reduction of discovery within site, the naming of this place. Site becomes place only through naming; naming fails to capture site when it encounters the groundlessness of its language. The border is no longer a place, but the discovery of place, a permanently endangered discovery of the silent civilizing moment in the ubiquity of madness, the Other's order.

Without a primal fact, or origin, that provides authority for a circle of interpretation, English Canadian philosophy can achieve no "again," or matching of recollected origin with present origin, that could outline a continuous tradition. Thus describing the site cannot be a matching of description and original experience. Philosophy cannot be knowledge or science – at least, not fundamentally or exclusively. It is continually thrown back to how to begin in this thick, extended present. It finds no place on a continuum and cannot be called progress. The real structure of this present remains opaque. Its temporal structure is not the past-present-future of tradition, but the before/after of emigration. This continually reinvented attempt to begin inaugurates the before/after that situates the multiplicity of our own. To describe this site, philosophy must risk the babble of the wilderness, which, stretched through the silent switching of the border, originates the naming of place. A first naming, it sidles up to poetry, exploring the primal metaphors rooted in social history. Radical homelessness cannot be overcome by inheriting a house, but only by building a home, making this place, here.

It is, of course, foolish to speak of English Canada; one can only speak of truth, and to speak truly we need silence. The forty-ninth parallel is not Canada; it lets Canada show itself as different. The border is not difference; it allows difference to appear. Still, the border is not silence; it is the site that allows the hearing of silence. In crossing, one may return both to the constantly reassuring murmur of anonymous belonging and to hysterical attachment to contingencies. The border suspends. It discovers place in the silent switching of madness and naming. With philosophy, this dallying with suspension, this site nowhere, the crossing is forever incomplete. But there can be no suspension, no loss of site, unless the Other is perceived. To perceive an Other, the border must be maintained. And to maintain the border, one must step back from involvements between the self and Other in order that the border may be manifested in its own light. English Canadian philosophy motivates this step back though its defence of particularity and articulates its ethics of preserving the Other though maintaining the border.

CHAPTER SIX

Multiculturalism as a Social Ideal

We live in an age in which the nation-state is being undermined from above and below by both political-economic and cultural influences. Globalizing tendencies stemming from the economy and regionalizing, or localizing, tendencies usually concerned with issues of identity coexist and are increasingly gaining ground that was previously organized through the nation-state. While the nation-state is not likely to cease to exist in the near future, there is not much doubt that its organizing power is receding and that this is no superficial development, but is based in long-term trends.We seem to be losing the key mediation that linked local and regional concerns to universal ones. In such a situation, the dangers of a resurgence of mere particularism – exclusive loyalty to the tribe – are apparent every day on the news. To counter such renewed us/them barbarism, the enlightened response is often to reassert the universality of liberal civil rights. However, the dominant tradition of individual rights cannot be exempted from contributing to the current impasse. By pushing the politics of identity formation out of the public sphere – or, more accurately, limiting public identity formation to a homogeneous conception articulated through the nation-state and centring on the civil rights of the individual – it removed all other identities from justification and surrendered them to irrational and decisionistic forces. Violence against the other is one major response to the perceived threat of the loss of identity. The present situation thus combines the mutually reinforcing dangers of the reassertion of an unsatisfactory universalism that ignores and marginalizes modes of group belonging with a return to particularism that denies any responsibility at all to the other. What is needed is a rethinking of the relation between particularity and universality or, alternatively stated, a recovery of particularity that is essentially connected to a discourse of legitimation with universalizing dimensions. The politics of multiculturalism is in a key location to address such a rethinking. It combines a recovery of a pre-rational sense of belonging with a claim to collective rights that must be articulated in universal terms.

Modern society is built upon a distinction between state and civil society such that private, voluntary beliefs and associations are left to the decisions of individuals. The state, on the other hand, is a compulsory organization whose decisions are made by the citizens as a collectivity. It is not merely a sum of private decisions and activities. The distinction between civil society and the state has undergone several mutations throughout the history of modern social and political thought, and it is not to the point to review them here. The main issue is that modern society has relegated once compulsory and collective forces – such as ethnicity and religion – from the collective sphere of the nation-state to the sphere of civil society. Thus modern nation-states are neither religious nor ethnic ones: religion is regarded as a matter of private conscience; ethnicity is usually regarded as irrelevant to the civil rights of the citizen. The recent resurgence of ethnic nationalism is thus a collapse of a defining characteristic of modernity since it defines the state as belonging exclusively to a given ethnic group as a result of that group's derivation from common ancestors and it castigates all others as outsiders without rights.[1] Similarly, contemporary developments that fuse the nation-state with a specific religion undo the modern separation of civil society from the nation-state and thereby undermine the sphere of individual civil rights. The same point could be made with reference to the fusing of state, party, and economy in communism, fascism, and other authoritarian regimes. It is no accident that the fall of communism was accompanied by a resurgence of both the theory and the practice of civil society, nor that the post-dictatorship period in Argentina was characterized by a new appreciation of ethnic pluralism.[2] It is important to guard within one's thinking about the nation-state the notion of its limitation: the understanding that the nation-state cannot legitimately extend throughout the whole lives of its citizens and that state action must be limited by constitutional guarantees of a sphere of individual rights.

There is a problem, however, with the way in which civil society has been seen as solely a sphere of individual rights limiting state action. Because of the important gain for individual rights that the separation of state and civil society achieved, the dominant liberal tradition has tended to regard all civil rights on the model of individual rights. Similarly, participation in the nation-state – through voting, the public expression of opinion, groups organized for political action, and so forth – has tended to be seen as solely an activity of individuals. Thus the whole idea of collective rights has been undermined by the separation between state and civil society. Any contemporary concern with collective rights must subject the modern state – civil society distinction to scrutiny. However, to revoke the distinction would be tantamount to the eradication of individual civil rights. The issue may therefore be defined as the necessity for a defence of collective rights to rethink the relationship between state and civil society, rather than undermine the distinction as such. The formation of social identity is a collective process that cannot be reduced to the choices and actions of individuals, and therefore a social and political philosophy oriented towards social identity must contain a defence of collective rights. Multiculturalism as public policy is one area in which the particularities and differences ejected by liberal individualism to the private sphere have emerged publicly. They require a defence of the public relevance of particularity through a theory of collective rights.[3]

Multiculturalism evinces a key feature that characterizes the attempt to bring particularities into the public domain: in emerging from the private, particularities are articulated as "rights"; that is to say, they are put in a universalizing form. The *right* to the retention and development of ethnic identity that is expressed in multiculturalism is not the same as the simple assertion of ethnic identity, nor the assertion that one will protect it. Expressed publicly, it becomes a right that is, in principle, extendable to other ethnic groups as well. Like other new social movements whose politics are oriented more towards activity within civil society than to capturing state power, multiculturalism is about the retention and development of ethnic identity in civil society and asks from the state the necessary means towards this end. The manner in which these necessary means are formulated suggests that a collective "right" has been recognized. The activity of new social movements as a reworking of the relation between nation-state and civil society leads to a centrality of the concept of rights in contemporary politics. The emphasis on identity, combined with the articulation of particularity in a universalizing discourse, leads to claims for the public recognition of rights.

The practice of multiculturalism in English Canada has proceeded further in its everyday, institutional, and policy contexts than it has as social and political philosophy. The present chapter develops the key philosophical concept of "particularity," which I claim can theorize a society committed to the public relevance of diverse collective identities based on ethno-cultures. In this way, I carry forward the tension between archaism and modernity in English Canadian thought by showing how the pre-modern sense of belonging contained in ethnic identity can be brought into the modern nation-state and given a universalizing form. To this end I begin with a sketch of the English Canadian situation in which the philosophical issue arises. The second section of the chapter addresses directly the relation between ethno-cultural identity in a multinational context and national identity. It includes a critique of the philosophical defence of collective identities by Charles Taylor, which was developed largely in the context of the place of Quebec within Canada and then applied to multiculturalism. Thirdly, I present the concept of particularity, which George Grant developed in order to criticize the ongoing pressure towards the incorporation of Canada into the American empire, criticize its polemical formulation in this context, and extend it in the direction of multiculturalism. Finally, I sketch the relation between ethno-cultures and the multicultural context in order to reject the common argument that the deep diversity promoted by multicultural politics necessarily leads to social fragmention, any more than the biodiversity of an ecosystem undermines the unity of that system. The concept of particularity proposed requires a reformulation of its relation to the universality to which philosophical discourse aspires. Thus, while the English Canadian context is such as to give rise to the philosophical issue, its relevance is not entirely circumscribed by the situation of its emergence, but pertains more widely to the radical democratic project of reconciling equality, collective rights, and social differences. Indeed, multiculturalism in Canada has been an influence in the spread of the term and the issues related to it in other countries.[4] Philosophical universalism is attainable only through such particular origins, and it would be a failure of traditional philosophical formulations if it were the case that the conditions for the emergence of universality were not sufficiently accounted for in theoretical articulations. These conditions pertain to the translation of ethno-cultural traditions and, for this reason, are socially concrete in the issue of multiculturalism.

THE ORIGINALITY OF THE MULTICULTURAL CONTEXT

The multicultural issue says something very important about what English Canada has come to be in fact and, even more significant, about who we *want* to be. Indeed, if English Canada has anything to offer social and political philosophy other than new examples for already defined concepts, it will likely be in large part through its developing ideal of multiculturalism. The term "multiculturalism" can be used in several ways. It may be employed to describe a *sociological fact* in the sense that, as a result of immigration, the population is composed of a multitude of diverse ethnic groups. It may be used to refer to *government policy,* particularly the federal Multiculturalism Act of 1988, but also the various provincial acts and federal and provincial policies. In addition, it may be applied to a *social ideal* that expresses how English Canada ought to conduct itself. It is in the third sense that I am concerned with multiculturalism in this chapter. However, these usages are not mutually exclusive even though they are different. For example, one might argue that, because of the sociological fact of diversity, we have had the political history that has led to current government policy and that, as a consequence, we need to become clearer about the ideal of multiculturalism that we want to pursue. Moreover, such a social ideal might allow us to act more justly in the sociological context and design government policy more effectively. Indeed, such an argument lies behind this chapter. But this connection is not automatic. There can be no direct and immediate passage from social history to policy to philosophy. It is possible to argue, by way of contrast, that the fact of social diversity has led to a lack of national unity that must be overcome by a policy oriented exclusively towards what we have in common and that our particular social history of diverse ethnicities requires no special concern when formulating a social ideal philosophically. Both Gad Horowitz and Reginald Bibby have argued in this fashion. Horowitz put it quite clearly: "Continuation of our strong emphasis on regional and ethnic differentiation perpetuates fragmentation, prevents the emergence of any clear Canadian or English Canadian identity, and leaves the door wide open for Americanization."[5] Bibby's claim is that multiculturalism leads to a mere "coexistence" that undermines any possibility of shared vision or goals.[6] Any argument with respect to multiculturalism as a social ideal will draw upon both the facts of social history and government policy, but it cannot be reduced to them. An argument for or against a social ideal requires a normative argument. For this reason it can be considered a part of social and political philosophy.

I have chosen to use the term "social ideal" rather than "political ideal" here because the ideal in question pertains to English Canadian society as a whole and is not limited to political institutions. This usage obviously depends on the meanings given to the terms "social" and "political," an issue that I do not want to engage here, but if the term "political" is understood as the symbolic condensation of ideals pervasive in the society (rather than as limited to issues circumscribed by political institutions), then the other term would do as well. My intent is to develop a conception of multiculturalism as an ideal that is relevant throughout social interaction. I do not suggest that it is the only ideal relevant in English Canada or even that it is the only ideal that draws upon the particularity of English Canadian social history. I claim only that it is an important social ideal because it regards as salient the pre-modern traditions that are rooted in social history and reformulates them in a manner appropriate to a contemporary polity. In this sense, the concern with the public relevance of particularities of blood, love, intimacy, and tradition normally relegated to private life in modern society is comparable in a theoretical sense to the argument by feminism that, in Chantal Mouffe's words, "the public realm of modern citizenship was constructed in a universalistic and rationalistic manner that precluded the recognition of division and antagonism and that relegated to the private all particularity and difference."[7] To this extent a rethinking of the role of ethnicity in public life is a crucial part of a critique of the homogenization and pure proceduralism of liberal public life. When particularities normally relegated to private life are brought into the public sphere, they become "multi"; that is to say, multiculturalism is about a plurality of ethnicities in the same polity, not a single nation-state organized along ethnic lines. It is distinct in principle from ethnic nationalism, which regards other ethnicities as aliens within that, more often than not, must be expelled to "cleanse" the nation. Multiculturalism as a social ideal is about how to conduct oneself in a society constituted by a pluri-cultural context and how to design a concept of national identity that is inclusive of the plurality of traditions.

A prior step towards articulating a social ideal of multiculturalism as a new relation of particularity and universality is thus a definition of the originality of the multicultural context. I want to elaborate this definition through a critical analysis that shows how current debates on multiculturalism fail entirely to capture this originality and thereby propose analyses that are ineluctably led to deny the salience of ethnic particularities for public life. Multiculturalism is misunderstood and reduced to other phenomena in three main ways. Often, culture is regarded as merely an individual possession. The Multicultural Act (1988), for example, attempts to derive the rights of ethnic, religious, or linguistic minorities from the civil rights of individual persons before the law as a necessity to "redress any proscribed discrimination," which Prime Minister Pierre Trudeau had earlier described as "basically the conscious support of individual freedom and choice." This position is hardly surprising since Trudeau-style liberalism has been the dominant tradition denying collective rights in Canada.[8] Culture is thus reduced to being of the kind of variation that is normal between different individuals, and it is suggested that adequately protecting individuals also protects ethno-cultures. A protection against discrimination, based on this misunderstanding, is certainly a contribution to individual civil rights, but has nothing at all to do with suggesting that ethno-cultural differences should play a positive role in public life. Ethno-cultures – indeed, any cultures – are based on social groups whose internal interaction constitutes a tradition of practices of sufficient duration and style to solidify into a style of life that may be distinguished from other groups. Consequently, culture cannot be conceptualized as the possession of a single individual, and, even more important, the characteristics of individuals must be understood as, in large part, formed through a cultural tradition.

A second misunderstanding occurs when multiculturalism is reduced to ethnicity or group belonging, which is the form of belonging within a single subculture. Ethnic cultures may have been whole cultures before the process of immigration, but their separation from their original context and transplantation into English Canada has rendered each one a subculture; that is to say, each ethno-culture exists within a context in which there also exists a plurality of other ethno-cultures. This plurality is absolutely essential to understanding multiculturalism as a social experience and thus to determining its salience in policy and philosophy. The third manner of misunderstanding multiculturalism is by reducing it to the question of intercultural communication, as if one were to be fully formed within a single ethno-culture and were then to encounter others – which would entail the question of how one can come to understand another culture. This is the model for Charles Taylor's hermeneutic account of the multicultural ideal, which I criticize in the section below. All these misunderstandings reduce the originality of the multicultural context to another, albeit related, phenomenon – to individuals, to ethnicity, or to intercultural communication – and fail to capture the sense in which one is formed within a social context populated by a plurality of ethno-cultures. Thus they also fail when they address the question of what it may mean to propose multiculturalism as a social ideal.

I can now proceed to define the originality of the multicultural context through the conditions of its historical emergence. There are three axes of significance within which the phenomenon of multiculturalism arises in the English Canadian context. The colonial connection with the British empire was the primary basis for the emergence of critiques of the ethnic exclusivity of the ruling class, which began with the "bilingualism and biculturalism" debate in the 1960s with regard to French Canadians and "multiculturalism within a bilingual framework" afterwards. The post-colonial phase of Canadian history

has increasingly criticized privileging the British connection and asserted the multiple immigrant origins of all Canadians. As a consequence, there is a duality inherent in the popular term "ethnics"
because of the conditions of its emergence. The term "ethnic" can
refer to all those of non-British origin, as it once did, meaning more or
less "those who are not like us," or, to the extent that the privileged
British connection fades, it can refer to the "ethno-cultural roots of
whatever group," including English Canadians.[9] The latter usage
pertains to multiculturalism as a social ideal, whereas the former
refers to its origins in a critique of the colonial past.

Canada shares the second axis of multiculturalism with all other
immigrant societies. The phenomenon of immigration slices off a
fragment of a culture and inserts it in another history as a subculture.
If we can define a tradition hermeneutically as a historical continuity
constructed as a synthesis of past and future through an active interpretation in the present, then immigration shatters this threefold temporal structure with a dualism of before and after. The immigrant
society is a *layered periodization* of such dualisms – for example, the
difference between the Jews or Ukrainians who came before the Rus-
sian Revolution and those who came after. Many ethnic communities
in Canada are fundamentally structured by traumatic political events
that occurred elsewhere and motivated their departure. Moreover,
our society as a whole contains a multiplicity of these layered peri-
odizations. Their temporal structures are dualistic but rooted in histories that go back to different events in different parts of the world –
plural dualisms, we might say. The common elements are the dualism
and the tendency to regard the new country as a kind of haven, often
– though by no means always – fitting into a rhetoric of salvation. But
this element of salvation, unlike in the United States or other revolutionary New World societies, cannot be fitted into a redemptive myth
of national salvation. Nor can it, as in the case of European nations
claiming a long continuous tradition, such as England or France, be
fitted into a rhetoric of national character. Thus the rhetoric of salvation tends to remain within immigrant ethno-cultures themselves and
has, perhaps unfortunately, not generally influenced English Canadian national identity.

Our self-consciousness as a nation is more tenuous than that. The
third axis has to do with the fact that Canada, especially English Canada, is a New World society that was not born in a revolution. Therefore it can indulge neither in the myth of an ancient nation from time
out of mind (as in Europe) nor in a revolutionary founding that might
forge a new nation in an act of radical institution of a new order (as in
post-revolutionary New World nations). The two main temporal rhet-

orics of nationhood are denied to us. We are left with, on one side, a rhetoric of historical continuity imbedded in the British tradition that emphasizes the United Empire Loyalist rejection of the American Revolution and the conservative virtues of order, tradition, and parliamentary sovereignty[10] and, on the other side, a rhetoric of the multiple origins of presently coexisting ethno-cultures. The problem is that each of these captures only a half the current reality of our multicultural society within an English-language (and institutions) framework. No mediation or synthesis seems possible. Certainly, every national myth tends to play up and play down selected aspects of national history. However, the two main myths of English Canada both contain aspects of our history that cannot be ignored, since they are central to current reality, and cannot be mediated, since they would require a strong and encompassing sense of nationhood to do so. We thus tend to lurch back and forth between these two versions. We seem to have no rhetoric that we do not experience as partial at the very moment that it is enunciated, which is perhaps just another way of saying that we have no encompassing sense of nationhood. Here is a deeper reason for the suspicion of the adequacy of language, and of intellectuals, that pervades English Canadian culture.

These three axes of (post-)colonialism, immigration, and a weak concept of nationhood constitute both the historical conditions of emergence for the politics of multiculturalism in English Canada and the social framework that multiculturalism as a social ideal regards as salient. For some time now I have toyed, semi-seriously, with a hypothetical historical law: Multiculturalism represents a strong internal plurality that can only appear and be accepted if there is no strong external unity to oppose it. Or, more directly stated: The stronger the national identity, the lesser the acceptance of multiculturalism, and vice versa. On a comparative level, notice, for example, the greater opposition to multiculturalism in the name of national identity in Australia, the United States, and Argentina (to mention only a few examples that I am familiar with) than in English Canada. When the objection comes, as it does in English Canada too, it is on the same grounds, though usually with a strong prospective dimension recognizing that we do not (yet) have a strong national identity.[11] It is notable that critiques of multiculturalism, both in Canada and elsewhere, almost always take this rhetorical form: "What's the point of stressing our differences? They're all in the past (or destructive, or irrelevant). What's important is that we're all Canadians (or Australians, or Argentinians, or Americans, etc.)." That is, multicultural affiliations are experienced as *competing with* national ones, which implies that they are seen as being in *the same domain of relevance*. It does seem that a weak sense of national identity was historically necessary for the practice of multiculturalism to appear in English Canada in its particularly strong form. Nevertheless, multiculturalism as a political ideal involves much more than the actual maintenance of ethnic ties, which exists to a greater or lesser degree in all immigrant societies, but rather the articulation of the right to the retention and development of such ties within a larger social context. In other words, the justificatory ideal pertaining to the whole social context has come to be altered by the practice of multiculturalism.

This change has occurred much more completely at the level of everyday, institutional, and policy practices than as social and political philosophy. It is now possible to add that a social ideal of multiculturalism, if it is possible at all, will have to differentiate the domain of relevance of ethno-cultural affiliations from national ones. An inability to do so amounts to claiming, or admitting, that multicultural and national allegiances are *necessarily* opposed and that, as a consequence, *one* national society committed to multiculturalism is impossible. Stated more directly, it would suggest, as opponents of multiculturalism always tend to do, that ethno-cultural affiliations always and by definition tend to weaken and destroy larger social ones. As pointed out above, this view has been argued by Gad Horowitz and Reginald Bibby. In an earlier essay I also succumbed to this temptation, though arguing in opposition to this dominant tendency in nationalism that (English) Canadian identity *is and should be* a black hole in order to allow for a plurality of ethnic identities.[12] Both negative and positive versions of this thesis, however, derive from the same source, which is to regard ethno-cultural and national identities as competing in the same domain, in which case one is forced into a choice between the two. Put otherwise, if the hypothetical law holds as *history*, with regard to the conditions of emergence of multicultural practices, it cannot hold as *philosophy*, with regard to the articulation of a general right, without dividing the society to the point at which it ceases to be in any relevant respect a single society. Perhaps this quandary explains why multiculturalism has been more successful as practice than as theory, thus far at least. In order for it to become a content of the social ideal, the two domains must be understood as on different levels and therefore as not necessarily competing. Multiculturalism as a social ideal requires that the plurality of ethno-cultures been seen as a *key content of a shared national identity.*

The rhetoric of opposition between multiculturalism and (English) Canadian national identity is, however, pervasive. A recent example is the debate between Neil Bissoondath and Sheila Finestone, secretary of state for multiculturalism. In his book *Selling Illusions: The Cult of Multiculturalism in Canada* and in various magazine articles and public appearances based on the book, Bissoondath argued that he has personally been ghettoized and that Canada has deprived itself of a national identity as a result of multiculturalism. "To pretend that one has not evolved, as official multiculturalism so often seems to demand of us, is to stultify the personality, creating stereotype, stripping the individual of uniqueness: you are not yourself, you are your group."[13] Finestone responded by saying on the CBC television show *W5* that "there isn't any one Canadian identity. Canada has no national culture."[14] I do not want to take sides in this argument but to point out that there is an identical assumption that underlies and structures both positions. The rhetorical opposition in which both are caught is clear: that there is an either/or choice between national and multicultural identity. Whichever way one choses, one reinforces the underlying presupposition of the opposition. Social identity is always about "identity and difference." It is interesting how the rhetoric of opposition that is pervasive in contemporary debates formulates the issue as "identity *or* difference."

A CBC television news special on multiculturalism in 1994 insisted on the same rhetoric. At the beginning of the show, the moderator described multiculturalism as being about "acceptance, accomodation and, of course that most Canadian concept of all, compromise" and went on to refer to "what many believe multiculturalism should be: a search for our similarities, not a promotion of separateness."[15] The important word here is "not." It is this little word that rejects the possibility that multiculturalism might be a search for both our similarities and our differences, that it might be a way of working out within our own social and political history the dialectic of "identity *and* difference," within which all social identity operates. It must be recalled that this rhetorical position is not merely that of a contributor to the debate. It is articulated by the moderator prior to his turning to commentators and remains as a structuring assumption throughout. Later, when Haroon Siddiqui, editor of the *Toronto Star*, was trying unsuccessfully to escape the logic imposed by the rhetoric of opposition, the moderator asked if he agreed with the statement of one of his opponents that multiculturalism "is about separateness, not about similarity." Various positions were debated, but the assumptions of the rhetoric of opposition were, if not exactly mandatory, impossible to question or reject within the confines of the show.

The rhetoric of opposition gives rise to related and derivatory rhetorics. Occasionally, opposition is presented as a continuum in which the issue becomes whether we have gone "too far" in one direction or another.[16] In this case, it is still a question of opposites, but one is not faced with a dichotomous either/or choice but rather with a "too much or too little" alternative. Another variation is the rhetoric of the slippery slope, in which "difference" is quickly redefined as "separation" and later "ghettoization." Any recognition of difference thus quickly becomes stigmatized as, in Bissoondath's words, "society's view of the individual's assigned place within its construct." It is just such a slippery slope that allows him to characterize the acceptance of diversity and difference by multiculturalism as leading to "a classic ghetto" and "a zoo of exoticism."[17] Here we still have an opposition, but one that is inflected as both more slippery – leading one to fall entirely to one side if one takes the first small step – and more coercive in that the recognition of difference is claimed, or assumed, necessarily to entail separation, stigmatization, marginalization, and ghettoization.

The rhetoric of opposition and its derivatives, whose scope I have been able only to indicate through these examples, structures contemporary public debate concerning multiculturalism. This critical rhetorical analysis should make one point clear: if a social ideal of multiculturalism is to become a key component of a social and political philosophy for English Canada, multiculturalism and national identity must be conceptualized as pertaining to different domains of relevance. They occur at different "levels," as it were, and thus do not (or at least, need not) come into conflict. From this point of view, one aspect of multicultural practice is key for the development of a philosophy of multiculturalism. The retention and development of ethno-cultural affiliations occurred in a social context in which, in order to succeed, it was articulated, not as a *particular right*, but as a *universal right*. This was not the case with regard to arguments for the inclusion of French Canadians, or Quebec, as one of two "founding nations," since the conditions presented for such inclusion could not be generalized to ethno-cultural groups. Neither would it be the case if First Nations were to attain a similar recognition as founding nations. Neither French Canadians nor Aboriginal peoples are an ethnic group in this sense.[18] The issue posed by multiculturalism as a social ideal is thus *the universalization of a right to particularity within a pluri-cultural, unilingual framework*, and it is in such a formulation that multiculturalism as a social ideal in English Canada may make a contribution to the extension of democratic theory to include the public recognition of particularities.

CRITIQUE OF HERMENEUTIC ETHICS

The retention and development of ethno-cultures is pursued by multiculturalism because it is claimed that individuals are not *just* individuals, but rather that the well-being of individuals depends on a sense of shared identity and that a major source of such collective identity is the cultural practices of ethno-cultural groups. Charles Taylor has argued in this vein, particularly with reference to Quebec, that the "horizon of meaning" provided by group membership is essential to an individual's discovery of his or her own identity. In Jürgen Habermas's phrasing, Taylor claims that a constitution must be "situated in the horizon of the history of a nation."[19] This Herderian view is by no means shared by all commentators, especially those whose focus is on the current ravages of ethnic nationalism and its demonizing of the other. Habermas himself, for example, contrasts national identity based in an ethnic community of descent with the notion of a nation of citizens based upon universal civil rights. He argues that "a political culture in the seedbed of which constitutional principles are rooted by no means has to be based on all citizens sharing the same language or the same ethnic and cultural origins."[20] The requisite commonality can be found instead in a common political culture. Citing the examples of the multinational states of Switzerland and the United States in this context – to which we might add Canada – Habermas argues that in a future Europe national traditions will be "related to and relativized by the vantage points of other national cultures."[21]

The distinction between ethnic and civic nationalism has been taken up by Michael Ignatieff, who also associates ethnic nationalism with other-directed violence used to sustain inner-group belonging and argues that the civilizing alternative is a civic nationalism shorn of any resonance to ethnic cultural traditions. In particular, he notes a phenomenon that he derives from Freud's term "the narcissism of minor difference" and claims that the violent assertion of differences often, or mainly, occurs when they are minor with respect to the whole ways of life of the respective communities. Perhaps closest to the present argument, he observes that "Quebec nationalists insist on the cultural and social distinctiveness of their society at exactly the moment it is losing so much of what made it distinctive."[22] This observation, and many others like it with regards to Serbs and Croats, for example, serves as an island from which Ignatieff unlooses many barbs against ethnic nationalism, embroiled as it is in so many irrational and unconscious processes. But he proposes no understanding of this phenomenon at all. Indeed, he uses the observation only to cast supercilious aspersions on any and all manifestations of ethnic solidarity. However, it is very important to understand how this phenomenon of the escalation of the perceived importance of differences (perhaps, to an observer's eyes, small ones) functions. How does it work? It is when a cultural identity finds itself threatened by possible extinction – perhaps by becoming indistinguishable from its neighbours – that the assertion of cultural distinctiveness emerges. If there is no other basis in history or current institutions for the preservation and extension of this identity, it is asserted as a violent movement of purification fuelled by a demonization of the other, *especially* the other who is closest and most difficult to distinguish. Even this short comment on the process of differentiation suggests two points that find no place in Ignatieff's analysis. First, it is not ethnic identity as such that leads to violence but the threatening situation, a situation in which many other institutional identifications are also precarious. Second, the violent turn occurs in the absence of alternative sources of confirmation of identity. Thus proposing civic nationalism as an alternative fails to address either the problem of general institutional failure at such times or, even more important in the present context, other processes of identification that might provide a buffer to the violent turn.

Outright rejection of the public recognition of ethno-cultural differences such is proposed by commentators in favour of civic nationalism cannot be expected to buffer the very violent turn of events to which they point as evidence of the dangers of ethnic nationalism. I by no means wish to minimize those dangers. However, when observers fail to see that it is not ethnic identity as such that leads in this direction, but rather threats to the maintenance of ethnic identity, a major source for a more civilized outcome is ignored and the contribution of civic nationalism to creating the perceived threat remains undiagnosed. The politics of multiculturalism in English Canada might be analysed as a source for alternative thinking at this point, especially if it can find some theory to match its practice.

The proponents of civic nationalism are partly right, of course, to the extent that a polity that guarantees individual rights independent of ethnic belonging is a key component of civilized intercourse between citizens whose ethno-cultural origins are diverse. This is the historic truth of liberalism, with its focus on the rights of individuals. It does not have anything to say, however, about the right to survival of ethno-cultures. Civic nationalism cannot adequately address the issues of ethno-cultural belonging, whose worst turn it names but does not explain. By denying public representation to ethno-cultural differences, it banishes them to the realm of irrational impulses. Habermas points, in part, to the relativizing of particular traditions that must be involved, but his adherence to civic nationalism must construe this relativizing as privatizing, as a cutting off from the universalizing aspects of public discourse. Thus, ironically, civic nationalism breeds, or at least cannot stem, the very reaction of ethnic violence that it condemns. But relativizing of traditions is only one side of the issue. The other is the lifting of particular traditions from mere particularism towards their universalizing dimensions. It is this process that I wish to highlight by distinguishing the concept of "particularity" from particularism. This possibility is cut off at the root by civic nationalism. The solution rather lies, in my view, with representing such differences in a context where their universalizing components are emphasized and developed. Thus the conception of "universalizing" that is proposed here is quite different from the concept of an already achieved (at least in principle) "universality" proposed by Habermas and other proponents of civic nationalism. Whereas in ethnic nationalism the differences of others are represented as outside the civic order, multiculturalism represents particular differences within a civic context of plural ethno-cultures. In civic nationalism such differences are excluded from public life in favour of the identity of all citizens. Multiculturalism as a social ideal is thus distinct from both ethnic nationalism and civic nationalism. It neither eliminates differences from within public life (like civic nationalism) nor places them outside (like ethnic nationalism), but rather transforms the relationship of inside and outside. The "outside" is brought in and, through its civic expression, thereby loses the demonized character that leads to ethnic violence.

The retention and deveopment of ethno-cultures is pursued in the present social climate because it is claimed that individuals are not *just* individuals, but that the well-being of individuals depends rather on a sense of shared identity and that a major source of such collective identity is the cultural practices of ethno-cultural groups. Multiculturalism is thus about the public representation of ethno-cultural differences and their significance for the formation of social identity, and though it is certainly not the only politics of identity in contemporary societies, it is nevertheless the specific political form that the retention and development of traditional cultures takes in contemporary societies. The politics of identity, as Charles Taylor argues in his essay on multiculturalism "The Politics of Recognition," is made up of both dignity and authenticity. Dignity is basically the democratic idea that human beings are worthy of equal respect, whereas authenticity refers to the notion that each human being has a unique way of being human. Taylor claims that since identities are formed in dialogue with others, a refusal to recognize the value of this unique way of being human can be seen as a form of damage needing a social remedy. As a consequence, there are two modes of politics. One, centring on the equality of rights, sets aside differences in individual identities, and the second, centring on recognition of particular identities, focuses precisely on these differences. The existence of these two modes leads to a significant tension with regard to particular identities. As Taylor phrases it, the "reproach the first makes to the second is just that it violates the principle of nondiscrimination. The reproach the second makes to the first is that it negates identity by forcing people into a homogeneous mold that is untrue to them ... The claim is that the supposedly neutral set of difference-blind principles of the politics of equal dignity is in fact a reflection of one hegemonic culture."[23] It is this claim that initiates multiculturalism as a major form of contemporary identity politics.

The burden of Taylor's argument is to defend a conception of collective rights against the procedural view of rights as solely individual that predominates in the United States, although it is certainly exists elsewhere. The procedural view is that "a liberal society cannot accomodate publicly espoused notions of the good" because it will necessarily be "a depreciation of those who do not personally share this definition."[24] In short, any public definition of collective identity will be repressive – itself constitute a harm – to those who do not share it, and at least in a democratic regime, any compulsion to share a collective identity must be excluded in principle. Procedural liberalism thus regards as illegitimate any legislation, such as Quebec's language laws, that would seek to protect and perpetuate a specific collective identity through public resources. In "The Politics of Recognition" Taylor simply asserts the cogency of a collective conception of liberalism, but the reason for this assertion is spelled out clearly in an earlier essay entitled "Why Do Nations Have to Become States?" "For each individual to discover in himself what his humanity consists in, he needs a horizon of meaning, which can only be provided by some allegiance, group membership, cultural tradition. He needs, in the broadest sense, a language in which to ask and answer the questions of ultimate significance."[25] Quebec's right to language legislation consists in the preservation and development of such a French-speaking horizon of meaning into the future. Federal support for "Canadian national culture" would do the same, even though language is not its main component. The liberal credentials of such a society consist in the tolerance with which those who do not share this collective identity are treated.[26] They are minorities in more than a numerical sense in that their identities are not recognized to the same degree in the public realm.

The defence of collective rights that Taylor developed largely in the context of Quebec's collective goals is also the basis for a conception of "deep diversity" with respect to Canadian national identity. He defines first-level diversity as pertaining to "great differences in culture and outlook and background in a population that nevertheless shares the same idea of what it is to belong to Canada." This diversity can be protected by a conception of individual rights such as has been institutionalized in the Canadian Charter of Rights and Freedoms. Such belonging "would not 'pass through' some other community, although the ethnic identification might be important to him or her in various ways."[27] According to Taylor, this is the model for multiculturalism in English Canada. He then goes on to argue that it is not a deep diversity such as that required for the inclusion of Quebec or Aboriginal peoples into Canada, in which each group would "belong in a different way" and be Canadian "through being members of their national communities."[28] He likens this deep diversity of modes of belonging to the new European citizenship, in which one is a European *through* being French, Spanish, Italian, and so on.[29] This model of deep diversity is important for conceptualizing plural modes of belonging that are, so to speak, on different *levels* and do not necessarily conflict with each other. Nevertheless, in our present context it is interesting that deep diversity is explicitly denied to multiculturalism in English Canada. Moreover, an essential part of the earlier argument was that the putative universalism of individualist, procedural conceptions of rights was not really universal because it incorporated a hegemonic culture into its actual functioning or, at the very least, did not embody within itself any brake on cultural homogenization. In Taylor's cautious phrasing, "while procedural liberalism doesn't seek to abolish difference, it is nevertheless inhospitable to difference."[30] Thus, if multiculturalism incorporates only such a shallow, first-level concept of diversity, it will not be capable of both preserving and developing ethno-cultures into the future. In short, the origin of Taylor's discussion in the language politics of Quebec with regard to Ottawa seems to limit its applicability in the case of multiculturalism in English Canada. This suspicion turns out to be warranted when we return to the key argument of "The Politics of Recognition."

In defining his own position more exactly, Taylor considers the claim often made in the context of multicultural discussions that we should recognize the equal worth of all cultures. He notes that his previous argument does not sustain this claim, but only that cultures can legitimately take certain public measures of self-defence and self-perpetuation. While the claim that we should recognize the equal worth of all cultures has a certain element of truth in it as a *presumption guiding actual investigations*, Taylor argues that the claim as such is not only false but demeaning. Recalling his defence of collective rights through the hermeneutic notion of a "horizon of meaning," he contends that intercultural understanding takes place through a "fusion of horizons," in Gadamer's sense, in which "we learn to move in a broader horizon, within which what we have formerly taken for granted as the background to valuation can be situated as one possibility alongside the different background of the formerly unfamiliar culture."[31] In the first place, the claim that we ought to recognize the equal worth of cultures is an attempt to dictate the result of an investigation before it takes place. Taylor's analysis has the ring of truth here. It certainly seems that one of the practical dilemmas to which the politics of multiculturalism has given rise is to provide the hermeneutic interpretive circle with a vicious twist: if all cultures are worthy of equal respect, each and every cultural investigation will come to the conclusion that "their" way of doing things is just as good as "ours," though from a different point of view. The investigator will be reluctant to register any deep differences with moral implications, and whenever it seems necessary to do so, we will be treated to shallow moralistic reminders that it only seems strange to us because, well, because we're us and they're them.

Thus cultural investigations are cut off from meaningful moral inquiry and can only result in superficial empirical knowledge of different practices whose difference cannot in principle impinge on the quality of perception of the human condition from varying cultural worlds. This all-too-common way of phrasing the problem of intercultural understanding makes it trivial on the one hand and, on a second look, really impossible: since I "know" in advance that cultures are worthy of equal respect, my inquiry will conclude that the other culture has equal resources and concepts in all important respects to my own and thus, on reflection, that I did not need to undertake the inquiry because I have not gained any knowledge relevant to my understanding of the human condition in the process. The argument that supposedly undermines ethnocentrism actually roots it more deeply. Moreover, as an unexamined prejudgment, such "recognition" of equal worth only succeeds in reducing all investigation to the confirmation of the prejudices of the investigator, in the style of a "Nietzschean" reduction of knowledge to power. As Taylor points out, a prior judgment of equal worth that is based on no knowledge or experience is actually condescending and demeaning. It presupposes that "we already have the standards to make such judgments. The standards we have, however, are those of North Atlantic civilization. And so the judgments implicitly and unconsciously will cram the others into our categories."[32] The irony is that this is not a necessary result, but derives from the malformation of the ethical postulate.

Thus the claim that we should accord equal respect to all cultures does not stand up to scrutiny, in Taylor's view. Nonetheless, it is reasonable to suppose that "all cultures that have provided the horizon of meaning for large numbers of human beings, of diverse characters and temperaments, over a long period of time" have something admirable about them.[33] As a presumption, this view is beyond reproach, but its foundation is not that we ought to give equal respect to all cultures, but rather "a sense of our own limited part in the whole human story."[34] On Taylor's account, claims for the dignity of all cultures cannot be extended beyond a presumption dependent for confirmation on subsequent inquiry to be a substantive moral claim in its own right. Respect is derived not from positive knowledge of all cultures – who could claim such a knowledge? no wonder its actual basis is an uninformed and misguided ethical demand – but from a reflexive sense of one's own limitation. From this position, one can turn outward to encountering other cultures in a way that is genuinely expanding of one's horizon. I have no argument whatever with Taylor's hermeneutic claim with regard to the foundation of intercultural understanding, but I do not believe that it adequately captures the originality of the multicultural context.

Let us attend closely to the us/them formulation in the above account. It is a lack of complete self-knowledge that leads "us" out to an encounter with "them." The assumed standpoint of the account is an "us" that is adequate to the case of intercultural understanding, since what does one have to start with but one's own culture? To state *inter*cultural understanding on these terms is fine, but a *multi*cultural society poses a different issue. First, one cannot speak of living within the single culture originally. It is not a "culture" in the sense of a self-sufficient formation with external borders, but a *sub*culture. It has been made such by immigration. Second, the sense of "us" is thus ambiguous in the multicultural context. Does it refer to the us that I share with those of my ethno-cultural group? Does it mean the us who inhabit the multicultural context as such, namely, all the members of the different ethno-cultural groups? Or does it refer to the ethno-cultural roots of the traditional elite that the policies of multiculturalism were meant to displace? And even, what if one's own culture is defined as "them" within the society? I think that these problems indicate that the key issue of multicultural understanding is an us/we relation, not an us/them one. By this I mean the "us" to refer to one's ethno-cultural group and the "we" to refer to the multi-cultural civic context of English Canada.

The issue is how can I be a member of an ethno-cultural group and at the same time a member of a multicultural society. An us/them relation in this context could refer to an attempt by someone from the traditional elites to expand the basis of their understanding when the conditions of their own belonging are not in question. Taylor's reference to "our" standards of North Atlantic civilization indicate that this is the standpoint of his theory. Such a standpoint pertains more to the historical conditions of the emergence of multiculturalism in English Canada than to its future as a social ideal. More to the point, a self/other relation could refer to an encounter *between* two or more ethno-cultural groups *within* the multicultural context, but even this case is complicated by the fact that the multicultural context is neither "owned" by only one of the groups (as in the first case) nor absent (in which case it would be reduced to the intercultural situation). The question posed by the social ideal of multiculturalism in English Canada pertains primarily to levels of the "self," not to the relation between the self and the other. The issue, then, does seem to be how one can participate in English Canada *through* involvement in an ethno-cultural group. Or, alternatively stated, how does one step back from one's involvement in an immediate and particular culture in order to uncover levels of participation in more universal dimensions? Taylor saw this issue in the context of Quebec and Canada, but in his earlier work he relegated the discussion of multiculturalism to the domain of individual rights. The essay "The Politics of Recognition" goes somewhat further in arguing for a presumption of worth in relation to other cultures. But in defining such cultures as "other" he fails to grasp what is crucial about the politics of multiculturalism in English Canada, which I have defined above as the *universalization of a right to particularity within a pluri-cultural, unilingual framework*. In order to do that, we need to begin from another angle, in which the issue is not one's access to the other, but rather the justification of what is "one's own."

A DEFENCE OF PARTICULARITY

The politics of multiculturalism suggests a process of identity formation within a context of differences that is not, at least in principle, in competition with a wider national identity common to all. Indeed, one key feature of this national identity that would commend it to the different groups would be its fostering of the retention and development of ethno-cultures. Such a multicultural context transforms the role of ethno-cultural tradition insofar as it is experienced *from the outset* as one possibility among others.[35] The uniqueness of one's own way of experiencing the world is immediately apparent. What becomes problematic and in need of development is the sense of the *validity* of this way and its *inclusion* in the common identity. Charles Taylor recognizes the "universality of particularism," in the sense that *every* identity and intellectual tradition is necessarily particular and that consequently what is at issue is the recognition of the right to particularity as a *universal principle*. Such a principle is universal in a different sense, however, than in the equal-rights version of applying in the same way to each and all. This interpretation implies that a recognition of particularity actually requires a rethinking of the notions of particularity and universality, and Taylor has not addressed this issue at all.[36] Thus, in the passage from the perception of uniqueness to its justification, the "us" is constituted; in the passage from the "us" to a multicultural context that includes many ethno-cultures, the "we" is formed. The issue of dignity in multiculturalism emerges not, as Taylor supposes, as a claim for the equal respect of all cultures, but in the first place, as that *my own culture* be accorded equal respect with those that are now recognized. It is not primarily an intercultural issue, but a self-justificatory one. The following discussion of particularity as the central concept for a social and political philosophy of multiculturalism is thus concerned primarily with these two issues: a *justification* of particularity, which must of necessity be retrospective, and the *formulation* of a universality inclusive of differences, which is projective and anticipatory.

George Grant introduced the term "one's own," or "particularity," in order to defend the existence of Canada against its incorporation into the United States. In his book *Lament for a Nation* he phrased the philosophical issue in this way: "The belief in Canada's continued existence has always appealed against universalism. It appealed to particularity against the wider loyalty of the continent. If universalism is the most 'valid modern trend,' then is it not right for Canadians to welcome our integration into the empire?"[37] Of course, the specific nature of this universalism can be opened to criticism as well, but even the greatest dissent on this score would not be enough to justify Canada's own way towards the universal. Why should one not merge one's criticism with the most positive trends available in the United States? Why should one resist incorporation into larger structures if there is not something about one's own way towards the universal that is of ultimate worth? Notice that in Charles Taylor's defence of the French-language "way" in Quebec, it was necessary to argue that an intellectual tradition and a whole way of life is compacted in language. This argument is current in contemporary philosophical accounts of the cultural and human significance of language such that a different language is enough to suggest a different way of life of sufficient depth and diversity to warrant protection. However, there is no language difference between English Canada and the United States, nor indeed in comparison with Britain. For that reason, the struggle for our distinctiveness has not centred on language. As Taylor and others have pointed out, this fact has tended to produce a shallow concept of language in English Canada, in which it is understood merely as a "medium of communication" without cultural significance for social identity. It has even led to viewing English Canada as mainly, or even entirely, committed to the doctrine of procedural individual rights that predominates in the United States. Certainly, the Charter of Rights, not to mention the FTA and NAFTA, have accelerated this component of English Canadian culture, and it was indeed at stake in the fiasco over the Meech Lake constitutional accord.[38] However, there is also a tradition of collective rights in English Canada, and the fact that it is not immediately tied to language differences may make it even more significant for understanding contemporary cultural identities.

By way of contrast to this reduction of English Canada, George Grant's concept of one's own is an attempt to capture the core of the defence of different cultural identities when it can not be self-evidently pinned on language. In a classic statement of the issue, he wrote: "To live in a world of these violent empires, and in a satellite of the greatest of them, presents complex problems of morality. The problems may be stated thus. In human life there must always be place for love of the good and love of one's own. Love of the good is man's highest end, but it is of the nature of things that we come to know and to love what is good by first meeting it in that which is our own – this particular body, this family, these friends, this woman, this part of the world, this set of traditions, this country, this civilization … In many parts of our lives the two loves need never be in conflict. In loving our friends we are also loving the good. But sometimes the conflict becomes open."[39] The immediate context to which Grant was referring was the Vietnam War, but the issue remains central for any English Canadian nationalism. If we are to justify our own way as separate from that of the United States, it must be because there is in this place a way towards the good that is justified because it is our own.

We know the universal *through* the particularities that make it concrete for us. But even more, we are cut off from such a passage towards the universal if we must sacrifice our own along the way. When a culture is sacrificed, when I must forget my own in order to pass on towards the universal, the universal remains without incarnation in my world. It becomes necessarily abstract, in the sense of lacking relation to the here and now, and my own becomes *merely* my own, parochial. This is the experience of all those who live in the shadow of empires. Within the United States or France or Britain, every place has its own uniqueness and yet partakes in the national identity. It is this *passage between* the particular and the universal that is blocked for those who live in a subculture which is not taken up into the larger identity. Thus the particular seems to be completely arbitrary and the universal a merely dry abstractness. In a phrase, the we/us relation is blocked. A philosophy concerned to address this situation must consider both the *justification of the particular* identity and a version of the universal that allows its *inclusion in universality* in order to restore the passage between the local here and now and the connection with humanity as such. This is the situation as described from within the sense of loss, of being cut off, experienced by identities that are not recognized by the larger social context. The description seems to me apposite to the situation of multiculturalism, which requires a rethinking of particular and universal from within the experience of the partiality and yet necessity of one's own ethnoculture. It begins from us, not from them. It is, so to speak, a double-sided turning towards the particular and towards the universal from a beginning in a mid-range position. This is the philosophical duty that one may expect from the concept of particularity.

George Grant's use of the term "particularity" is tied to the polemical context in which it was formulated. His main allegiance in this regard was Canadian nationalism, and it can fairly be considered a continuation of the Loyalist version of a conservative, communitarian Canada in the face of the liberal individualism of the United States.[40] The concept of particularity is used by Grant, I believe without exception, in order to defend a particular allegiance at a moment in which it is perceived as threatened. This is why it is relevant to the development of a political philosophy for multiculturalism. But like multiculturalism itself, the concept of particularity has to develop beyond its conditions of emergence and stand on its own feet. It must go beyond being formulated as *against* a deficient concept of universality towards a formulation of a new particularity-universality nexus. In what remains of this chapter I will develop the concept of particularity beyond its polemical formulation in Grant's work into a basic concept for contemporary political philosophy.

Clarification of the concept of particularity can begin by distinguishing it from the concept of contingency, which is widespread in contemporary philosophical discourse. The discourse of contingency and its defence as a proper concern for philosophy was most force-fully argued by existentialism. The first appearance of the term "con-tingency" in Jean-Paul Sartre's *Being and Nothingness* is in the context of explaining human being as always existing in a "condition which it has not chosen." Humans are thrown into a "situation" insofar as one's being is bound up with factuality and does not provide its own foundation. Here contingency refers to the fact that "the explanation and the foundation of my being – in so far as I am a *particular being* – can not be sought in necessary being."[41] The immediate structure of human being is in its presence to a world that cannot be derived from structures of universality. The term "contingency" is thus a way of in-troducing into philosophy a concern with non-necessary, non-univer-sal elements of a particular being's situation – in fact, of bringing philosophy down from the level of what is everywhere and always the case to issues that arise for a temporally and spatially particular-ized concrete being. It is not too much to say that the term is part and parcel of a critique of traditional philosophy and a turning towards particularity. "Contingency" itself, however, is especially derived from "non-necessary," in the sense of that which cannot be accounted for or explained. There are actually two different inflections here: one, the contingent cannot be *derived from* the universal; it is more than a mere example; and two, it cannot be accounted for or explained. These two inflections appear to be identical if the accounting for or explaining is understood on the model of derivation from the univer-sal, that is, a mode of explanation characteristic of the traditional phi-losophy that is here being criticized. Therefore we may say that, to the extent that a new mode of philosophical discourse is achieved and "accounting for" no longer takes this traditional form, the differ-ence between the two inflections becomes more marked.[42]

Sartre's use of the term "contingency" compresses two meanings that it is now necessary to distinguish. In the terminology that I would like to suggest, particularity is more than an example of uni-versality; it refers to the fact that a temporally and spatially bound be-ing is thrown into a situation that it does not create. Contingency, by way of contrast, refers to the non-derivability of particularity from traditional modes of philosophical discourse. The notion that particu-larity cannot be accounted for or explained is based upon Sartre's maintenance of a traditional version of what philosophical explana-tion would consist in. Thus his use of the term "contingency" inflects the concept in the direction of non-accountability, inability of expla-nation, and arbitrariness. To the extent that philosophical explanation can, or has been, turned towards human situations – as Sartre himself recommended – and the model of explanation itself reformulated as a result, then "contingency" is no longer appropriate. The particularity that requires philosophical articulation is cut off from that articulation if it is interpreted as *purely contingent* in the manner of Sartre. The distinction between particularity and contingency, in sharp contrast, opens up the particularities of human situations to philosophical articulation and, in the same moment, implies a reformulation of the concept of philosophy. From this standpoint, Sartre's role was to have opened up a new conception of philosophy that his own formulation prevented from emerging properly. Particularity need no longer be defined as against universality, but as the very *condition for* whatever universality the human being may be able to apprehend.

The more recent use of the term "contingency" by Richard Rorty in *Contingency, Irony and Solidarity* contains a similar slide between particularity and contingency,[43] even connecting the terms with idiosyncracy, thus suggesting that it is a characteristic of contemporary philosophy to identify the two, not merely an individual proclivity. Rorty introduces the term "contingency" in order to oppose the notion that there is a "core self" to all human beings regardless of their spatial and temporal location. He claims that "what counts as being a decent human being is relative to historical circumstance, a matter of transient consensus about what attitudes are normal and what practices are just or unjust."[44] All human characteristics are plunged into a social and historical relativism such that the question of why not to be cruel to other human beings is denied the possibility of any non-circular answer.[45] Sartre would certainly not have gone so far; nonethless, it does seem to be a consequence of making contingency basic to philosophical discourse. The interpretation of morality as a language and languages as historical contingencies has, Rorty claims, the consequence that moral action is a matter of "identifying oneself with such a contingency."[46] The action of identifying with a contingency, however, does not have any particular force. The contingency simply remains a contingency.

This limitation occludes at a deeper level one of the key components of the distinction for which I am arguing. While the components of socio-historical location are contingent, in the sense of non-necessary and non-derivable from universals, identification with such components renders them essential for recognition of the identity of the individual or group in question. Identity comes about through precisely such processes of identification with practices and components of a world. They no longer merely surround the actor, but become part of the self-definition of the actor. Rorty's conclusions only appear to follow because contingency, in his view, is necessarily opposed to universality. Thus he denies any meaningful possibility of identification with the universal category of human beings as such, claiming that any "we" is necessarily contrasted to a "they."[47] In the case of multicultural-alism, this view would lead to the consequence that any ethno-cultural group is only definable as against another group and that identification with the multicultural context as a common good is impossible. The origin of this error can now be defined clearly: first, in the slide between the meanings of particularity and contingency and, second, in the failure to account for the *effective power of identification*. These components are central to the concept of particularity that I want to develop in the context of a political philosophy for multicul-turalism.

If I can generalize from these two examples, it seems that contem-porary philosophical discourse is paralysed by a contradiction. On the one hand, it wishes to open up the realm of the specificity of spa-tial and temporal location to investigation as opposed to the straight-forward universals of traditional philosophy. But on the other hand, it opens up this territory solely in contrast to traditional philosophical categories and thereby misrepresents the phenomenon. As a conse-quence, contemporary philosophy tends to take a sceptical and rela-tivist turn. The distinction between contingency and particularity would avoid this consequence by paving the way for a renewal of the particularity-universalizing (as articulation of situations) nexus in-stead of remaining within the contingency-universality (as necessity) dead end. Grant's polemic against universality has a certain similar-ity to that of Sartre and Rorty in its critique of deficient universals, but with the crucial difference that it is concerned to justify the legiti-macy of mid-range identifications. For this reason it contains the pos-sibility of a further development beyond the polemical context that can address, rather than succumb to, the contradiction of contempo-rary philosophy.

The distinction of particularity from contingency provides the philosophical basis for distinguishing the exclusive tribe loyalty al-luded to at the beginning of this chapter from a defence of one's own that opens out to justification of the legitimacy of others' identities also. Moreover, the respect demanded for one's own culture – as a result of the multicultural context in which it is articulated as a uni-versalizing justification – tends to become a moral justification of the worth of all cultures. The definition of this concept of particularity requires that one take a "step back" with regard to one's everyday involvements in a collective identity in order to recognize that it *is* endangered, that it *should* be preserved and extended, and that this project requires that such a right be extended to *others* as well. It is thus a continuation of the concept of the border that was developed in the preceding chapter. Such a reflexive step back concerns the common origin of ontology and axiology. It turns the purely inherited, or socially formed, character of collective identity into a project capable of rational justification. Such reflection is concrete in the sense that it does not pulverize the belonging upon which it reflects but rather articulates it and preserves it in a new form. In this sense the reflexive turn constitutes a new mediation between particularity and universality by originating the possibility of a rational discourse concerning belonging. It is a reflexive turn from within social action, not epistemology, and therefore occurs within the realm of love and hate, suffering and joy, and concerns their opening out to philosophical articulation.

Particularity thus involves *embracing* ethno-cultural identity, not just inheriting it. The step back begins from the experience of affective belonging that is one's own, which requires that other belongings be seen from the outside and justified in a moral discourse of equal worth. The multicultural context establishes the difference in one's own case between being seen from the outside and experienced as one's own from within. This distinction allows the transfer to others of the necessity for affective belonging of ethno-cultural components that do not have this meaning for me. The transfer is itself more affective than rational; it concerns the domain that was traditionally called empathy in the human sciences. The interplay between inside and outside occurs both for myself and for the other though in a manner than cannot be mediated by a dialectic because the positions cannot be made reversible. It thus does not culminate in a synthesis, but in a respect for the Otherness of the other, a recognition of difference not an *alter ego*, a letting go of the desire to be completely in charge of human universality. To state this more precisely: every human individual exists as a relation between particularity and universality. But the universality is only available through the mediation of the Other's particularity, which I can only see as practices from the outside, as it were. Thus the relations may be stated this way: I *feel* my own belonging; I *know* the other's difference; I *justify* my own belonging; I *justify* the other's belonging; we *understand* that human life is about identities; we *engage* each other in the construction of a common culture that illuminates human universality. In this way, an us/them relation that always contains the possibility of turning violent as a result of its exclusion of the other is mitigated and surpassed through a we/us relation.

This mutual relation does not supersede affectivity with reason in the same way for both sides. It therefore shows a way around the zero-sum identity game that is described on the us/them model by civic nationalists. Against Michael Ignatieff, it is not the case that "we are only likely to be more tolerant of other identities if we also learn to love our own a little less."[48] Love, or even respect, is not a zero-sum game. Rather, to the extent that I am drawn into a universalizing discourse justifying my own identity, then precisely to that extent I will be drawn out to recognize the identity of the Other. The Other remains Other, as I remain attached to my own in a manner distinct from the cultures of Others. It cannot be a dialectic, and it cannot issue in an identity of feeling and reason. Thus it involves, necessarily, a tragic sense that something of what is essential to humanity will escape me, that this is the very condition of experiencing the collective identity that defines human life. The step back discloses that the condition for the appearance of any universality is the particularity that can connect one to the universal only through others. Access to the universal requires respect for otherness. Particularity is not the opposite of universality but its condition, as universality is not the transcendence of particularity but its articulation. Philosophy is thus not a universal, but a *universalizing*, discourse.[49] This conception thereby leads towards a conception of universality that is not homogenizing in the sense of ejecting all particularity and difference from public life, but that is a basis for sustaining particular traditions while not merely "relativizing" them in Habermas's sense but rather leading them on towards their universal dimensions.

If it should be discovered subsequently that I cannot (continue to) deem that another (sub)culture deserves equal respect, this discovery will be acknowledged in a reflection retreating from the universalizing claim. It is experienced with sadness and tragedy. The justificatory discourse extends, in the first place, to a claim for the equal worth of all (sub)cultures. Perhaps it may have to retreat, in the second place, to its denial in a specific case. But the situation is the reverse of that described by Taylor. A first presumption leading to, in some cases, a positive knowledge of equal worth is not morally sufficient for a multicultural society. First comes the universalizing postulate of equal worth; second, if necessary, the reluctant retreat based on the discovery of one's inability to accord it in a given case. This retreat is itself based on one's own identity – what I/we cannot accept and still be ourselves. This is the point at which a we/they relation may distil out of a failure of the we/us relation. Taylor's account reduces the multicultural context to one of intercultural knowledge. The present one restores its originality as a moral practice that requires a postulate of equal worth.[50] Only this is sufficient to put in its key place the multicultural context itself and not to substitute for it either a non-ethnic civic context or an intercultural one.

AN ETHIC OF RESPECT

An ethics based upon one's own particularity and moving outward to its abjection in respect for the Other occurs within a multicultural context that comprises ongoing ethno-culturally derived everyday practices, historically derived institutions, and justificatory discourses. The main justificatory discourses in English Canada, as elsewhere, stem from the institutional power of the capitalist economy and the central government. Multiculturalism is significant insofar as it constitutes a critical current centring on collective rights in opposition to private-property rights and market exchanges. It can be made effective insofar as it becomes part of the defined content of national identity. In English Canada, the tradition of collective rights – though certainly endangered by the current slide towards individualist procedural rights under the influence of the United States, the free trade agreements, and the Charter of Rights – can both support a multicultural social ideal and, in turn, find an additional source of renewal in multiculturalism.

That the philosophical concept of particularity can be separated from contingency and articulated as a component of national identity is due in large part to the new multicultural context that has emerged in English Canada. Every society, multicultural or not, is comprised of practices, institutions, and justificatory discourses that persist in both space and time. These practices, institutions, and justificatory discourses normally belong within a tradition that unifies past and future through an active interpretation in the present. Modern nation-states have been built upon an assumption that the normal basis for a society is a shared ethno-cultural tradition, and this assumption has silently entered into the large part of modern social and political thought. To the extent that ethno-cultural plurality has been addressed, it has been generally argued in a civic-nationalist manner that citizens must rise above their particular and different allegiances to appreciate the universal claims of the modern liberal state.

If we take the historical development of English Canada as the starting point for theory, however, these three components must be carefully distinguished. The plurality of everyday practices goes back not to a single tradition, but to a plurality of ethno-cultures splintered off from continuity through immigration – plural dualisms, I called them above. Institutions, by way of contrast, go back primarily to the colonial connection to the British empire and have unfolded continuously without revolution. Justificatory discourses have shifted in relation to these other two factors. To simplify history for the sake of philosophy, we may say that "originally" the justificatory discourses were articulated primarily on the basis of institutional continuity, while the plurality of everyday practices was relegated to the private realm (and some of them were actively discriminated against). At "present," we have reached a situation in which such a writing out of everyday cultural plurality is no longer possible. Justificatory discourses tend, therefore, to be articulated upon the plurality of everyday practices rooted in ethno-cultures. Thus it is difficult to see how the society can retain enough unity to be a single entity. It is often asked, "Can all social institutions be understood as relative to (multi)cultures and their internal resources of justification?" This apparent dilemma, it can now be shown, only occurs when we overlook the factor of institutional unity that remains. Unity is not necessarily opposed to diversity and may be crafted from an interaction of different parts, as in the ecosystemic concept of biodiversity, for example. This overlooking of institutional unity is the basis for the dangerous tendency of what we might call, adapting a phrase of Rudolph Bahro's, "actually existing multiculturalism": it tends to retreat into mere pluralism and relativism such that social unity seems threatened or impossible. Thus, on both the popular and the academic level, multiculturalism is posed as an alternative to national identity, rather than as a component of it, and even further, multiculturalism is itself, as we have seen, often blamed for the tendency towards dissolution. This argument leads nowhere but to an impossible backward utopia of Anglo-conformity that is certain to exclude other ethnic groups. As I have argued, the way out of this dilemma of pluralism-relativism versus Anglo-conformity is to think through the philosophical implications of multiculturalism as a component of national identity through the concept of particularity.

Contemporary justificatory discourses legitimate the plurality of everyday practices rooted in ethno-cultures, but they do not imply the dissolution of the institutional commonality rooted in shared history. These institutions can change under the influences of critiques stemming from the plurality of justificatory discourses, but they change as public institutions, which implies both that an institutional commonality is maintained and that in intersecting with institutional commonality, plural justificatory discourses come to forge a "tradition" of public discourse within the multicultural context. In contrast to the threefold past-present-future temporal structure of tradition, immigration is constituted by a dualism. Institutional change, based upon historical continuity and multicultural criticism, is composed through an intersection of a threefold temporal structure with a dual one. Thus our tradition of public discourse is comprised of a complex temporality in which claims to genuine universality are always displaced into the future because it is always possible to claim that a given institution is rooted in partial, and thus discriminatory, practices. Insofar as a given institutional practice survives criticism, however, it has been lifted from contingency to particularity and therefore to an always pending universality. Justificatory discourses are structured differently again. They borrow from the claims to universality in justificatory discourses from around the world, though they gain relevance to our situation through intersecting with the immigrant dualisms of our own history. The problem is not that multiculturalism shatters all commonality, which is impossible within a single society and continues to inhere in institutional continuity. There is nonetheless a problem with contemporary debates, both pro and con, with regard to multiculturalism insofar as they seem to skip over this component of institutional continuity directly from the plurality of ethno-culturally based everyday practices to the plurality of justificatory discourses. Such an elision of institutional solidity will indeed lead into a dead end. My argument avoided this pass by beginning from an analysis of the three historical axes of significance from which the institutional solidity is historically determined.

It is not sufficient to claim, for example, that parliamentary traditions *might* involve an ethno-centric bias or that it *must* because of the specific group who designed them. Such a bias must be pointed to, explained, and criticized in order for changes to be made. In short, criticism must draw attention to contemporary ethno-centric *effects*, not particular *origins*. Through this process the changes will be concrete and will contribute to an institutional continuity, not devolve upon an indefinite plurality. It was suggested above that contemporary philosophy is paralysed by a contradiction with regard to the way that it has opened up spatio-temporal specificity to investigation. We may now say that contemporary politics seems to be paralysed by a similar contradiction: institutions are the very realm where the "contingencies" of a given history are open to discourses of criticism and justification and, for exactly this reason, are not merely contingent but particular. They do not cut us off from human universality, but are our entry into it.

In summary, the multicultural social ideal comprises a relation between the particular practices of interaction within an ethno-(sub)culture and the rules of interaction in a socio-institutional context defined as multicultural. But these are not merely separate levels of social interaction. They interact in such a way that at any moment either one can be the context for the other. Particularity refers to the ethno-culture as discovered within the multicultural context such as to justify publicly its own validity – what I called above the constitution of the "we." The multicultural context, however, does not pre-exist the ethno-cultures. It is formed through them such that, and one of them may open up a criticism of the multicultural context such that, it is not (sufficiently) universal – this is the constitution of the "us." The particular ethno-culture may thus become the context for judging the multicultural context. Context and content are therefore not pre-defined, but are continuously reformed in a reflexive relation in which each may become content to the other's context.[51] This is the new relation of particularity and universality that is required by a social and political philosophy of multiculturalism.

Perhaps the relation between multicultural context and ethno-cultural content, and the reversal of this relation, can be illustrated through a story. Suppose that a person from an Anglo-Scottish background meets a person from an Argentinian-Jewish background. Certain understandings of culture, politics, and individual life have been learned through these different traditions. To begin with, then, one can say that their relationship is the content that occurs within the context of one tradition for one person and another for the other. While there is a similar content, the contexts are not shared – they are private, as it were. As a relationship develops, presupposed understandings based in these separate traditions become problematic through disagreements or misunderstandings. The two people then discuss the formed beliefs of one or the other, which amounts to a critical thematizing of an ethno-cultural tradition. The common life of these two individuals is formed by the working through of such differences so as to forge a new unity. In this way, their relationship becomes the context for the ethno-cultural traditions. The relationship of content and context has reversed. While initially the ethno-cultural traditions seemed to be the largest context, through the forging of a *common reflection*, the new shared life becomes the context for the contents of ethno-cultures. It is from this shared reflection that common institutions emerge. To use the terms of the previous chapter, when the experiential content has been forged metaphorically into a mythic form, then the prior mythic forms appear as the experiential contents of prior cultures.

This analogy of a personal relationship points to what is crucial in understanding the multicultural context: what is context and what is content do not remain static; they reverse places through the process of common reflection and institutionalization. At times the multicultural society is the context for the experience of one's own ethno-culture. At others one's own ethno-culture is the context for the evaluation and criticism of the multicultural society. It is the interchangeability of content and context through critical reflection that provides an alternative to both homogenizing universalism and self-enclosed particularism. As Chantal Mouffe has described it, "contrary to liberalism, which evacuates the idea of the common good, and civic republicanism, which reifies it, a radical democratic approach views the common good as a 'vanishing point,' something to which we must constantly refer when acting as citizens, but that can never be reached."[52] Every particular articulation makes a claim to define the universal even though it cannot be definitive and is open to critique by other articulations, which themselves originate from a particularity. In this way is solved the apparent problem that ethno-cultures seem merely external to one another and thus appear to give rise to mere coexistence (Bibby) and loss of national identity (Horowitz). Ethno-cultures are not simply external to each other but come into a process of mutual translation and criticism through the critical reflection involved in designing institutions. Thus, also resolved is the issue that is posed critically against multiculturalism that "it fosters the attitude that Canada must change, not the immigrants who come to Canada."[53] The common-sense answer to this criticism is right. Obviously, both will change. In any unity that is constructed from a plurality of different parts, the whole is altered as the parts, or their relations, alter. Immigrants will adapt to their new country. What Canada becomes will be influenced by the successive waves of immigrants. There is only a problem here if one wants to preserve a Canada that is impervious to the influences of new immigrants. Multiculturalism as sociological fact and as government policy has proceeded through compromise in this regard, which is not a bad practice, but a philosophy of multiculturalism needs something more definite. It requires a conception of content and context, of particular and universal, of experiential content and mythic form, of part and whole, of theme and horizon, that can back up the practice.[54] This chapter has attempted to provide such a philosophical justification through the concept of particularity.

The multicultural context thus opens the possibility of revising the starting point of social and political thought in order to radicalize a relation of tradition and criticism into a complex threefold relation of particular practices, multicultural institutions, and plural justificatory discourses in which the commonality of the institutional component is continuously open to criticism and revision without dissolving into mere plurality. But the politics of multiculturalism in English Canada has never gone so far as to question the use of English as the language of everyday interaction, commerce, and politics. To the extent that this remains a baseline assumption, it may be claimed that multiculturalism cannot be a deep diversity. I will conclude with a few remarks on this issue.

First of all, the dominance of English was not simply a given in Canadian history. It was established through the power of the Anglo-colonial elite. For instance, James Peggy MacDonald told me that in the early years of this century on Cape Breton Island the speaking of Gaelic was forbidden in the school grounds and that children were sent home if it was heard by the teachers.[55] This is a traditional strategy to spread a sense of shame among a subordinate population and to separate the young and the educated from their community. Furthermore, Manoly Lupul has documented how the Ukrainian agenda of "cultural retention through bilingual education" has been systematically rejected in multicultural politics.[56] The tendency to reduce multiculturalism to folk arts and affirmative action for individuals is indeed powerful. One might well remark that it would be better for the realizing of a multicultural social ideal if the common language were not that of a partial group. Leslie Armour has suggested the revival of Chinook, the west coast trading language – the second language of all and the first of none – for this purpose.[57] It does not seem likely that things will develop in this direction in the future. However, I do think that a genuine multicultural philosophy will want to keep the issue alive.

The goal of a fully multicultural philosophy is to open all aspects of the common institutional axis to critique from the particularities of plural cultures. This is not the same as randomly suggesting that anything could be simply a result of bias or the history of power. It involves a process of specific critique and concrete suggestion for reform that contributes to and does not negate an evolving commonality. The totality must not be superimposed upon the particular identities, but must be continually open to criticism from within them. The relation between language and culture is close, but it is not simply a given fact. It may be argued for in some instances, surely, but in the general discourse of the human sciences, language is the *figure* for the discussion of culture, neither its guarantee nor a certainty of its loss. What is important is that the question remain an open one. To the extent that it does so, English Canada will have decided to go the full distance in its embrace of multiculturalism.

Multiculturalism requires the philosophical defence of one's own and respect for the Other. This relation must be philosophically comprehended in the relation between particularity and universalizing understood as a dynamic tension. I have argued that the *multicultural context* shifts the manner in which the issue of the survival and development of ethno-cultures should be posed. The plural context does not cut off a universalizing discourse, but is the very condition for its new emergence as a translation of ethno-cultures, a practice of crossing borders, that defines a whole through the diversity of its contents, not in opposition to such diversity. Consequently, there is no necessity for regarding social identities other than ethno-cultural ones – such as national, regional, gender, or political identities – as on the same level and thus as necessarily competing. Rather, the preservation and development of ethno-cultural identities might be a key mediation between national and individual identity. The contemporary world requires that we participate in a plurality of allegiances, not that we choose between them. Multiculturalism is embedded in our political practice in English Canada for sound historical reasons. It is as yet an open question whether we should pursue it all the way as a social ideal, especially in the context of continued uncertainty concerning national identity. In order to decide this question, it is essential that we explore its philosophical ramifications to the largest degree possible. This chapter has attempted to contribute to this task. To the extent that plural formations of social identities are an ineluctable feature of contemporary societies, the success or failure of this task has ramifications for democratic theory beyond the conditions of its emergence in English Canada.

CHAPTER SEVEN

An Ecological Relation
to the World

At the present time, the available resources of learning and thought suffer a profound discontinuity when brought into the public arena because of the formation of concepts of analysis within the existing intellectual division of labour of the industrial world. As Hegel said at an earlier turning point, "a shape of life has grown old."[1] Thought that takes its public responsibilities seriously is at a turning point. One can, and must, retrospectively attempt to sum up the previous form of life, as well as the repressed possibilities strewn in its path. This task requires that one use large, newly constructed concepts such as "industrialism," with all the consequent dangers of false generalization and oversimplification. These dangers are not avoidable, but are negotiable. One must also look ahead into more murky territory and allow one's thought to be an anticipation. As in all momentous times, there must be an election of position, an acceptance of risk, that perhaps clarifies the risk that is thought itself as it seeks consciously to inhabit its world. Today this risk is to speak of an ecological relation of self and world when one does not know, and perhaps can never entirely *know*, what such a relation means, in the same way that one cannot *know in advance* that another culture in the multicultural society is really worthy of respect. The risk is an entry into a site of discovery, an anticipatory thinking, that seeks to embrace the world more firmly by entering a moment in which it is lost. It is this loss, or abjection, that one may find in the contemporary turning, that takes us beyond the conservatism of the Red Tory critique of industrialism as the imposition of a homogenizing uniformity on social locality and plurality towards a justification of (biological and social) diversity as the cement of a sustainable whole.[2] A thinking that is both retrospective and anticipatory is founded through taking a risk. This risk was defined in chapter 4 as a "decisive act" that takes the historical formation of English Canadian identity as its source for philosophical articulation.

BEYOND A STRATEGY OF CONTAINMENT

Why look for an ecological relation to the world that has specific reference to English Canada? Surely, problems of ecology, nature, and the environment are world problems. Perhaps it is simply the accident of our location here that we must consider. After all, serious world problems must be addressed in Argentina, in Kenya, in Yugoslavia, and in Canada too – perhaps even in the United States and Europe. Ecological problems raise questions of the whole, of the totality of human relationships as they are interconnected with non-human nature. These interconnections now span the globe, and it seems reasonable to anticipate that they can be adequately addressed only by a thinking that focuses on the planet as our common home.

Nevertheless, we can take the notion of "world" in another sense as well – the world as a network of involvements, such that we may speak of my personal world, the business world, or the world of the Aztecs. A person, a group, or a culture has a certain style of belonging in and inhabiting its world that distinguishes it from other worlds. This sense of world pertains to the origin of a human cultural environment: from what root experiences it springs, what characteristic style is maintained throughout changes in content, and what goals and aspirations are brought forth within it. In this sense, the ecological question is not only *in* English Canada, but *of* English Canada. To put the same point differently, English Canada is indeed a place in relation to others on the planet. But it is also a history, a characteristic cultural style, and a certain, or perhaps still uncertain, set of aspirations.By putting the point about world in this way, I do not mean to imply that there is a homogeneity to English Canadian history and culture. In fact, my argument is that the question of "plural origins" is characteristic of its multicultural context. Nevertheless, to talk about English Canada at all implies that the totality of these origins, as well as their reciprocal encounters, through this common history becomes itself a characteristic style of life, or world.

In the first sense of "world," it is a question of one place in relation to a totality of other places. In the second sense, it is a question of the origin of a place, what gives it a certain kind of unity such that it can be considered to be a single place. To simplify slightly, before there can be a relationship between places, there must be a division of space and a cultural formation of the separate place through a specific style of practical life. Henceforward it can enter into relations with other places, but only through the distinctive style of its locality. In this sense, the ecological question is not only concerned with the planet, and therefore with

Canada as one part of the planet, but with the origin and style of our world, and therefore with the *type of interaction* that we can have with the other worlds that populate the planet.

Planetary ecological issues will be addressed, or perhaps fail to be addressed, from many different worlds. There is thus an interaction between the diagnosing of the ecological issues – that which we see – and the perspective from which they are diagnosed, the seeing itself. Moreover, there is a further interaction: that which we see also needs saving, or preserving. Interwoven here are three senses of ourselves: that which is seen, that which is saved, and that which sees, in reflection, in order to set up a productive relationship between the seen and the saved. Already we can glimpse the danger here that some ways of investigating may not allow and foster this relationship. We are called to *accomplish* a productive relationship between seeing, saving, and the seen. This accomplishment is ecological thought. It also, by virtue of the particular world in which this accomplishment is demanded, English Canadian thought – not simply thought in English Canada, nor only thought about English Canada, but thought of English Canada, belonging to English Canada. To enact this thought, we need to draw upon traditions from the social history, intellectual style, and public life of Canada in order to speak forth from academic disciplines and divisions towards the issues facing our common world.

These two senses of "world" can be connected with the two Canadian thinkers – Harold Innis and George Grant – who have made distinctive and far-reaching contributions to a Canadian thought that constitutes this place and for this reason have been our signposts throught this work. The increasing interconnection of the planet that has been accomplished by industrialism was called "control over space" by Innis. The orientation to space is characteristic of writing and print for him, though it has been furthered even more by telecommunications and microelectronics in our own day. Media of communication contain a "bias" that emphasizes spatial or temporal relationships and thereby shape the totality of everyday practices of a society. The space orientation of industrialism in Canada emerges from the emphasis on transportation necessary to a dependent colonial economy based on the extraction and export of staple resources to be processed in the imperial centre and returned as manufactured products. Both resource extraction and consumption tie the dependent economy to industrial production by virtue of its cultural continuity with Europe, but the historical relation is to an external industrial base. Thus, though English Canada is certainly hooked into the dominant space orientation of the planet, the directing power of its industrial development is experienced primarily as deriving from elsewhere.

As a consequence, the economy is subject to continuous boom-and-bust cycles originating in external industrial conditions. This instability over time was diagnosed by Innis as an over-reliance on media oriented to space and developed into a defence of oral tradition as an undervalued time-oriented medium of communication. His analysis allows us to appreciate a fact of Canadian social history that he did not investigated: the central role of ethnic communities in settling and developing Canadian society. The bias towards time is characteristic of decentralized institutions, whereas space favours centralization. Though undervalued, time-oriented media of communication have provided the temporal stability without which the dominant push to control space could not have survived, Innis's theory of communication points towards an ideal balance between spatial and temporal dimensions. We are at present overbalanced towards space, inhabiting a highly developed planetary system that is subject to endemic crises. Thus the healing dimension of communication theory is to justify and extend the concern with time, with the diversity of decentralized and local institutions that are presently dominated by the imperatives of world-system management.

If we can interpret Harold Innis's communication theory in this manner as a critique of the planetary order brought about by industrialism, it is similarly important to recall George Grant's use of the term "one's own." As he put it in the justly famous statement already quoted earlier, "In human life there must always be place for love of the good and love of one's own. Love of the good is man's highest end, but it is of the nature of things that we come to know and to love what is good by first meeting it in that which is our own."[3] This term functions as a critique of the industrial domination of nature and the massive socio-economic institutions that it requires. In an age when industrial space domination draws the planet into an increasingly larger and more tightly knit system, any critique or resistance requires the justification of a form of allegiance of a less universal scope. The term "one's own" was used by Grant mainly to justify Canadian sovereignty, but also as the philosophical concept of particularity that theorizes local attachments in the midst of the drive to universality and homogeneity characteristic of modern technological empires. The particularity that is one's own is that with which one is involved such that it cannot be treated as one among many. One's own is what is loved, prior to reflection.

The condition for the unleashing of the domination of nature was the undermining of traditional conceptions of meaningful world order that kept technology within defined limits. Modern science and

philosophy criticized such conceptions of world order as anthropo-
morphic projections and thereby provided the foundation for a scientifically based technology armed with both a theoretical justification and
a research program. Thus industrialism consists in the assertion of
human will against nature understood as a lawlike mechanism without moral order. Human purposes could no longer be derived from
nature, or indeed from any factual state, and could be founded only
in the activity of their assertion itself. Consequently, we speak of "values" as chosen or asserted by human subjects because the ground for
any justification of human ethics in the order of Being has been sheared
off. The condition of modern technological empires is a restless conception of subjectivity continuously unable to provide grounds for itself
juxtaposed with the lawlike necessity of objectivity in nature and society.[4] In this context, the concept of particularity is a critique of the language of "values" that is inherent in the domination of nature. Grant's
philosophical intervention was to turn back the drive to universality in
both political and philosophical affairs towards one's own world –
towards the world understood as a place for belonging, not as one
place among others.

This is not parochialism, though Grant was often enough accused
of it. In the era of space-dominating industrialism, we are urged to
give up our own, that is, to treat our world as merely one place
among others on the planet. It is easy enough to see why a defence of
particularity would be interpreted as a mirror-image rejection of universality. Nevertheless, Grant's defence is not a justification of particularity as against universality, but rather a claiming of one's own as
the "first meeting" with the good, which therefore cannot be simply
dispensed with. Thus we may derive from Grant a characterization of
industrialism as homelessness that complements the analysis of the
space-oriented planetary system of the industrial domination of
nature by Harold Innis. From this perspective, we may define industrialism as based on the subject-object relationship, in which all purpose and value are deemed "subjective" and what is objective is
viewed merely as a resource to be utilized for these purposes. Industrialism is the practice of this subject-object *separation*, which then
involves a subsequent *relation* of the domination of the world, understood as a store of natural resources, by human will.

It is significant that both Innis and Grant situate themselves as critics of the dominant industrial capitalist trend of European societies
since the seventeenth century. English Canadian thought, as an
expression of English Canadian identity, has never entirely accepted
the assumptions of "possessive individualism" (in C.B. Macpherson's
phrase) inherent in this dominant trend.[5] In contrast to the emphasis

on progress, industry, and individuals in the United States, Canadian thought has tended to centre on history, tradition, and community, though its relation to industry has been more equivocal, both in public life and in thought. Innis's argument for a "balance" of space by time still accepted the desirability and/or inevitability of the industrial form of organization. Grant's defence of belonging became increasingly remote from public life exactly to the extent that it came to be directed at contemporary technological society as a whole. For this reason, both can be interpreted as conservatives in the classic sense, that is, as critics of industrial capitalism on the basis of traditions and ethics that precede the modern revolutions and that subsist, though to a neglected extent, afterward. In short, they were red Tories, or backward-looking critics who nevertheless accept that there is a certain inevitability in industrial development and argue a kind of "strategy of containment," of limitation, of conservation. This strategy of containment is no longer possible, and I want to sketch the basis of another strategy.

But first, let me state a hypothesis: that the conservatism of Innis and Grant, and perhaps by implication that of much of Canadian society and thought, can be better interpreted at the present juncture as *conservationism*. In other words, their critique of industrialism is fundamentally an attempt to conserve and recover traditions of social community and less destructive relations to nature, and such a recovery is not inherently politically conservative in the sense of tending to preserve hierarchy and inequality. In recent years, new social movements – such as ecology; anti-nuclear activism; feminism; ethnic politics; local, regional, and national autonomy movements; human rights organizations; and the Aboriginal people's movements – have implied that the old right-left political spectrum is inadequate in present circumstances.[6] This spectrum pertains only to criticisms of inequalities *within* industrial society, not to the present juncture, which requires a *critique of industrial society* as such. Certain important connections arise: the concern with time and history is related to the theme of "responsibility to future generations" in the ecology and anti-nuclear movements; "balance" suggests the argument for a less destructive interaction of humanity and nature; the concern for the place of human life in an overarching world order – out of place in Western thought for hundreds of years – has been rediscovered, or reinvented, in ecological thought. These connections indicate a new formation whose difficult emergence involves elements of both socialist and conservative thought – a combination of substantive equality with conservation – that is unsettling the bases of argument axiomatic within the industrial order. We may call ecological thought the attempt to render clear and rigorous the suspicion that underlying these connections is a shifting of the dominant industrial relation of self and world. My hypothesis in a formula: English Canadian conservatism, minus the acceptance of industrialism as inevitable, can be a key conservationist element in an emergent ecological thinking of our world with sympathetic resonances to the new social movements.

SOCIAL MOVEMENTS

The two most powerful institutions of contemporary life are the economy and the state. The era of left-nationalism in English Canadian political life was tied to the possibility of the nation-state as the most significant locus of social identity and as the main force capable of protecting society from the effects of transnational corporations. In the current free trade era, the economic concentration of capitalist enterprise into global economic forces more powerful than some nations enables them to define the limits of many practical public alternatives according to their own interests. Commercial mass media, which is a product of these same immense economic power blocs, rarely holds their assumptions up to public scrutiny. While the nation-state was once more or less the regulator of the social prerequistes for the pursuit of profit and the locus of social protection from these same forces, more recently it has tended to be dominated by a social plan formed by alliances between economic power blocs and the interests of the nation-state in a global economy. Public deliberation on the role of powerful institutions in key social issues thus encounters pervasive forces tending to confine reflection within the very assumptions that need to be held up to scrutiny. Environmental and ecological problems tend to be defined with respect to "corporate misconduct" and "adequate regulation" within the ambit of continued corporate and state power – whose legitimacy is not held up to question. Even so, there is a significant undercurrent of popular opinion, which has been expressed in the new social movements of recent years, to the effect that environmental and ecological problems are endemic to industrial society and require a substantial reorientation of social goals. New social movements are the active force in society that encourages such a rethinking and reorientation.

Social movements are called new in comparison with the socialist and Marxist movements that preceded and for a short period coexisted with them. Both historically significant branches of Marxism were oriented to gaining power in the nation-state as the key stage towards the transformation of society as a whole. The social democratic branch was committed to gaining state power through parliamentary means, whereas the Leninist branch was oriented to seizing power by military means. This separation in Marxist politics goes back to the Leninist critique of the Second International in the period immediately prior to the First World War. It is often confused with the distinction between reform and revolution, with which it certainly overlaps. Nonetheless, that distinction depends on the goal of the social transformation, and the choice of requisite means is a subsidiary question. A revolutionary social movement is oriented towards changing the basic structure and more of organization of capitalist society, whereas a reformist movement wants only to ameliorate the worst excesses of the system. From a contemporary standpoint, the common features of these two branches of Marxism are more significant than their differences, especially with regard to examining their contrast to the politics of the new social movements.

Both branches of Marxism were oriented to the state as the key moment in the transition of power, even though their program involved the transformation of capitalist society as a whole. Similarly, both were "productivist," in the sense that they regarded the productive apparatus of society, or industry, as the key component of the society, and thus its specifically capitalist form of organization was thought to define the whole society adequately. Social transformation was therefore to be from the capitalist form of industry to a socialist form. This change, in turn, would be sufficient to define the whole of the succeeding society as socialist. The form of industry was a condensation, or metonymy, of the social form as a whole. The third component of Marxism as a social movement was its conception of the key location of the working class as the social agent capable of overthrowing the capitalist system. In the terms introduced in chapter 2, Marxism defined itself as a social movement through an institution, a rhetoric, and a social actor. The institution was industry in its capitalist and proposed socialist form; the rhetoric was of class struggle and of conquering state power; the actor was the proletariat, or working class, who was deemed capable of carrying through the transition. These three features of Marxism as a social movement were incorporated into English Canadian left-nationalism. What I defined in chapter 2 as the core of left-nationalism – its argument that the capitalist class no longer had a nation-building vocation – was the basis for linking these features of Marxism to a specific analysis of Canadian social economy. This argument strengthened the state orientation of Marxism by making the nation-state into the key actor – which is why there were endless debates about the relationship between the working class and the nation. "Real Marxists," as it were, rejected left-nationalism because of its substitution of the nation for the working class as the key actor.

Left-nationalists were obliged to produce reasons for linking the two. The possibility of this linkage was based in the definition of the nation as the key social actor by the "permeable Fordism" that defined the political economy of the era. Left-nationalism was thus the critical current that linked the classic Marxist conception of social change to the defining characteristics of post-war capitalism in English Canada.

The new social movements are distinguished, in English Canada but also around the world, by their abandonment of this model of social change, a characteristic that also implies a different analysis of the nature of the system to be changed. In place of the emphasis on the state as the key stage in social transformation, these new movements operate within civil society. In place of the productivist orientation of Marxism, they propose different definitions of the society depending on their particular orientation: for feminism, the system is patriarchal; for Aboriginal and other minority movements, it is Eurocentric; for the peace movement, the system is exterminist; for the environmental and ecological movement, it is industrial and humanist (in the sense of exalting human values in the domination of nature). Similarly, in place of the class actor of Marxism and the nation-class actor of left-nationalism, the social actors of the new social movements are defined in relation to the analysis that they propose of the system. For example, for feminism, "woman" is the actor; other movements propose other social actors – and consequently new social identities – that are the basis for much internal discussion and definition within the movements themselves. But it is now an established feature of contemporary society that new identities such as environmentalists, gays and lesbians, women, ethnic groups, and so forth have become actors in events and interpreters of the nature and direction of society.

The key fact about the new social movements is their plurality, which is why every discussion (including this one) tends to define them at least in part by listing them (an enumeration that is, virtually by definition, incomplete). As Diego Martin Raus has put it, "in the map of social structures, the heterogenization of social demands implies the appearance of new social aggregates, new modalities of the constitution of social identities."[7] This plurality, and the new model of social change that is implicit in it, derives from the location of new social movements in the heterogeneity of civil society as opposed to the homogeneity of class and nation. Jean Cohen and Andrew Arato suggest that "the current 'discourse of civil society' ... focusses precisely on new, generally non-class-based forms of collective action oriented and linked to the legal, associational, and public institutions of society. These are differentiated not only from the state but also from the capitalist market economy."[8] Understanding the emergence of a plurality of new identities in civil society is thus the condition for defining the relation of new social movements to the system that they criticize and therefore for clarifying their crucial role for the project of social criticism and change in the era of globalization.

The distinction between the state and civil society pre-dates Marx. As sketched in the previous chapter, it is characteristic of modernity as such and must be maintained by any contemporary theory that wishes to preserve the gains for individual civil rights that it has enabled. While the new social movements do not attempt to erase the distinction between state and civil society, they do try to change it in a manner that would allow the particularities previously relegated to civil society to take on public relevance. Again, this point can be clarified by comparing it to the trajectory of Marxism. In his early work, Marx criticized the distinction of the state from civil society that he had inherited from prior modern thinkers. In an important early (1843) essay, *On the Jewish Question*, he criticized the "rights of man" brought into being by the French and American revolutions as egoistic ones, that is to say, rights that refer to "an individual separated from the community, withdrawn into himself, wholly preoccupied with his private interest."[9] The "species-being," or common good, by way of contrast, was supposed to reside in the state. Marx regarded this separation of individual, egoistic interest from the common good as alienation and defined his conception of human emancipation as complete "when the real, individual man has absorbed into himself the abstract citizen."[10] The means for overcoming this self-alienation, or separation between individual interests and those of the community, were not addressed in this early work. Its main critical conclusion, however, was significant for the Marxist critique of capitalist society. "The political revolution dissolves civil society into its elements without revolutionizing these elements themselves or subjecting them to criticism."[11] In other words, the previous communal bonds within civil society have been dissolved; the individual within civil society appears as purely egoistic; the modern political revolutions recognize these individual rights without asking about why they appear in this egoistic way and without proposing a manner of changing them.

The next step was taken soon afterward, however, in the period from 1843 to 1845. Retrospectively, in the preface to *Contribution to the Critique of Political Economy* (1859), Marx summed up this new position thus: "the anatomy of civil society is to be sought in political economy."[12] But there is still a further element. During this period he discovered political economy to be based on a fundamental contradiction between the working class and the owners of capital. This is the most characteristic aspect of Marx's thought and the one that became the key thread to all his future work on the nature of the capitalist system. The proletariat, or working class, was defined as "a class in civil society which is not a class of civil society,"[13] which is to say, its members do not enjoy the rights of egoism and voluntary association that are normal to civil society even though they are part of it insofar as they labour. Thus, though "the possessing class and the proletarian class represent one and the same human self-alienation,"[14] the working class is in a crucial location within capitalism such as to be able to change this relationship and to bring about a new society. By virtue of this location, it will not bring about a new form of class society but will overcome class society altogether. Its members suffer "not a particular wrong but wrong in general," as a "total loss of humanity ... which can only redeem itself by a total redemption of humanity."[15] Marx's subsequent work after 1845 thus dealt, not with the relation of civil society to the state, but with a contradiction within civil society between the working class and the owners of capital. It is a defining characteristic of Marxism to regard this class relation within civil society as the basic relationship of capitalist society as a whole. Thus, while the theory of capitalism, and its relation to other epochs of human history, is developed in an increasingly sophisticated way throughout Marx's later work, this starting point for Marxist theory is never revoked.

There is a threefold reduction in his analysis of civil society. First, civil society is reduced to egoistic self-interest. Marx argues that this reduction is accomplished by capitalism or, more precisely, the modern political revolutions, but it is actually only a tendency of capitalist society. Second, social relations within civil society are reduced to those between the proletariat and the owners of capital. Third, all relations in and through the state are reduced to being mere expressions of the basic class division within civil society. Only through this threefold reduction is it possible to claim that the particular interests of the proletariat represent universal interests within capitalist society capable of transforming it into a classless one. I will argue that this threefold reduction is unacceptable and that the set of issues connected with civil society remain pertinent today. The new social movements can thus be defined as the inheritors of the basic question for social change: How can particular interests give rise to a universalizing, or general, critique of the system?

With respect to the first reduction, one may recall an argument made in chapter 1 that the nation-state should not be simplistically considered as only "a committee for managing the common affairs of the whole bourgeoisie," that it is also an identification with the gains that the movement of social protection made against the capitalist forces through using the power of the state. In order to make this argument, I relied on Polanyi's description of capitalist society as a double movement between the reorganization of society by the capitalist market, on the one hand, and the self-protection of society from this first tendency, on the other. Marx's analysis of capitalist society captures only one-half of this movement. Indeed, this whole book has made the argument that the nation and the state cannot be considered purely as reflexes of capitalism but must also be seen as a locus of action often oriented towards limiting the otherwise unrestricted power of capital. I do not want to repeat that argument here, but rather to point out that the reduction of civil society to egoistic self-interest cannot be sustained in the face of this double movement. Douglas Brown has summarized the import of Polanyi's thesis in this way: that "the emergence, at least in embryonic form, of a self-regulating market economy was not at all an organic process and that its destructive ramifications for the social fabric of society were so great that it was met simultaneously with protest and reaction by victimized social groups."[16] The protective response of society against its reorganization by the market thus meant that disenfranchised *groups* within civil society fought back and, in so doing, constituted and consolidated social identities within civil society.

From the failure of this first reduction follows the failure of the second and third. The social relations within civil society are not reducible to those between the proletariat and the bourgeoisie. There is a plurality of social identities based on the specific histories – mainly, but not exclusively, national – of the protective response. Moreover, the partial successes of the protective response as articulated through the state had the consequence that the proletariat did not congeal into a homogeneous social identity as expected by Marx. Brown summarizes the conclusion that the Budapest school drew from Polanyi's analysis. "There were not only 'class' interests involved but a whole spectrum of subordinate social groups whose existence cannot be adequately characterized as that of the proletariat. The winning of the franchise for propertyless groups, factory legislation, union recognition, welfare for the poor, income maintenance for the disabled, price support for farmers, loan credits for small businesses, housing loans, free public education and so on, all testify to the diversity of the protective response. All of this legislation and policy by the state thwarted the consolidation and homogenization of the proletarian class."[17] The result is a stratified society that is still capitalist but is based on representative democratic government and includes a multititude of social identities and partial powers that may be summarized as "the self-protection of society from the market." These protective responses often occurred through the state, which requires a rejection of Marx's third reduction.

It should be noticed that this argument requires neither a rejection of Marx's work in its totality nor a denial of the continued power of capital in contemporary society, but rather demands that it should be interpreted as one side of a contradictory double movement between the market and society. The balance between these two opposing forces at any moment depends on the history and contemporary forces interacting, but it is always illegitimate to reduce the society as a whole to the force of capital operating through the market. There is a continued vitality of movements within civil society, often affecting the state, that is effaced by Marx's threefold reduction of civil society. It is my argument that new social movements are the contemporary expression of the protective response acting through the historical and contemporary identities formed in the double movement. They operate within the stratified and unequal power of civil society in an attempt to influence market forces, often through the state. In the contemporary era of globalization, when the power of the nation-state to hegemonize social identity has been reduced, new social movements are the main forces acting against the global power of capital. We have passed from the era of left-nationalism and the nation-state in a transnational economy to an era of polarization between global capital and the new social movements with the nation-state in-between. At present the protective aspect of the nation-state is being brought to heel by the argument of "fiscal responsibility" in a time of drastically decreased corporate taxes. It is the task of the social movements to influence the nation-state towards a new protective response though the formation of a new historic bloc.

The theory of new social movements is based on a recognition of the capacity of civil society to produce new social identities through voluntary associations and the possibility that they can influence the nation-state and thereby reinforce the protective response against the power of capital exercised through the market. The Marxist model of social change through revolution, in which the key power shift was gaining control of the state, was based on the opposed interests of the working class and the owners of capital within civil society. The basic struggle was thus within the factory, and the uniformity of the tendency of capital was matched (in theory) by the increasing consolidation and homogenization of the proletariat – a consolidation which has not occurred historically and which has, exactly contrary to Marx's expectation, been stronger in recently industrializing and modernizing societies rather than in highly developed capitalist ones. Polanyi's critique of Marxism suggests that it is the relation between market forces and the protective response of society that is the main locus of social conflict and therefore the possibility of social change. Thus the strong reaction against industrialization and market forces in the initial stages as they undermine pre-capitalist community structures can be explained, a historical fact that has been better understood by anarchism than Marxism. For Polanyi the self-protection of society occurred mainly, or even exclusively, through the state and encompassed the plurality of social relations endangered by the tendency to subordinate them to a reorganization by the market. "To remove the elements of production – land, labour and money – from the market is thus a uniform act only from the viewpoint of the market, which was dealing with them as if they were commodities. From the viewpoint of human reality that which is restored by the disestablishment of the commodity fiction lies in all directions of the social compass."[18] Thus, while the tendency of the market is towards uniformity, the counter-tendency of the protective response is necessarily plural. While Polanyi's emphasis on the nation-state as the key locus of the protective response is accurate as a historical generalization, it is important to point out that the state does not, even in his view, originate this response but rather itself responds to social forces. In the contemporary period, the new social movements are the originators of the protective response. Each of them has influenced the nation-state to some extent, though it is yet to be seen whether a new historic bloc will emerge that could congeal and solidify the counter-tendency to capital.

The basic conflict in contemporary society can thus be defined as the self-protection of community versus the reorganization of social relations by the market. I use "community" here because it is the sociological term that expresses social relations formed "organically" outside of market forces, whereas "society" usually refers to market-type relations of self-interested individuals. I do not deny that there is a conflict of interests between wage-workers and owners of capital, but only that this conflict can be understood as the *general and defining social opposition* of contemporary society. Moreover, it is possible in certain social conflicts that these two groups find themselves on the same side – if the workers accept the necessity of social adjustment to market forces – against environmental or citizens' groups acting in protection of the community, for example. In other words, the labour-capital conflict becomes part of the general and defining opposition only to the extent that the workers are aligned with the anti-capital, anti-market tendency. We might call the self-protective tendency of new social movements *anti-mercantilist* in the sense that they oppose the reduction and reorganization of social relations by the exchange relations of the market and thus promote their own visions of community. Harold Innis referred in this vein to "the penetrative powers of the price system" in corroding and reorganizing non-market social relations.[19] As Marxists have pointed out, this mercantilist conception of the influence of the market is more indebted to Adam Smith than to Marx insofar as it focuses on the exchange relations of the market and much less, if at all, on the coercive structure of the capital-labour relation in industrial production.[20] Marx criticized mercantilist political economy because it "sees in value only the social form, or rather its insubstantial semblance," and not the origin of value in labour.[21] Of course, I am not recommending a return to mercantilist political economy. I am arguing that the basic contradictory relation of contemporary society, as expressed by the new social movements, is between market relations and community. This locus of tension, or contradiction, is defined by the *reduction and reorganization of social relations by exchange.* It is not primarily a question of the origin or quantity of value but of the manner of social organization that focuses primarily on the critique of exchange relations, or the reduction of community. The importance of new social movements is that they are the social forces that originate the self-protection of community from exchange relations through their construction of new social identities.

The Marxist tradition called the locus of social tension in the capital-labour relation a "contradiction" and understood this to mean a systemic conflict that requires resolution and the establishment of a thoroughly different system in which the workers rule production. Such an overcoming of the systemic contradiction is the very definition of revolution. The model of social change that emerges from the practice of new social movements is not based on an definitive overcoming, or revolutionary overthrow, but rather on the assertion of a counter-tendency that will not, or cannot, entirely supplant its opposing tendency. That is why I call it a "locus of tension" rather than a contradiction. It attempts a subordination of market exchange to the self-organization of communities. Polanyi already saw that such a strategy does not require doing away with market relations altogether, but only their subordination to the community, or plurality of communities, that is affected by them. He defined socialism as "a tendency inherent in an industrial civilization to transcend the self-regulating market by consciously subordinating it to a democratic society."[22] In this context, it is interesting that the most influential party of the left in Canada, the CCF–NDP, was built on a farmer-labour alliance and was never a purely proletarian party. In a similar vein, Gordon Laxer has recently described this approach as a strategy of displacement as opposed to a definitive overthrow or revolution. "In place of the traditional socialist policy of 'nationalization,' a strategy of displacement of corporate capitalism is a possibility. An alternative to private corporate ownership is democratic social ownership by wage-earners and communities that have 'location commitment' to immobile labour and to territorially defined communities."[23]

From this point of view, it seems unnecessary to mention wage earners separately from communities; they can be understood as a specific community, defined by their common condition in a particular industry. This strategy also has much in common with Samir Amin's notion of "delinking," whose two main features are "a model of 'alternative development' based on expanding the scope for non-commodity and self-management activities" and "rejection of blind surrender to the demands of international competitiveness."[24] Politics now is not about finding the "primary contradiction," but about the importance of all struggles for the maintenance and extension of community over the reorganization of society by global market forces. Rather than looking "beneath" the plurality of social movements for a basis for unity in a supposedly more fundamental relation, such as that of capital and labour, the plurality can attain a certain unity as a historic bloc by forging relationships between the different movements. After all, no one is completely described through a single social identity. The plurality of social identities proposed by social movements overlap and interrelate. Ernesto Laclau and Chantal Mouffe call this new politics of the social movements a practice of "forging equivalences" that sets up relations between different movements and identities in order to expand the space of democratic action.[25] It is not foundationalist, but hegemonic. Its plurality is not a problem, but a solution. Its unity is derived from diversity, not opposed to it. Social change is not overcoming and a new foundation, but displacement and acceptance of the Other.

As one of the new social movements, the environmental and ecological movement participates in the attempt to displace the hegemony of market forces by asserting the forces of community – the local communities designed by humans, but especially those in which humans are imbedded with other beings. In so doing, it must propose its definition of the system that should be displaced. As Alain Touraine says, "The subject exists only in the form of a social movement, of a challenge to the logic of order."[26] Up to this point I have simply called this system of social order "market forces," but it must now be determined more precisely.

THE SYSTEM AND ITS EXCESS

At the present juncture, a thinking that accepts the challenge to be ecological must incorporate both a retrospective and a prospective dimension. It must sum up the past in a way that may be of use in thinking forward: not planning, but allowing us to respond freely to its demands. In a retrospective mode, I want to suggest that one may characterize the uniformity and homogeneity of industrial capitalism as a "system" and as a "representation." There were, of course, markets before capitalism and may well be after. Capitalism becomes the dominant mode of production when *all factors* of production are organized through markets. In particular, land and labour become regulated through exchange values. As a consequence, the mode of production becomes a "system" in the sense that it aims at being self-enclosed and self-regulating through the relationships defined by exchange. Moreover, this system extends beyond production as such to become the central organizing system of the social order as a whole as a result of the inclusion of the productive, or wealth-producing, factors upon which the system of production depends within the economic system itself. Commodities have value both as useful goods and as an exchange, or money equivalent, of other goods. All goods produced for the market have this dual character. In the capitalist system, this duality extends also to land and labour. Their use value is, as in all modes of production, that they are the fundamental productive forces which create wealth; that they become exchange values is indicated by the fact that in the capitalist system, land and labour are regulated by money and in that sense become comparable to other commodities. Michel Henry interprets the significance of Marx's critique of political economy in this way: "With respect to the market economy and to the concept that serves as its foundation – namely, value – it has been shown that the origin of value in human praxis cannot be transformed into a rigorous determination, nor, for example, can it make exchange possible, unless for the subjectivity of praxis is substituted the quantifiable objective equivalents on the basis of which value will itself be able to be quantified."[27] The capitalist system can be defined as "capitalist" and as a "system" because that which is really productive itself is treated as a factor of production that is "in principle" like any other factor, made comparable through money equivalents for land and labour. Stated briefly, the origin of wealth, productive activity itself, is organized as if it could be simply internal to the economic system of exchange that it originates. This occlusion of origin is the condition for the emergence of a system.

This economic system, which attempts to incorporate within itself its own conditions of origin, is closely allied to the presupposition of modern science as it arose in the late Renaissance – that the world be viewed as standing apart from a subject who represents that world cognitively to itself. The standard culprit in this story is Descartes, though he is really in this respect simply an emblem of the inaugura- tion of the epoch of the modern world. The subject withdraws from direct participation in the world to ask about the truth of received knowledge of the world. In this reflective state, the self-knowledge of the withdrawn subject becomes the linchpin for any knowledge of the world. By arraying the world in front of the subject, one may take a view upon the world and design representations of it. This radical doubt of previous knowledge that was intertwined with the world opens up a style of knowledge that is not so intertwined, and instead throws a scheme of representation over the world. Thus the world can be interpreted as if it were an "objective" order, since the know- ing subject has been subtracted from participation in the world, and thus the world can be represented in front of a knowing subject who can master it conceptually.[28]

When we look back from within the present turning point, it is nec- essary to gather together an understanding of the capitalist "system" with modern scientific "representation" into a single concept, since both of these are important to the set of contemporary issues that can be designated as ecological. Here the key issue is the emergence of the very notion of a self-enclosed and self-regulating system. This notion of a system occurs both in the modern representation of the world as an object of knowledge and in the economic representation of all factors of production – especially land and labour – as desig- nated by exchange equivalents such that unity arises from the equal- ization, or homogenization, of parts rather than through the coordination of concrete diversity. Such a system became constitutive of human knowledge during the Renaissance and constitutive of the ordinary practices of the modern world when land and labour became commodities. It would be attempting too much to try to give a satisfactory account of the relation between scientific representation and economic system here, but for present purposes it should suffice to notice that the root issue is the same: the very idea of a self- enclosed, self-regulating system. Descartes thought that there was a location in which subject and object were connected in the pineal gland. Whatever one may think of this suggestion, some such connec- tion between the system and the lived, experiential domain for which it emerges is necessary. The human body is the locus of this connec- tion – it is neither simply object nor simply cognitive subject, but a

source of motility. The body is that from which every system abstracts
in order to become self-enclosed. But, we may ask, why only the
human body? Labour is the productive activity of the human body.
Land is also a productive source, including the productive activity of
generating beings and things that populate the world. The human
body and the body of the world continually overflow the system of
representation.

There is always an excess. This excess is the productive origin that
enables any system to be articulated. *The very idea of a system consists
in turning this productive origin inside and representing it as simply
another factor within the system.* When land and labour are given prices
within the economic system, when the human body is viewed as subject to scientific knowledge on the same model as its knowledge of
the external world, that which makes the system possible is represented within the system as a discrete factor. In this way, the system
of representation projects a self-enclosed and self-regulating scheme
that obscures the conditions of its own origin. The productive origin
of the system of representation is itself treated as a representable element within the system. In this sense, a system is always parasitic; it
depends upon an origin whose originary character it denies. This
conception of thought and practical action brings to an apogee the
domination of nature for the production of wealth, which was supposed to be the means towards a society based on the liberal ideal of
freedom and equality for all. Looking back, we may say that modern
industrialism obscures its own origin, indeed, obscures the very
notion of origin. Industrialism consists the entrapment of land-labour
and knowledge – or productive origin – in a relation of reflective certainty that enables their exploitation as resources. In this sense, it confers a central role on thought, understood as representation within a
system, though not as opposed to practice, but as itself a practical
relation of production that reduces productive origin to an intrasystemic equivalence.[29]

The very idea of systemic representation is characteristic of modernity and must be displaced by an ecological alternative. It is this conception which stands behind the social and economic system of
industrial capitalism and which the ecological movement needs in
order to define the specific nature of the alternative that it proposes.
In the above description I used both the Marxist (broadly speaking, in
a sense that includes Polanyi) focus on the extension of exchange to
land and labour and the Heideggerian focus on the representation of
the world in front of a sovereign subject. From the perspective outlined here, there are clear continuities between these two analyses.
But I must now clarify that they are not, strictly speaking, equivalent

or compatible, but rather represent two historical stages of the critique of industrial society: Marxism through the notion of capitalism and Heideggerian phenomenology through the notion of technology. The core of the difference between these two stages is the extent to which one can conceive of the excess as capable of reintegration in a new system of order – one might say, the extent to which the concreteness of lived experience can be the foundation of a post-industrial order.

For Marx, concreteness – which we might also call the incomparability, or diversity, of concrete difference – resides in use as opposed to exchange. When wealth is viewed from the side of its use-value, it is concrete in the sense of *qualitatively different* from all other use-values. Similarly, "the useful labour contained in them is qualitatively different in each case."[30] In this sense, concreteness denotes the specificity and irreducibility of the characteristics of a given thing or activity. It is contrasted by Marx to "comparability," or the determination of a plurality of things or activities by a common standard that is at the origin of exchange. In discussing the origin of exchange at the beginning of *Capital*, he writes that "if we make abstraction from its use-value, we abstract also from the material constituents and forms which make it a use-value. It is no longer a table, a house, a piece of yarn, or any other useful thing. All its sensuous characteristics are extinguished."[31] He goes on immediately to call this common element – which is the basis for exchange – a "residue," a "phantom-like objectivity," and "crystals of this social substance, which is common to them all." The criterion for the "materiality" of the thing is clearly the existence of immediately experienceable qualities that make tables and houses simply concretely different things. Insofar as they are uses, they are incomparable. This is the basic meaning for the "concrete" in Marx. It is the immediacy of qualitative difference in an experiential and phenomenological sense. When the comparability of exchange is called "abstract," and "abstract labour" is described as producing exchange values, the abstractness in question is arrived at through the contrast between the heterogeneity of immediate qualitative difference and the imposition of an abstract standard. The fact that a coat can be sold for $100 is possible through the imposition of a calculus of comparability that abstracts from all concrete, qualitative determinations. This conception of concreteness as qualitative difference establishes the continuity of concern between Marxism and new social movement theory as successive historical stages in the attempt to appropriate the heterogeneous world of qualitative difference.

The circuit of exchange and commodity production, insofar as it includes land and labour power, can become a system only to the extent that as it abstracts itself from the heterogeneity of concreteness. Marx showed this fact in the opening chapters of *Capital*, where he was concerned to revive a sense of the utter strangeness of this comparability to which concrete difference had become subject, in order to render it needful of explanation. The comparability of concretely different commodities is established by creating a standard of equivalence that is shorn of concrete characteristics. On this basis, comparability can be generalized into a system of reckoning and further into the science of political economy. Systematicity is a product of this process of abstraction. It is for this reason that Marx was always critical of the legal and moral conception of equal right. Such a conception of right renders comparable that which is concretely heterogeneous in a way that parallels the relations of exchange. As he said in *Critique of the Gotha Program*, "right by its very nature can consist only in the application of an equal standard; but unequal individuals (and they would not be different individuals if they were not unequal) are measurable only by an equal standard insofar as they are brought under an equal point of view."[32] His conception of communism, which is the solution to the problem of the regime of equalization of concreteness by exchange, is thus of a society that recognizes qualitative difference, that is based not on equality but on "each according to his needs." Such a concept would mean the emancipation of the senses, which are our organs for perceiving qualitative difference, and a social order based on the reciprocity of sensuous concreteness. As Marx said in the *Economic and Philosophical Manuscripts of 1844*, "Assume man to be man and his relationship to the world to be a human one: then you can exchange love only for love, trust for trust, etc. ... Every one of your relations to nature must be a specific expression, corresponding to the object of your will, of your real individual life."[33] We may thus say that Marx's work is a critique of exchange that proposes a new regime based on the reappropriation of the concrete.

Stanley Moore has argued that there is a thoroughgoing contradiction in Marx's work insofar as his acceptance of "philosophical communism," which occurred in 1844, was maintained throughout his life, but his political economic works were never able to establish the necessity for a post-capitalist communist system. Marx's critique of political economy could only establish the necessity for overcoming the private appropriation of profit by capitalists but not the abolition of all forms of exchange – to which he nevertheless remained committed as a "higher" system than a post-capitalist "socialist" one that still tolerated exchange. Moore concludes, "The persisting influence of his moral argument [for communism] apparently blinded Marx to a consequence entailed by his economic arguments – that the only workable complex classless economies are socialist economies with competitive markets."[34] Here we see an important convergence with an earlier argument. It is because Marx interpreted equal right and exchange economies with civil society as described in Hegel's *Philosophy of Right* as referring only to the rights of abstractly equal egoistic interests that he sustained a preference for a regime that would recognize concrete sensuousness.[35]

To generalize Moore's argument with respect to the role of markets in Marx's thinking, we may say that it remains indeterminate whether the critique of abstract equivalence can usher in a new regime of the concrete: while Marx definitely remained committed to this possibility of a concretely sensuous communism, nevertheless it cannot be derived directly from the critique of exchange in his critique of political economy. While political economy and exchange have presuppositions (which is Marx's point), this fact does not guarantee that these presuppositions can themselves be appropriated in a way that could generate a new regime of concreteness. The concrete that functions as a presupposition of abstract comparability is only concrete because of a heterogeneity that belies systematicity. It is for this reason that Marx's work can be called the *first critique* of the paramount conceit of modernity to be self-founding. It is a *critique* because it shows the necessary failure of the system of exchange to include its excessive origin within the system itself. And it is the *first* because this critique coexists with an assumption that the goal of critique is the outright replacement of this system with another regime based on concrete, sensuous, qualitative difference.

But the difficulty is that the project of a (re)appropriation of the concreteness of human need cannot be accomplished with the same systematicity as the internal articulation of abstractions that occurs in the system of exchange. Thus I would suggest that the critique actually asserts the *limits of systematicity* as such. The presuppositions of systemic representation mean that every system *in its actual concrete functioning* is parasitic upon qualitative difference. The dependence of the reproduction of the wage labour force on unwaged domestic labour in the home is a key case in point. But the more one looks around from this perspective, the more unwaged labour in kitchens, gardens, and parks is essential for the reproduction of the system of systemic representation. This is the point at which its project is related to that of the new social movements, each of which (but heterogeneously because concretely) asserts a certain qualitative experience against the tendency to systematize and regard such differences as dispensable. The embrace of plurality is the first step in recovering the concrete. Its image would be more a dispersal, a cascading river, an excess, emphasizing the impossibility of return.

This interpretation of the project of Marxism and the new social movements as asserting and exploring the limits of systematicity has several notable implications. First, it implies that the question of the failure of the working class to constitute itself as a unity confronting capital that has plagued Marxism is an intractable issue. Real concreteness is heterogeneous. Unity is thus a political task that can only be accomplished in a temporary form through forging equivalences. This conclusion suggests that the heterogeneity of new social movements will never be theoretically bridged as such and that politics consists in building alliances between them to construct a historic bloc. Second, the interpretation raises the issue of whether the limits of systematicity imply (as Marx thought) an overcoming of systematicity as such by a *regime of the concrete*. Such a regime is not possible as a social formation since any such formation implies an overarching organization that itself implies systematicity (of some sort, not necessarily capitalist). This would explain the replacement of the Marxist project of revolution by the new social-movement strategy of building reforms within civil society and by a respect for representative democracy.[36] Third, the interpretation suggests that the differences between Marxism and new social-movement theory represent historical stages of the project of appropriation of the concrete. In this connection it is important to note that it was an essential aspect of Marx's starting point that the concreteness of use as such was not considered problematic. His project was to explain the origin and limits of the system of exchange. In his words, "so far as it is a use-value, there is nothing mysterious about it."[37] At the historical stage of the new social movements, however, it is the question of use, or concreteness, itself that has become problematic. Fourth, the interpretation may serve to assert that the question of the limits on social movements posed by the existence of capital remains an inportant theoretical and practical issue. It cannot be shunted aside with the assumption that the question inevitably returns one to the politics of orthodox Marxism. Rather, the project of the new social movements can be theoretically understood as the protective response of society to the domination of systemic representation (of which one major form is market exchange).

The first stage of the critique of systemic representation by Marxism supposes that it can be replaced by a new sensuous regime called communism. Communism thus may be called the idea of the concreteness of qualitative difference organized as a system. It contains a logical contradiction in that it claims to put together in a viable fashion the features of abstract systematicity with qualitative heterogeneity. In the second stage of critique it has become apparent that the excess which is presupposed by any systemic representation cannot itself be the basis for a new regime. In fact, the claim to internalize the excess – to make it intrasystemic – is what characterizes the exchange system, or technology system, itself. Concreteness evades not only this system, but all systematization. Thus the project of social change in the new social movements cannot be thought of as a definitive revolutionary overcoming. Indeed, one can interpret the idea of revolutionary overcoming as itself part of the project of modernity to be self-founding. If the concreteness of qualitative difference cannot be organized as a system, it can be conceptualized as that which always escapes in any systematization, an excess that the social movements embrace, to which they give partial and plural definitions, and through which one can neither be resigned to nor definitively reject, but rather "twist away from," the system. Gianni Vattimo has explained this conception of change with the Nietzschean concept of convalescence and the Heideggerian concept of *Verwindung*, which he calls "a going-beyond that is both an acceptance and a deepening" through which "we become open to the meaning and richness of proximity."[38] We twist away from the system to the extent that we criticise its claims to self-founding systematicity, analyse it through its concrete effects, and propose our own sensuousness in opposition without predicating it on a definitive overcoming.

I have argued that every system is haunted by an excess which is its origination and which it attempts to turn inside and treat as an element within the system. Social movements twist away from the system to the extent that they recover this excess, even though their definition of it can be only partial. There is a plurality of movements, since any name for the excess is insufficient. The limits of systemic representation have become visible in the failure of the system to sustain its own environmental conditions for functioning. Thus there has emerged a public debate and considerable literature on "sustainable development." Sustainable development was defined by the report of the United Nations World Commission on Environment and Development, also known as the Bruntland Report, as "development that meets the needs of the present without compromising the ability of future generations to meet their own needs"; the report argued that "living standards that go beyond the basic minimum are sustainable only if consumption standards everywhere have regard for long-term sustainability."[39] Sustainable development is thus interwoven with important issues of inequality and the form or type of development.[40] However, the basic idea concerns the extent to which the relation to nature predominant in industrial society is unstable because of the social and environmental uniformity that it creates, thereby endangering the human relation to nature upon which our survival as a species depends. Sustainable development is therefore a concept critical of the domination of nature which proposes a new type of development "based on forms and processes that do not undermine the integrity of the environment on which they depend."[41] It requires that the diversity of the ecological system be maintained in the process of human interaction with nature.

The widespread perception of the unsustainability of the present system based on the market-dominated practices of what I have called "systemic representation" has led to a social movement known as the environmental and/or ecological movement. The terms "environment" and "ecology" are not, however, interchangeable. "Environment," like its equivalents in other languages – *Umwelt* in German, *milieu* in French, and *medio ambiente* in Spanish – refers to the world that surrounds humans. It includes the natural world, but also refers to the urban environment in which environmental issues such as roads and transportation, for example, are important. Both "environment" and "ecology" propose ways of understanding contemporary issues that go beyond the entrenched dualism between humanity and nature and therefore attempt to address problems in that relationship that have led to current unsustainable practices. But they do so in different ways. The term "environment" continues to put humans, and thus their interests and concerns, at the centre. Everything else – non-human animals, living and non-living beings, the world, all of Being – is defined in relation to human-centred concerns. They surround us. The term "ecology," by way of contrast, attempts to insert humans within the diversity of relations of all other beings in the world without putting them in a central, or privileged, place. As Stan Rowe has explained, "the essential insight of the ecosystem concept" is "that all life participates in a complex and interactive system where boundaries between living and non-living are vague or non-existent. The largest ecological system, the Earth Ecosphere, is the reality of which people are one part; they are imbedded in it and totally dependent on it. Here is the scientific source of the environment's intrinsic value."[42]

The ambivalence in naming the environmental and/or ecological movement thus corresponds to a real issue that pertains to the current fate of systemic representation of the world. The dangers that the failures of this system present to human life have become increasingly apparent and have therefore spawned a social movement aimed at the self-protection of humans. Such self-protection requires that the conditions for human life be sustained, and the term "environmentalism" describes the way in which non-human life is important, from this perspective, as the *sustaining ground for human life*. The ecological movement, by way of contrast, aims at a more radical decentring of human life and displacement of systemic representation insofar as it suggests that non-human beings are important not only to the extent that they sustain humans but also *in their own right*. This divide may be expressed with respect to the key concept of diversity: environmentalism defends diversity as the necessary biological ground for human life. Thus humans remain central and are not fully given over to the concept of diversity. Ecological thought is more radical in this respect insofar as it subsumes humans within the diversity. While in practice, environmental and ecological concerns inevitably overlap, the nature of their critique of the system of systemic representation is different. The ecological movement may be defined as the self-protection of the community of Being, which includes humans as participants, but which, rather than placing them at the ˙centre, regards them as thoroughly immanent to ecological relations between species and non-living beings. The community of Being derives its unity from its diversity and the self-sustaining character of the interaction of diverse parts. Thus the ecological movement responds to the transformation of ethics rooted in Being to "values" chosen by human will. In chapter 4 it was suggested that overcoming technology implies an ontology of participation and an immanent concept of the sacred. We may now find this in ecology, if we understand it not as a scientific discipline but as the self-protection of the community of Being.[43]

Ecology thus responds more radically to the excess presupposed and purportedly internalized by systemic representation. The distinction between environmentalism and ecology overlaps considerably that between deep ecology and social ecology insofar as the role of humans is again the central issue. Social ecology claims that it is unequal relations between humans – of class, gender, and, perhaps we could add, other forms of dependency – that are at the root of problems in the human relation to nature. Deep ecology, on the other hand, claims that these problems cannot be reduced to intrahuman inequalities and that the relation of humans to nature has itself engendered systemic problems.[44] While the ethical and political orientation of social ecology, by virtue of this analysis, tends to be continuous with the radical social movements that have addressed issues of inequality between humans, deep ecology requires a new ethical and political orientation. Arne Naess, the founder of deep ecology, suggests several features of this new ethics, of which I will mention only the two that diverge from social ecology. He argues for a "rejection of the man-in-environment image in favour of the relational, total-field image," such that "an intrinsic relation belongs to the definitions or basic constitutions of A and B, so that without the relation, A and B are no longer the same things." To this relationist definition of human being Naess adds the ethical principle of "biospheric egalitarianism," which refers to the equal right of all life to live.[45] In ethical terms, it implies that every living being, and perhaps every being, has a right to persist in its being, that every being has an intrinsic worth independent of its use by, or relation to, human beings.

Environmentalism and ecology, social ecology and deep ecology, have been pitted against each other because of their differing emphases either on social inequality between humans or inequality between humans as a species and non-human nature. These different emphases stem from the basic distinction between humans and non-human nature, which it is, ironically, the aim of the environmental and ecological movement to overcome. I want to suggest that the previous analysis of systemic representation allows for a synthesis of these two emphases by developing a more basic concept that subtends them both. The focus of social ecology is continuous with traditional Marxism in describing the process of capitalist industrial production as the exploitation of labour, that is, as the appropriation of the surplus that labour produces above and beyond its wages by the owners of capital. I will suggest that a similar analysis can be applied to describe the exploitation of wild nature.

Gary Snyder has claimed that "human beings are still a wild species (our breeding has never been controlled for the purpose of any specific yield)," and he has suggested that language is also wild because its "basic structures are not domesticated or cultivated."[46] Humans have captured the productivity of the wild by domesticating and cultivating it, that is to say, by subordinating its yield to human ends. Wilderness is excess. It produces weeds as well as fruit. Wilderness always produces more than seems to be needed; it produces prolifically, though not in an ordered way – at least, not in a humanly ordered way. There is a wild order, a balance between species and habitats, a limit to the unbalanced growth of any one species, but it is independent of human needs and goals. Snyder calls this wild order "all-age unmanaged – that's a natural community, human or other."[47] In the absence of an imposed order, the wild is composed of all ages – of trees, wolves, all beings – a diversity in which each sustains and replaces the other continuously. When the wild is subjected to human order the first act is a weeding out. Some species are more useful than others; they give more fruit, offer a tastier meal, or make a stronger rope. Natural diversity is thinned down depending upon the prevailing human goals. The all-age character of continuous replacement is thinned down; reaping and planting are regulated according to human needs. Human domestication of the excess that defines the wild shapes the wild order into a humanly convenient one, reduces diversity, and takes the excess for itself.

Uncontrolled excess gives way to a yield, that is, a domesticated excess that appears within the imposed system as wealth that can satisfy human needs. Understood in this way, the domestication of the wild does to the wilderness exactly what the exploitation of labour power does to human labour or uniculturalism does to the plurality of human cultures. Human labour also produces an excess, but not necessarily one that is of use to the owners of capital. Industrial capitalism is the domestication and cultivation of the working class such that the previously unmanaged excess can appear within the system as profit. Thus we must revise Snyder's statement that humans are a wild species. There is a conflict within humanity such that some attempt to domesticate others for their own purposes. It is true that the species as a whole is not domesticated, but there is a process of domestication within humanity that is coextensive with the exploitation of labour. Thus the process of domestication can describe not only the relationship of humans to non-human beings but also intrahuman conflict. The concept of domestication of the wild therefore subtends both social ecology and deep ecology. The taming of excess, the turning inside of excess to make a profit or a yield, is the core of an ecological critique of industrial society that can maintain a continuity with Marxism and English Canadian left-nationalism, but which opens out towards the social movements.

Domination, whether between humans or of humans over wild nature, consists in the domestication and control of excess. The concept of excess is thus a truly ecological one in the sense that it is prior to the distinction between humans and nature and roots human activity thoroughly within nature. The phenomenon that I have called "turning inside," or bringing the excess into the systemic representation, is the process of domestication that turns wild excess into the productivity without which a self-enclosed system of exchanges would simply grind down. Excess keeps the system going, but finds no recognition within it, only the belated and diluted recognition of a yield. English Canadian philosophy has thus far interpreted the border in the wilderness as the imposition of a human limit on nature, that is, as domestication. The new social movements push for the twisting free of excess, but there can be no human regime of excess. It may be possible for philosophy, however, to articulate this blooming excess of the wild and to return human life to it as to a sacrament.

BUILDING A HOME

When we look ahead, how stands it with the relation of self and world such that this relation might be called "ecological"? An important step outside the assumptions of industrialism was made when key currents of twentieth-century philosophy affirmed the primacy of practical life over issues of scientific knowledge, since modern science and technology are key components of the industrial domination of nature. Though, I should add parenthetically, science and technology can themselves be called to play an anticipatory role in this turning. In particular, human reality was defined by Martin Heidegger as being-in-the-world, rather than in terms of a subject-object relationship. This is not a spatial relationship of being-contained-in, like groceries piled in a basket, but a relation of mutual definition in which the characteristic of human reality as being-in ties it essentially to practical involvements with the world. In the world, humans are not simply alongside, or next to, other beings, but (as Heidegger puts it) their "Being towards the world is essentially concern."[48] The self cannot therefore be defined *as against* the world of things, other beings, tools, and so forth, but gains its identity precisely through its involvement with a world that it inhabits. Thought, or reflection, is founded upon this more fundamental practical involvement; consequently, the self is not primarily defined through thought, but is rather a centre of focus in what may be called, in Neil Evernden's words, a "field of care."[49] Reflection, when it occurs, is not upon a subjectivity estranged from worldly entanglements, but upon the whole field of care in which the self is enmeshed.

The self as a centre of focus is not fixed. For example, it may expand or contract: often I speak of "my arm," indicating that "I" am perceived as more localized and my appendage taken to "belong" to, and thereby not to be a part of, myself. On other occasions, such as when "someone" bumps into "me" – that is, another car hits my car – I perceive myself as spread out into my practical involvements with the world.[50] The experience of the self is directly related to the extent to which tools and other practical involvements are experienced as embodiments (and extensions) of human capacities. We may say that the more one is involved with the practical world, the more one's sense of self is spread out into those activities. Thus the subject-object relation of systemic representation on which industrialism is based consists in the first place in a withdrawal from practical concerns in order, in the second place, to design an abstracted method of thought, which subsequently establishes a magisterial dominance over the whole field of practice. The emblematic example of this double (or perhaps triple) move is still Descartes. Both the *Discourse on Method* and *Meditations* begin from a withdrawal from practical involvement, design a method of knowing, and continue through the application of the abstracted method of knowing on the whole field of experience.[51] In this sense, industrialism is a product of thought; it incorporates a form of reflection with practical antecedents and consequences – which implies that the standpoint and role of reflection must be fundamentally questioned in ecological thought.

We may expect to find a more ecological relation of self and world within this description of the inhabiting of the world by an involved self and to address the problem of reflection from this starting point. But a fundamental complication arises at this stage. The phenomenological description of the self-world relation, while an important move beyond industrialism, incorporates an assumption that leaves it at a distance from the central experience of English Canadian identity. Moreover, this is exactly the same assumption that underlies the Red Tory strategy of containment.[52] Human reality, described as a totality of practical involvements in the world, suggests a self that is "at home" in the world, that dwells in and inhabits a world with which it is familiar and to which it is accustomed, as the fundamental experience.[53] It is the notion that this being-at-home-in-the-world subsists undisturbed beneath the dislocation of industrialism that is precisely what must be held up to question in the present turning point. To return to the hypothesis with which this chapter began: the red Tory critique of industrialism can pursue a strategy of containment because of two related assumptions, first, as I have shown, of the inevitability of industrialism and, second, of what we might call the "superficiality" of industrialism, in the sense that it does not penetrate "all the way down." Thus it is assumed by both Harold Innis and George Grant that there remain experiences of oral tradition and of our own – in short, a fundamental experience of "being-at-home" from which their critiques can be developed and which therefore underlies their conservatism.

Within the assumption of a primordial being-at-home, we can discern a mutually confirming relation between interpretation of our current situation, implications for action, and philosophical insight. The belonging of practical life can be seen through a hermeneutic reflection that confirms and clarifies practical belonging in order to continue and preserve it. In the terms introduced earlier, the fusing of the seeing with the seen produces a saving relation. In this interpretive circle, the judicious action brought forth by reflection would be a continuous expression of belonging. What, then, would be the motive for the disruption of unconscious belonging by the act of reflection?

The motive must be exclusively outside this interpretive circle of mutual confirmation. External disruptions of our history of belonging motivate a conservative reflection that pushes away the disruption and terminates in a recovery of being-at-home. Following Heidegger, this reflection may be called an interpretive circle of the Same since it brings together the seen and the saved through the temporary interruption of a seeing that effaces itself. "The Sameness of thinking and Being that speaks in Parmenides' fragment stems from further back than the kind of identity defined by metaphysics in terms of Being as a characteristic of Being."[54] Thinking, Being, and the relation of belonging are moments of the Same continuous process of self-understanding.

This circle of the Same provides the basis for the mutual confirmation of the two senses of world with which we began. Innis's focus on the world system of industrialism provides the external disrupting motive, while Grant's thinking of our own provides the moment of recovery. This mutually confirming interpretive circle, rooted in our red Tory tradition, is deeply ambiguous. It has clearly served to defend and extend the practical belonging of our home. Nevertheless, it has done so by defining all disruption of the serenity of belonging as external, thereby obscuring the disruptions and divisions within our borders and, most fundamentally, the encounter with wilderness that is characteristic of Canada as a New World society. They have defended Canada only through imagining it as a continuation of Europe, and in this sense, their imagination is that of the dominant ruling class. The disruptions of the wilderness are pushed outside as we are imagined to inhabit the house of the Same.

Within this imagined being-at-home, disruptions appear as external. In particular, the disruptions and crises brought about by industrialism appear to be only external threats. It is this assumption of English Canadian experience as a primordial belonging that I now want to displace in order to develop English Canadian roots for an ecological relation of self and world that is conservationist, but not conservative. To do so, disruptions must be recognized as also internal to industrial society, the New World as a discontinuity, and we must open to an abjection that blows away the security of interpretive self-confirmation within the Same. As in chapter 5, the security of hermeneutic interpretation must give way to a deconstructive wind.

The fundamental level of our practical inhabitation of the world in Canada cannot be characterized as being-at-home. The history of inhabitation is the story of the *construction* of settlements in the wilderness, or domestication, and therefore of a fundamental tension between wilderness and building a home. When one later embraces in reflection the prior-built sphere of belonging, one must also turn to embrace the wilderness. Here we re-encounter the polarity between archaism and modernity that characterizes English Canadian thought. Innis and Grant, in embracing solely the belonging in our inhabiting, have incorporated a falsely European conception of being-in-the-world as being-at-home. In the New World, being-at-home can not be regarded as either fundamental or unproblematic. The primal experience is of *building a home* and thus also of wilderness and homelessness. A difference between humanity and wilderness that does not attempt to tame the wild undoes the closure of humanity within its socially constructed reality and opens us to the affections of the embodied environment. We must construct a home and place it alongside the homes of others, but we must also accept the wind that shakes all foundations, uncovering the inevitable locality of all constructions. Our abjection is revealed by this wind.

From this standpoint, we can reinterpret the Red Tory interpretive fusing of seen, saved, and seer. We need to take a "step back" with regard to this interpretive circle; that is, not simply to deny it, but rather to cease from engagement in it in order to see it more clearly. This step back reveals that the interpretive circle of the Same occurs through domestication, which has meant the construction of cultural continuity *against* nature. It presupposes and extends the division between nature and culture and, for this reason, cannot address adequately the concerns of contemporary ecological thought – centring on the concept of excess, which is beyond the nature-culture division. But when we uncover the presupposition of domestication upon which English Canadian philosophy has been articulated, the possibility of re-encountering the wilderness also arises. Such an encounter with wilderness would undo the opposition between nature and culture and develop a conception of civilization that does not depend on the repression of nature.

In order to clarify the relation between seen, saved, and seer revealed by this step back, I will conclude by developing the concept of particularity beyond that which was possible within the Red Tory interpretive circle. Both Innis and Grant actively *embrace* particularity in their thinking, a "particularity" understood on many levels, from one's own body, through local oral traditions to Canada itself, and perhaps beyond. Particularity is not a defined arena of social life, but a concept that pertains to the character of one's *encounter* with any given arena of that life as a legitimation of a less universal, but necessary and good, moment of belonging, or being-at-home. It is because it is not a defined sphere of social life that particularity must be actively embraced. We may say that particularity is a mode of concern in which the specificity of initial encounter is deemed worthwhile precisely insofar as it is one's indispensable way towards the universal. Innis and Grant performed this embracing in order to begin their thinking of Canada. The result of the thinking is clear enough. But the embracing itself, which is the prior condition of the thinking, has been occluded. What is embraced has been thought, but not the embracing itself. This claiming, or embracing, of one's own needs to be further clarified in order to make plain where one's own is blown away by the wind of abjection.

Claiming one's own is not the same as simply having it or living it through. Particularity is embracing one's own as a first meeting with a belonging that extends indefinitely beyond towards universality. In this sense, as the last chapter has shown, it is not a contingency that could be dispensed with, but an initial encounter without which no reaching towards universality is possible. The conditions for apprehending universality include inhabiting a particular world, which is a matter of contingency, but also of "embracing" this world as mine – as the locus in which I can be myself – and therefore in recognizing that it is not the world as such, but one world among others. It is one among many, but cannot be treated as simply contingent because it is *this particular way* towards the good that demands public recognition. Such a formulation suggests that there is an important distinction between inhabiting and embracing which is occluded in the work of Innis and Grant and which has to do with the reflective activity in which we grasp our prior involvements with the world. If we think through the nature of embracing itself, we come upon the character of the self as an embracing of elements of one's lived condition. The self is not a thing in the world, but an embracing, or identifying with, selected features of the world. The step back allows the self to identify in a deeper and more extensive way with one's environment, a growth of the self to a larger self that may also be called a death of the original self. As Arne Naess says, "the intensity of identification with other life depends upon milieu, culture and economic conditions. The ecosophical outlook is developed through an identification so deep that one's *own self* is no longer adequately delimited by the personal ego or the organism."[55] In identifying with one's sustaining ecology, the egoistic self may die (become abject to the Other), but the larger self lives on (expands its sphere of belonging).

English Canadian philosophy must also embrace a moment of wildness, of loss, and of absence, for wilderness is precisely what cannot be captured. In the same moment that we reflect on our construction of a home, the ineradicability of the wilderness must be brought inside as an acceptance of the locality of all belonging. This means acceptance of a kind of abjection, an abandonment of the world in which one belongs. Underneath all home-making is an absence of belonging, an absence of being a particular self. Thus in a reflection that is oriented to the whole history of inhabiting, there must be also an experience of the limits of recapturing, a limit of thought insofar as it can claim to dominate its object. In this moment, English Canadian philosophy recovers wildness without subduing it, discovers in its own thinking a thought of the limit of thought, an abjection stumbling blindly at the edge of wilderness. This analysis implies that the metaphors that have guided thought in European philosophy, particularly "reflection" (the water/mirror) and "light" (the sun/seeing), need to be rethought in English Canadian philosophy. Especially central are the metaphors of wilderness and border. I have been able only to touch initially and tentatively on this project here. It is in the tension between the embracing of one's home-making, which initiates a higher consciousness of belonging, and the recovery of abjection, which bathes us in the stream without a source, that an English Canadian ecological philosophy is stretched.

It is because we have not succeeded in building a home, in really belonging, that we have needed the red Tory defence and lament. It is also why drawing of a border in the wilderness has been understood as domestication and thereby has fuelled the domination of nature, rather than drawing us on towards ecological ethics. Either in imagined purity or in unlimited domination, we are entrapped within the circle of the Same. But the recovery of abjection opens the Same to the Other, where even the Same is our loss of the Other. Even our most profound loss is our belonging; even our closest belonging is haunted by loss. Here there is seer and seen, but no saving. The deconstructive wind cannot be counted on to preserve our houses. For an ecological thought that does not force identity through the assertion of itself against the wilderness, the slogan must be "No more of the Same."

To sum up: ecological thought now must centre on the relationship between belonging and abjection. These are both ecological concepts and experiences; that is to say, they are prior to any conceptual division into human versus nature. Understood in this way, the relation between wilderness and civilization is not that of an opposition. Both wilderness and civilization are forms of order; the difference is that one is oriented towards human interests and the other is not. If we remain within the interpretive circle of belonging, whose presupposed condition is domestication, then belonging and abjection seem to be opposites. But the deconstruction of domestication shows that it replaces order with order; the similarity between belonging within a human order and belonging within an ecological order becomes

204 A Border Within

palpable. The condition of this awareness is that we loosen the desire to be saved and open to an abjection towards the Other. Or, to say it differently, one may identify with what is beyond the self and thus must allow for the death of self to provide for the birth of Self. Perhaps this is how we should structure the university: a Faculty of Belonging, exploring all the varieties of being at home in the world, and a Faculty of Abjection, investigating forms in which belonging is lost and the terror and pleasure of such loss. Most professors would probably need cross-appointments. In searching for English Canadian roots for an ecological relation of self and world, we have come upon an ineradicable tension between culture, or home-making, and wilderness, or excess. In seeing ourselves as *becoming* ourselves through home-making, we see also beneath "ourselves" into a great wilderness before the distinction between humanity and nature. We see too the constitutive relation of our humanness with this wilderness. And the thinking of this wilderness is itself plunged into this tension between belonging and abjection. This border is not a philosophical articulation of domestication but the embrace of an wild order beneath human intention. In an anticipatory thinking that risks a departure from the reign of knowledge, looking beyond humanity is also a being looked at. The more we discover and create ourselves, the more we find ourselves on the border of an extensive unknown. It is an unmeasurable sea, both Atlantic and Pacific, that supports the world as Atlas supported the universe and with which we must make our peace – a peace that can be no contract, but that we may uneasily approach when we take our responsibility for the world beyond ourselves.

CHAPTER EIGHT

Conclusion

This book has attempted to think through the philosophical significance of the historical and geographical formation of the English Canadian identity. It is an initial formulation of that task. Basing itself on English Canadian social and political thought as represented in the work of Harold Innis and George Grant, it has attempted to move beyond this tradition, and also a particular moment of it represented by the discourse of left-nationalism, through an immanent critique of its main tenets. This critique has allowed a connection to the tradition and consequently, one hopes, to the national-popular collective will of a nation whose unawareness of itself is legendary. It has also enabled a prospective formulation of two themes – multiculturalism and ecology – deeply rooted in the self-conception of English Canada as a result of their convergence on a recognition of the strength of diversity. This diversity does not require a rejection of universality, or unity, as much so-called postmodernist thought implies nowadays, but rather a new hegemonic and phenomenological conception of unity that is articulated through, rather than against, diversity.[1] It is not suggested that these are the only themes amenable to this treatment or to an emergent social and political philosophy for English Canada. Much work remains to be done.

The immanent critique encountered a special difficulty, however. The era of permeable Fordism that succeeded the Second World War, in which the orientation to national identity was crucial, has come to a close, as indicated by the Free Trade Agreement and the North American Free Trade Agreement. The current era is one of polarization between globalizing free market forces and new social movements. Thus the emergent theory proposed here had to argue for the closure of the left-nationalist option and to outline the basis of theory of the new social movements. While immanent critique constructs a

206 A Border Within

continuity, the closure suggests a break. The entire text has attempted to negotiate the relationship between continuity and break sufficiently to claim adherence to a tradition while departing from it in key aspects. At a more philosophical level, the break signifies a shift from a defence of one's own towards a recognition of the constitutive status of the Other; in ethical terms, from belonging to abjection. In short, the defence of diversity by previous English Canadian thought was necessary to legitimate a difference of English Canada from the United States, but it stopped with the conception of national identity and thus did not recognize crucial aspects of internal and more radical diversity. The current argument radicalizes the concept of diversity, or plurality, but does not abandon national identity as a site for political opposition and philosophical articulation.[2]

English Canadian thought was moulded by its defence of a difference from the United States, which has meant a critique of modernity, technology, industrialism, and individualism. It can be fairly said that this critique implies an archaizing tendency, a suggestion that history ought to be rubbed in the other direction. It is, of course, a tendency, not the entirety of the thought. If it were all, one might legitimately speak of a dangerous romantic abandonment of the gains of modern enlightenment. No such implication follows, however, from an awareness of what has been lost, repressed, or exploited by modernization. What it does imply is a revaluation of those remaining remnants of pre-modern traditions and archaic encounters, in order to bring them into a reformed political and philosophical project. The incorporation of pre-modern ethnic traditions into a transformed context by multiculturalism and the recovery of the intrinsic worth of nature by the ecology movement are not one-sidedly archaizing tendencies. They incorporate a retrieval of pre-progressive and archaizing tendencies within the gains of modernity, thus rerouting an otherwise one-sided modernity.

The critique of modernity, technology, industrialism, and individualism is thus maintained, radicalized, and reformulated in the present argument. The metaphor of the border was proposed as the key mediation between the tradition of defence of one's own place and the emergent theory. An elaboration of this metaphor was essential to the task of bringing English Canada to philosophical articulation. A certain conception of philosophy is presupposed by this project. Philosophy is the thinking through of the particularities that form the destiny of a people towards its universal dimensions. It is characterized by its continuity with social and political issues, but also it transcends them towards a characterization from a certain angle of the human condition as such.[3] That this is not a conception of philosophy that is current within the branch of the academic division of labour often referred to by the same name is not a matter of overriding importance. This fact may, however, be partly responsible for the relatively primitive state of the task, compared to French, German, American, or Chinese philosophy, for example. The rest of the blame may be laid on dependency itself. In this, English Canadian philosophy shares its condition with that of Latin America, Quebec, and other peripheral societies. In the future, a lot may depend on the extent to which these "minor" traditions can gain some purchase on the definition of the universality of the human condition. The deepest condition of dependency is to believe that the thought which constitutes our humanness must belong somewhere else and that that which constitutes our own condition is necessarily parochial. My entire argument is an attempt to escape the horns of this dilemma. English Canadian intellectuals must face the difficult tasks involved in speaking out of the academic division of labour to a general audience if our future is to take on any clear definition. The sense of one's own inadequacy is no excuse; neither is the illusory consolation of value-free social or natural science, which achieves its illusion by reinforcing the assumptions of the historical epoch and its dominant forces. Crafting a public discourse concerning our destiny is a crucial component of the responsibility of the intellectual to criticize and confront dependency. There are no institutions within which this is a favoured task, though the university still has a historical legacy to discharge in this respect.

The cruciality of the border is revealed by a step back with regard to the orienting ideas of Harold Innis and George Grant – Innis's attempt to define the "here" of a dependent colony and Grant's to articulate the loss of "one's own." A meditation on belonging here is the whole of English Canadian social and political philosophy. I have not entered directly into debate about what it is to belong here. Rather, I have concentrated on the constitutive role that this preoccupation has had. In examining it, one must "step back" from one's engagements in order to describe the place in which the involvements occur.[4] Any arguments emanating from this territory are thus not straightforwardly one's own. They grow from the landscape and give it its distinctive appearance. Philosophy is owned by no one. It is a wild creature. The step back comes upon one in the wild and cannot be an act of gaining control. In this moment one can discover philosophy here, and not through any importation. It is the philosopher's job to hear and to give voice, not engage in arbitrary invention.

Maintaining the border allows one's own to be preserved and provides a glimpse of the other as Other, as beyond one's clutches. Here the history and collective formation of English Canada turns into an ethics in which preserving one's own requires accepting the Other. Paradoxically, it discovers itself in abjection, because it finds itself in the critique of self-assertion. English Canada is a weak nation, and a certain weakness may open the door to wisdom. If there will be anything left of this nation, it will not be preserved through demands for exclusive loyalty. I have attempted to explore the significance of this non-exclusivity, or constitutive Otherness, through the recognition of the ethical claims of diversity in multiculturalism and the ecological movement. The future will be a struggle between those who locate the other within the assertion of the self and those who accept the Other in order to discover themselves. What kind of struggle could this be, since it will obviously not be a test of strength? Philosophy cannot predict this, or any other, event. It cannot command experience, but rather articulates it. The condition for preserving one's own is that the Other be manifested through the border. The coming-to-be of manifestation itself is excess, which overflows any definition. This refusal to be captured may be called "wilderness." It may also be "our own" to the extent that we participate in a unity that we do not control, but for which we must take responsibility.

Missing Links in Canadian Theoretical Discourse

The following is an analysis of the edited collection *Canada: Theoretical Discourse/Discours théoriques*, which was the first book that attempted to assess the scope of Canadian theoretical discourse as a whole.[1] It is a selection of eighteen essays from the Association for Canadian Studies conference on Theoretical Discourse in the Canadian Intellectual Community held in Saint-Jovite, Quebec, in September 1992. As in all multidisciplinary and thematic collections of this sort, the essays range over a multitude of topics and are difficult to assemble into a comprehensive and coherent framework. Such is perhaps especially true in this case, given the very large scope of the topic. The difficulty of circumscribing the theoretical discourse of any one discipline, such as Canadian literature, folklore, sociology, or geography, is notorious enough: one tends to achieve coherence precisely to the extent that one is willing to rule certain approaches actually present in the discipline out of one's theoretical scheme and thereby to risk "disciplining" in Foucault's sense. Especially in the case of multidisciplinary collections and interdisciplinary inquiries, the task of classification seems impossible. Nonetheless, it is important to this collection beyond all others. The conference, and the collection of essays assembled from it, attempted to define theoretical discourse in Canada. "What is a community of scholars?" ask the editors in the first sentence of their introduction. Perhaps it is an impossible question to answer, but it is inevitably of great interest to anyone who is committed to the investigation of Canada. One cannot avoid the question, vexing as it is, of Canadian distinctiveness. While a question such as this virtually drips with hubris, the distinctiveness it seeks must be articulated, or at least implicitly assumed, in any defence of Canadian Studies. The explicit asking of this question is thus an index of the maturity of Canadian Studies, a willingness to risk the possibility of an insufficient answer, or perhaps a gamble that even a lack of definitiveness will produce a discourse rich enough to stimulate further investigation.

Canadian Studies as an interdisciplinary association and as a teaching and research enterprise in Canadian universities drew for justification upon the left-nationalist discourse that preceded it. It is notable that this discourse had sufficient appeal, not only in university circles but also in government and to some extent business, labour, and public ones, to create sources of funding and benefit that often provided a wedge against recalcitrant university administration and faculty. Staple-theory political economy, combined with cultural nationalism, provided an argument that Canadian history was unique enough to bother investigating and salient enough to our identity to be important intellectually. Harold Innis and George Grant were the stars in this firmament, around which many others could be arranged, such as Marxist critiques of staple theory and socialist critiques of Grant's conservatism. Put together with an individual's own interests, often formed in a particular discipline, this combination proved diverse and persistent enough to sustain the discourse of "Canadian Studies" that has emerged over the last twenty-five years or so. Left-nationalism's vision of a conservative past and a socialist future opened a complex discursive space for investigation that, interestingly, excluded liberal themes and writers from its purview. Thus, when Jill Vickers finds that Innis and Grant were often cited in Canadian Studies publications and only very rarely were others such writers as Frye, Trudeau, Scott, and McLuhan, one is hardly surprised (356, 360). Many of the papers in the volume under discussion reconsider this founding left-nationalist discourse, which is both a timely and important task for thinking about Canadian theoretical discourse and where it might go in the future. In order to confront this task, one must first define a "theoretical discourse" as well as what specifically characterizes the "Canadian" one, and the richness and diversity of this volume is an excellent place to start.

The editors suggest in their introduction (6) that the article by Claude Couture and Claude Denis, "La captation du couple tradition/modernité par la sociographie québécoise," can propose an organization for the volume. The tradition-modernity distinction, whose influence in Quebec they trace to the Chicago school of sociology, is pervasive throughout the social sciences and has many other sources as well, such as Max Weber. These authors argue that this sociological distinction led to the misunderstanding of key features of Quebec society as "monolithically traditional" and the ignoring of its dynamic, mercantile, liberal, and utilitarian features (121–2). Nonetheless, they continue, the Rioux-Guindon sociology that was formed in the 1950s used the tradition-modernity distinction to oppose the traditionalism of Duplessis and to this extent surpassed its formative concepts towards a notion of "political reason." This excellent argument, whose implications are suggested only briefly in conclusion, indicates an important characteristic of intellectual life in peripheral societies. Even when concepts are taken over from dominant formations, they may be used in a way that surpasses their original formation and thereby changes their meaning. Moreover, this modification can occur even when such concepts lead to misunderstandings of the peripheral society itself. This analysis suggests, in opposition to Jill Vickers (367), Robin Mathews (287), and the editors' own account of Couture and Denis's argument (6), that there is more at work in dependent importations than mere repetition of intellectual concepts and misunderstanding of the local context. The point is that the *meaning* of theoretical concepts is *not internal* to either their original context of articulation or the theoretical system itself, but arises from contact between these and the *context of application* in which they are deployed.

It is ironic, then, that the editors suggest that Vickers's and Mathews's papers can be situated also with respect to the "crux between tradition and modernity" (7), especially since these two contributions seem to have polarized the conference (6) and they represent, respectively, hostile critique and impassioned defence of the left-nationalist founding discourse. Mathews argues that the terms "empire" and "imperialism" have been central to the formation of a distinctively Canadian intellectual discourse and are being systematically ignored today as part of a general treason of the intellectuals that is "contributing to the destruction of a better system on behalf of a very bad system" represented, now as in the past, by the United States (288). He defends precisely the moral, anti-modern tradition of Canadian Studies that Vickers regards as the main obstacle to it becoming a "normal field" defined by the "conceptual agreement" of a "cognitive community" (368, 353, 368). The editors pose this conflict as an issue of adherence to a Canadian community versus a commitment to internationalist concepts such as feminism (7), but surely this is too simple a polarization, as the Couture and Denis argument has shown. "Empire," after all, was surely not in the first place a Canadian concept, even though it is certainly possible to agree with Mathews that it has been constitutive of the Canadian nationalist discourse. Feminism, which certainly has an international dimension, is nevertheless capable of different local formations that respond to specific components of its context. Susan Knutson, for example, demonstrates in a careful analysis of Nicole Brossard's intervention with regard to the use of the word "woman" that the situation of Quebec feminism at the nexus of both French and American feminisms has led to a very theoretically sophisticated movement (188). Nevertheless, however theoretically developed the analysis may be, it has not been influential outside Quebec and English Canada (197). A dependent intellectual formation thus also contains hidden sources of power, even if they are not often appreciated outside that formation.

The underlying issue here is one of borders, how they are constituted, and what are their effects – all issues that pertain primarily to the context of application of a theory. To look for the distinctive features of the Canadian intellectual formation by searching for concepts that appear nowhere else is a vain enterprise – as much so as concluding that because concepts always appear elsewhere, there is no distinctiveness to the Canadian theoretical discourse. The posing of the issue in this way is an effect of the tradition-modernity distinction itself: one is confronted with a choice of either a self-enclosed, local society or an international, open one. Innis rephrased this classical sociological distinction in terms of time-bound or space-bound aspects of media of communication. It was thereby transformed from a global alternative between types of societies to aspects of a single social formation that could, at least in principle, be harmonized or balanced. Thus it led to another theoretical agenda from that of European sociology and also from that of American modernization theory, which was directed at the "underdeveloped societies." In this rephrasing, Innis *repeated* the tradition-modernity doublet, which derives from the notion of industrialism as a break from previous societies, but put it in a way that also *transformed* the distinction and opened a path for new theoretical developments that may well have a specific relation to Canadian historical experience.[2]

Is there, then, a way of conceptualizing the structure of this volume, and by implication, the Canadian theoretical discourse, in other terms than the tradition-modernity doublet affords? First, one must note that an intellectual discourse can not be understood through the notions of consensus or agreement, which will always be partial and thus simplifying and/or imposed. An intellectual discourse is also open to debate and disagreement and remains a "discourse" even so. For disagreement to occur, a certain "frame," or field of discourse, must already exist; otherwise we do not have disagreement, but rather simply different statements without any relation to each other. In fact, for a theoretical discourse to persist effectively (except in the case of authoritarian control), it must contain sufficient internal complexity to create problems and open new areas for investigation. Thus, while there has been a certain continuity in the Canadian left-nationalist discourse associated with hostility to the assumptions of empire, technology-industrialism, and progress-liberalism, it has also provided a rich enough field to stimulate both internal debates (often bitter ones) and plausible claims for distinctiveness from other national traditions. The question is therefore: How is a space for agreement and disagreement constructed, a space that is neither infinitely wide (and thus without any definite characteristics) nor so narrow as to be simply a single theme (and thus not a field such as Canadian Studies, but a topic such as staple theory). In short, how is a field of discourse constructed, especially in regard to its context of application?

With this question in mind, the article by Leslie Armour, entitled "Canada and the History of Philosophy," is of considerable interest. He distinguishes between the history of philosophy understood as the self-unfolding of an inner logic versus philosophy understood in relation to history and culture in general. While there are certainly proponents of the first way of viewing philosophy in Canada, Armour argues that the development of Canadian philosophy itself cannot be understood in these terms. He interprets Quebec's Cartesian philosophy as produced by "struggling to establish a community in a new world in which they must confront new [i.e., aboriginal] cultures," in which "they sought to return to what is common to all human beings" (29). English Canadian philosophy, in the hands of Watson and John Clark Murray, was concerned with the fact that social unity "could only thrive so long as certain kinds of plurality were honoured" (34). While it is certainly possible to view philosophy in isolation, one is likely to miss "the significance of what is going on" (39). This is a good part of what is at issue in the question of Canadian philosophy. Armour defends the importance of such philosophers, *even if they are bad philosophers*, because "they cast a good deal of light on our plight and on our adventures" (35), whereas it is fairly common for those who are concerned with the internal history of philosophy to put our locals alongside Plato and Hegel and judge them wanting and therefore without interest. (Never mind that a good many widely read U.S. philosophers would be found wanting by the same standard.) This posing of the issue as between "local interest" and "perennial human themes" is deeply rooted, and Armour's defence of Canadian philosophy in this regard is a version of the defence of "our own" made famous by George Grant. It explains our need to stress our difference from Britain and the United States, which, in the view of Jill Vickers, is part of the abnormal character of of Canadian Studies as a field of inquiry (355). The motto might be: Even if it's bad, it's ours, and we're important, at least to ourselves. And why not? Surely this captures at least part of the motive for Canadian Studies, at least for us. If it is abnormal in academic affairs, is not that just the worse for academic affairs, as Mathews concludes (287)?

The thrust of Armour's argument is thus to connect a contextual understanding of the history of philosophy in general to the necessity of the Canadian context to understanding Canadian philosophers and, moreover, to suggest that the reason for one's interest in philosophical questions derives from, in some way, sharing the context of the philosopher. Significantly, we share our context with Canadian philosophers, so that they cast light on our context. It is a powerful argument, and while Armour does not speak of empire, as Mathews would like – indeed, only Richard A. Cavell (83) and Misao Dean (157) do so – he certainly has a lot to say about community, which is its antithesis in the context of American individualism. The article by Sheldon Wein is very interesting in this connection. He notes a significant difference with regards to social-contract theories of justice in Canada versus those in the United States. In Canada, economic contractarianism predominates. It seeks "amoral reasons for convincing individuals to become moral persons" (377). By way of contrast, social contractarianism predominates in the United States and uses moral reasons, such as fairness, in the specification of the initial situation in which a contract is formed. Thus the social-contract *theory* of the United States is more like the *political culture* of Canada, and vice versa. Wein seeks to explain this difference by the importance of political rhetoric and moral exhortation in the United States, whereas Canadians look for a theory of justice that is based on self-interest because "we confront legitimate concerns that the basic structure of our social arrangements is at risk" (387). The article shows that a theoretical discourse may not directly reflect the social order of which it is a part. Because theory is a product of imagination, it is also diagnosis, critique, and projection of the society in which it occurs. It may reflect the order by reacting to it and imagining alternatives, in other words. Armour, however, is not a social contractarian, and his theory of community is in continuity with the Canadian political culture.[3]

The relation between theory and social order, or text and context, is thus a complex one. I have one problem with Armour's analysis, however, which might pertain to his own doubts about its validity (25, 37) and his apparently exasperated claim that "surely, there must be a dialectic involved" between history and philosophy (40). His analysis involves an unwarranted connection, or confusion, between perenniality of themes and isolation from context. "As long as philosophers continue to ask the same questions and to reorganize the same concepts, it is not necessary to know anything much about the external history involved" (37). Armour assumes that if philosophers remain concerned with the same issues, then the context in which the issues arise is not of importance. Why? Probably because they arise in each and all contexts. But this is not really the same thing. While he provides a version of "our own" that is a powerful defence of Canadian Studies, it does so at the very high price of cutting us off from the perennial themes. Even with perennial questions, there is a *necessity of entry* into the issue, and this is provided, not by the philosophical discourse itself, but by the opening of the philosophical text onto a specific context. This opening allows access. Now, it is perfectly possible that philosophical texts are about universal themes regarding the human condition and yet that our access to that discourse requires an opening to our context to be available. That opening would be Canadian Studies. In short, not exactly "our own," but our own *way in*. So universality of theme and the significance of context are not opposed, and there is no reason to choose between them. One need only regard the context of application of a theory, as I called it above, as constitutive of the theoretical discourse.[4] Armour's phrasing of the issue in terms of an opposition between perenniality and locality is the same theoretical posing that looks for Canadian distinctiveness in something that does not exist anywhere else, that is, something which is distinctive in a merely empirical sense and which therefore implies an *identical* theoretical discourse to ascertain it. The distinctiveness of a *theoretical discourse*, by contrast, may contain identical *elements*, but it is constituted through the manner of their arrangement. We may then ask: What are the *axes*, or themes, whose arrangement constructs the Canadian theoretical discourse, and how does this discourse lend itself to a certain *context of application*?

The notion of a discursive space for (dis)agreement constructed through the intersection of several axes that defines the significance of our context of application seems superior to a tradition-modernity doublet as a theorization of the field of Canadian Studies, or indeed of any single thematic focus. Tradition/modernity would be only one, inadequate, formulation of "significance" from this point of view. Historically, staple theory has been the major thematic focus through which significance has been articulated in English Canada. It has made the connections to colonial status, cultural continuity with Europe, and economic nationalism that have seemed crucial to the continuance of Canada. Several authors in this volume question the continued applicability of the model provided by staple theory. Patricia Marchak argues that it is outmoded because of recent globalizing trends (261). Robert C.H. Sweeny claims that it has always been a misleading account of Canadian capitalism because of the arbitrariness of its distinction between internal and external markets (333). Richard A. Cavell argues that it has been burdened with an abstract concept of space, suggesting that we "substitute the notion of heterotopia for the notion of utopia which has largely governed thought about space in Canada" (88). David Crowley and David Mitchell suggest that the communication theory of the Toronto circle (Innis and McLuhan) is problematic because "hegemonic control emanating from the messages that these technologies systematically circulate is increasingly undercut today by evidence that the reception and use of mediated messages are much less under the control of organizing groups and special interests than we previously thought" (149). It is clear enough from this volume generally that wholesale criticism of staple theory and its relation to contemporary Canadian theoretical discourse has become widespread.

Cultural nationalism, the other main thematic focus of Canadian Studies, fares no better in the volume. While it is not the focus of explicit criticism as is the staple theory, the articles addressing cultural issues tend altogether to avoid traditional topics such as national identity, cultural imperialism, and French-English dualism. The outstanding exception is the argument by Misao Dean that recent literary criticism has adopted a postmodernist orientation that has taken as its main target left-nationalist criticism (154). In the course of "revaluing the concerns of women, aboriginal people and members of cultural groups other than English or French" (154), postmodern critics have rejected a "monolithic" concept of the nation that, they claim, characterizes left-nationalism and in particular the literary criticism of Robin Mathews (155). This seems to be the case, judging from this volume, anyway. David Leahy shows that discourse analyses predominate in the study of male identities (212). Lianne Moyes's interesting account of feminist fiction/theory as a genre mixing mentions it as "an important site of inquiry into questions of national, cultural, and historical as well as gender specificity" (307), though only the latter is discussed in the article. Pauline Greenhill and Diane Tye analyse the appropriation and dismissal of the work of non-academic women folklorists by the academic establishment (172). Marie-Andrée Bertrand argues that feminism has provided more to criminology than the reverse and that postmodernism demonstrates the richness of the vision of minorities in comparison to modern scientism (66).

All these articles, as well as the one by Knutson on Brossard mentioned earlier, are informative and carefully researched accounts of processes of exclusion within domains of social and cultural studies, and by pointing out that none of them deal with the concept of nation, I by no means want to imply differently. However, it is significant that all these articles, as well as some of those mentioned above as critical of staple theory (Cavell; Crowley and Mitchell), have two things in common. First, they do not reinterpret, criticize, or deconstruct subject matter previously understood to be within the founding discourse of Canadian Studies; rather, they pass it by altogether. Second, their theoretical legitimation is some version of postmodernism. I therefore conclude that a polarization has been set up between postmodernism and the founding discourse of left-nationalism and that between these polarized opposites there exists only an empty space. It is an interesting question as to whether this theoretical either/or is a necessary one and how it has come into being. Dean seems to be right about this: postmodernism, evenwhile it defends diversity and dependent formations, seems to have assumed that the left-nationalist founding discourse is *necessarily* hooked to a unitary and repressive concept of the nation. And, reciprocally, the remaining left-nationalists seem convinced that postmodernism necessarily entails abandoning the nation as a significant site for cultural defence and/or emancipation (Mathews, 283; Marchak, 264).[5]

It is only in Jill Vickers's article "Liberating Theory in Canadian Studies" that this polarization is directly addressed.[6] She argues that the founding left-nationalist discourse of Canadian Studies is grounded in a majoritarian, European, and anti-American perpective based on the anti-modern, antiliberal, and anti-technology theories of George Grant and Harold Innis. Vickers contends that Canadian Studies has not generated a cognitive community because it has never become a normal field, and therefore it has not been subject to the generational revisionism that other, presumably normal, fields undergo. Instead, it has been stuck at its foundational moment, whose "antimodernism is about the defence of cultural identity understood from an elite, male-centred and white perspective" (365). This formation has, it is claimed, both distorted attempts to deal with new issues within Canadian Studies and also excluded marginalized "others" from entering the field. Vickers mentions Barry Cooper, Philip Resnick, and myself, among others, as contemporary representatives of this establishment intellectual formation (359). In an essay of mine published in the *Canadian Issues/Themes canadiens* special issue on ecology and culture, I apparently "recycled" Grant and Innis, repeating the dichotomies of anti-modernism between spirit and nature that justify gender, racial, and environmental dominations. Vickers seems to have missed the central claim of the essay that Canadian conservatism can become useful to environmentalism *if it is transformed* by questioning and rejecting "the assumption of industrialism as inevitable" – even though she quotes precisely this phrase (362–3)! It is of course possible that my claim is nonsense, or not sufficiently radical, or based on a faulty analysis of Innis's and Grant's work. But she attempts to show none of these things. It seems that my use of Grant and Innis is sufficient to indicate an adherence to the intellectual formation she criticizes. Actually, my claim seems very close to Marchak's critique of staple theory for assuming the superiority of a manufacturing economy by equating "development" with "manufacturing," a claim that seems to me a well-argued and important critique of the founding discourse (262). One can add that the work of Barry Cooper and Philip Resnick, whatever their respective merits, also amounts to more than a recycling of Innis and Grant. It is precisely the generational revisionism that Vickers claims has not occurred. The question then becomes: How does one distinguish between "recycling" and "generational revisionism"? For her, counting citations seems to be sufficient (356, n. 8).[7]

The deeper problem here is the mare's nest that emerges whenever one tries to define a national identity. Of course, one can argue over whether a proposed definition is the right one, but a more fundamental issue can be raised with regard to the attempt at definition itself. Any definition will exclude some possibilities, a number of which are being actively pursued within the boundaries of the nation. So one is in the tricky position of defining a national identity that is not comprehensive in an empirical sense and thereby excluding some works and writers. Dean describes Mathews's dialectical paradigm of national identity as a "struggle between the liberal/individualist and conservative/collective vision of Canada [which] is not only the master narrative of Canadian intellectual history but a specific pattern in individual novels" (159). As a consequence, this definition "has allowed him to identify works by Canadian citizens as non-Canadian – works by Kroetsch, Richler, Woodcock and Atwood are the most controversial examples" (161). The debate has shifted from addressing whether Mathews is right in his characterization to rejecting the idea of any such characterization at all. Any definition is taken to be repressively homogenizing and therefore to be avoided at all costs. This claim, which is largely unexplored, has come to stand as a cardinal assumption of postmodern criticism and social theory. It is this postulate that is behind both the contemporary postmodern rejection of left-nationalist discourse and the general tendency not to discuss issues pertaining to national identity at all.

It seems to me that there is one common thread to the postmodernist position and the left-nationalist one. Both would agree, I think, that the position of the speaker is a key constitutive component of any discourse (Dean, 157; Mathews, 276; Greenhill and Tye, 169; Moyes, 312; Melançon, 302; Vickers, 365). In fact, the "politics of the speaker/reader in theory" could have been a subtitle for the whole volume. The postmodern claim is that the left-nationalist position is a homogenizing one based on some form of privilege that allows the speaker to silence, marginalize, or appropriate the many voices of others.[8] Thus the intellectual project is to promote as many diverse voices as possible. The left-nationalist claim is that talk of diversity without any reference to the commonalities that have sustained Canada as a nation is merely an abandonment of a central arena for struggle to the dominant international forces, mainly the United States. The polarization is thus between diversity and unity, and there is no middle ground.

I want to suggest that this polarization is unnecessary, at least in this form. I do not want to invent a middle ground or to reconcile incompatibles, but rather to point to the way that the polarization has been constructed in order to suggest an alternative posing of the issue. It is important to recall that the left-nationalist position did not claim that the nation-state is never internally repressive, but only that *in the present context* of economic and cultural domination by the United States, it is an arena that cannot be abandoned. In other words, the left-nationalist speaker's position situated itself within a field of discourse that included other speakers also. Postmodern critics who charge that the left-nationalist founding discourse was "the *basis* of the sexism, the racism and the Anglo-Canadian, ethnic chauvinism that has characterized much of the underlying thought in Canadian Studies" (Vickers, 364; emphasis added) need to show that these effects are actually a result of the left-nationalist speaker and not importantly related to other speaking positions, such as patriarchy, class society, colonialism, and so on. The postmodern position, on the other hand, has indeed pointed to diverse experiences that have not made their way into the dominant discourse. To suggest, as left-nationalists sometimes do (Mathews, 278–9, 283), though not always (Dean, 155–6), that postmodern talk of diversity must necessarily subvert the project of an independent Canada is to *naturalize* the nation-state. Such claims, like the postmodern ones, also need to show that the *specific interventions* pointed to in the discourse are the responsible ones.[9] Why is it not possible to say that, in the context of international power issues, the dependence of Canada is a significant phenomenon, that, in the context of internal Canadian issues, the class-linguistic-gender-racial-ethnic power formation is significant, and that, in the context of the formation of Canada, the colonization of aboriginal people is fundamental? All of these are sensible statements. The interesting thing is that in the polarization that inhabits this volume and, one may suppose, the larger field of Canadian Studies, it has not been possible to say all these things at once. Why not?

The error that underlies this polarization consists of two interrelated aspects. First, *statements* within a discourse are conflated with the discourse itself. Thus the postmodernists collapse the discourse of the Canadian nation-state, and Canadian Studies as an academic field, with left-nationalist speakers, often even a particular author.[10] And left-nationalists often, though not always, assume that a focus on internal diversity necessarily occludes the international field. But no single statement or author dominates an entire discourse. Silences within discourses are indeed important, though not attributable to a single author; but silences within a single text or author's work (statements) do not have any particular significance as such – a single text can say only a very few of the many worthwhile things that could be said. Thus it cannot be concluded that, because something is not said, it is therefore rejected or denied, a conclusion that can often lead to *ad hominem* attacks. Debate nowadays regularly tends to shift from what is being said to who is saying it. The exclusions of the past indeed justify investigating the closures of *discourses* and the way that they have been structured through such exclusions. Who is talking thus becomes a key issue, but does it have to be manifested in the all-too-common reduction of intellectual debate to reciprocal diatribe? Only if one fails to notice that "who one is" is defined in large part by what is said, how one positions oneself with regards to the subject within the discourse as a whole. The reduction of subject matter to speaker that is so common nowadays is only possible if one refrains from problematizing the subject or speaker at the same time that one problematizes the construction of the discourse itself. This approach is not theoretically defensible since it is precisely the same intellectual currents that have illuminated the social construction of discursive formations by showing that the construction of identities occurs within these formations, not prior to them. The recourse to *ad hominem* attacks stems from the attempt to accept the first part of this lesson while ignoring the second.

By conflating a statement with a discourse, Vickers manages to accuse me of suggesting that Aboriginal people should learn from Grant and Innis about environmentalism. She regards it as self-evident that, because I do not discuss the contributions of Aboriginal people to environmental thought, I think that there are no such contributions (362). Again, this is a common, but unjustified presumption. It is often supposed to be a criticism of a work to point out that it does not mention x or y, but this could only be a valid criticism if it were shown how the bringing of x or y into the discussion would significantly alter the articulated position in relation to the subject matter addressed. After all, one cannot mention everything, and, even more fundamental, mentioning something by no means guarantees genuine inclusion. If I were to represent Aboriginal knowledge concerning the environment within an essay that attempts a reflexive account of how European culture in Canada might discover some resources within itself to change in an ecological direction, then this would be a case of merely appropriating native cosmologies for my own purposes – a case of cultural appropriation. It is not because I have not thought about this issue, but because I have, that I made no such mention. It is important for Euro-Canadians to work their way out of forms of domination such as capitalism, industrialism, patriarchy, imperialism, and colonialism. As the self-critique of the culture develops, it will be possible to enter into dialogues with other traditions and to learn from them. But if the self-critique is not prior, the result will be a cultural appropriation of other contributions within a framework presumed to be superior. Thus the critique that my essay performed was, I believe, a more genuine entry into anti-colonial, post-colonial dialogue with Aboriginal views than any mere mentioning could possibly be.

The motive behind Vickers's "interpretation" is revealed in the claim that "it is hard for anyone other than white males of the majoritarian culture to find a sense of identity in the discourse represented by the founding consensus" (363). Thus my presence in the elite formation of Canadian Studies can be "proven" quite quickly by showing that I am a white male, but the relevance of my white maleness to the discursive formation in question needs to be shown, not assumed as given.[11] White maleness is not a pre-existent identity, any more than woman or Aboriginal. This slide between viewing some concepts as socially constructed (such as "Canadian Studies" as an anti-modernist formation) and presupposing others as merely natural (such as white maleness, whose significance therefore requires no elaboration in tying it to a privileged position) is very common nowadays, but it has no intellectual validity and is a mere ideological perversion.

Many of the authors in this volume are aware of this issue. Several make the diagnosis of this type of error a key part of their analysis. For example, Marie-Andrée Bertrand points out that feminist deconstructions of the penal system sometimes resort to the same punitive model that they normally criticize when addressing cases of men guilty of crimes against women (61–2). David Leahy states that when he uses the term "straight men," it is a "strategic essentialism which should not be naturalized" (204), and the same point is made by Susan Knutson (191–2).[12] When Greenhill and Tye argue that the "very presence of these women [folklorists] – situated outside the academy – is critical and alternative" (167), their analysis avoids a naturalizing essentialism by intersecting the gender issue with the institutional one.

Only – and this is the second aspect that constucts the polarization – if one social relationship, such as nation, gender, race, and so forth, is *naturalized*, does this reciprocal diatribe become inevitable. When one social relationship, or "identity," is naturalized it does not require explanation of its social construction. All other relationships can then be (apparently) explained in their social construction with reference to this assumed natural centre. But all social relationships are socially constructed. It is for this reason that an investigation of the influence of power in the construction of one social relationship cannot be assumed necessarily to imply *anything at all* with regard to the others. It is a false universalization. We can see how it plays itself out in Vickers's text. She argues, first, that there is an equity issue, that some stories have been left out, and, second, that, as a consequence, there has been a "fundamental inability to comprehend our subject – Canada and the Canadian experience" (364). Indeed, Canada, like all other nations, has been defined by historical exclusions and silences. But it is not at all clear that the exclusion of Aboriginal people can be rectified by bringing them into "Canada." It is apparent that at least some Aboriginal people maintain that they are not and do not want to be part of "Canada." Many want independence and self-government. It is not the place of either me or Jill Vickers or anyone else from white settler society to decide this issue. It can only be properly addressed – that is to say, in a way that might genuinely begin to undo the exclusion based on military superiority, government double-dealing, sociocultural indifference, and racism – by beginning to negotiate with native people themselves, based on a presumption of their ability to decide what they want for themselves. This task requires that "we" Euro-Canadians turn our attention to our own traditions, their critique, and their reformation, not that we perform tiny and irrelevant gestures of accomodation that will only lead to new forms of cultural appropriation. In short, it is precisely this, our own, tradition that is at issue. It is indeed diverse and criss-crossed by exclusions, but exclusions so deep that they cannot be healed by a supposed inclusion established by one writer's mentioning of them. This is the real failure of liberalism, whether in its traditional or in its postmodern guise. There is a deep failure here to comprehend the role of the writer and thinker in the face of such historical exclusions. They cannot be made up for by mentioning them in texts; the texts must be understood in the context of a much larger field of discourse that includes government, capital, the media, and the public (at least). It is not necessary to mention everything; it is important to intervene in a way that pushes things along in a direction (call me old-fashioned) that increases the chances of general human emancipation. Such a universality can only be achieved by self-criticism of one's historical formation, combined with the refusal to speak for others. The texts have to prepare "ourselves" for a new kind of encounter with the "other" that will not occur only in the texts. We must work on *our own*, as the black civil rights movement said to its white sympathizers, not "accomodate" the others. It is quite fine by me if Aboriginal people want to enter into "Canadian Studies" and transform it, but it seems to me that they are more interested in starting programs of First Nations studies. And why not?

Vickers reveals the kind of patronizing inclusion that she has in mind when she comes to discuss the exclusion of women, arguing for the "possibility that experiences of the Canadian environment differed as profoundly by gender as they did by race" (365). The notion that it is "race" that is the basis for the different views of Aboriginal people to the environment is a reduction of profound differences of history, culture, and experience onto the figure of race – which is precisely what was used to exclude these cultures in the first place. In other words, it is a racist version of the reasons behind their exclusion. Moreover, it is, at least to me, an outrage to suggest that women of the white settler society are as profoundly excluded as Aboriginal people were. This is not to deny exclusion based on gender, nor the necessity for uncovering its bases; but this kind of inflation, it strikes me, is characteristic of a certain establishment feminism that is particularly powerful in universities today. It is merely an ideological appropriation that suggests that the diverse and heterogeneous exclusions that have marked Canadian history can be summed up through the discussion of women. Culture, Vickers says, is "primarily an activity of women" (365), and while it is not said what culture is, the reduction of a whole way of life to the activity of women is as imperialistic as the patriarchal bias itself. Of course, this reaction can be understood – but precisely as a reaction and a symptom – and there are plenty of reasons to suggest that it bodes ill for the future. Feminism, it is often said, is not anti-man but anti-patriarchy. As long as it is so, I have no problem at all with the undoing of the exclusion of women from history and Canadian Studies, though it is not primarily my task to pursue. But there is altogether too much willingness nowadays – especially by male academics seeking to be "politically correct" or, rather, safe – to accede to a reduction of the problem of exclusion to one of women, itself a heterogeneous phenomenon, in a way that masks the different tasks of historical and cultural critique.[13]

Can the defence of Canada as a nation be put together with a critique of the exclusions through which this nation was defined as a unity? The polarization between postmodernism and left-nationalism suggests that it cannot. In this case, we would be left with the alternative of either abandoning Canadian Studies as inherently reactionary (insofar as the "Canada" of its name is an imposed unity) or defending it at the cost of accepting a repression of internal heterogeneity. This would be an unfortunate pass indeed. But the opposition seems to me, for the reasons outlined above, to be a caricature of both left-nationalism and postmodernism. While it is a significant tendency, it by no means characterizes all the contributions to this volume, nor to Canadian Studies generally.[14] So, to return to where this argument started, is it a problem that Mathews regards some works by Canadian authors as non-Canadian?

Let us note that this problem is not unique to the politics of national identity. It raises its head in any politics of identity. Feminists claim to speak for "women," but all women are not feminists. Quebec nationalists claim to speak for the people of Quebec, but not all Quebeckers are separatists. Socialists claim to speak for the working class, but not all working-class people are socialists. The list is endless precisely because any social identity *as articulated by an active voice* must base itself on a *social position as already given* within a wider discourse, but nevertheless intends to *transform that discourse as a whole* through its articulation. Thus it must claim to "sum up" the social position in question and "project it forward" into a new situation. Any such summing up is inherently controversial. It sums up, not in an empirical sense, but in a political one. This duality in social identities give rise to an extensive *politics of representation* that is as active in the academic world as in the social world generally. By the politics of representation I mean, first, *what* individuals and groups are represented, including what is marginalized or unrepresented; second, *where* they are represented – whether on a powerful social medium such as television or in a coffee-shop conversation or a street-corner argument; third, *how* they are represented – which perceptual and cognitive characteristics the medium of communication emphasizes; fourth, *who* represents whom; and fifth, perhaps summing up all the rest, *why* the representation in question has the impact that it has on the society as a whole. I suggest that this politics of representation is a better way of theorizing the volume under review and the current debates in Canadian Studies. One consequence is that the mere pointing to an example which is empirically present in the field as an exception to the theoretical-political totalization is not a convincing criticism as such. In short, there is no problem if Mathews defines some Canadian writers as "out." Every theorization of Canadian literature will, either implicitly or explicitly, do the same thing. In fact, it is to his credit that he is quite explicit about his grounds for doing so, and this extends to left-nationalism in general. Why should everything in Canada be expected to exhibit Canadian distinctiveness?

The only way in which one could avoid this problem of "defining out" would be to engage in no definition at all. One could limit oneself to deconstruction of certain discourses, leaving others alone (for reasons not articulated, since one's theory is based solely on deconstruction) and proposing nothing in one's own voice. There is a certain version of postmodernism that delights in blowing things to pieces precisely in order to leave them in pieces. It is a turn in contemporary thought that has been called sceptical, relativist, and non-political, which it is, but more important, it is a failure of nerve and a lack of courage. Every intellectual production that proposes a theory and, at least implicitly (but better, explicitly), a politics will seek to totalize a field when it cannot empirically succeed. It is common nowadays, in this sceptical climate, to associate such leaky totalizations with totalitarianism, but doing so is merely a defence of meekness. Proposed totalizations by theorists are not discourses, but statements within discourses (as was explained above). There is, in general, no danger that one author, or one position, will dominate the entire discursive field. There will always be other literary critics besides Robin Mathews. If it is really the case that a given position is hegemonic over the entire field, then it is reasonable to suggest that it is guilty of exclusions, that is, of becoming totalitarian, if its hegemony is not won by consent. But only in this extreme case is the equation of totalization with totalitarianism credible. In general, this equation functions to undermine the commitment that is vital to any kind of intellectual activity.

There is, of course, another version of postmodernism, and it is well represented in the volume under review. One can recognize that all proposed definitions *could* be shown to be partial and repressive in certain circumstances, but proceed to take all (or most) speaking positions into account and intervene in defining the field the best one can, and in the direction that one wants, nonetheless. This postmodernism reminds us of something key to all intellectual activity: that it is born of commitment and imagination and that it does not seek consensus, but intervention. To the extent that previous intellectual discourse hid this truth under meta-narratives of science or artistic freedom, or indeed national unity, the reminder is a needed purgative. It seems to me that left-nationalism demanded exactly this commitment and that a certain thanks should be retained within Canadian Studies to the imagination that became its founding discourse. However, the assumption that any focus on other sorts of power relations necessarily detracts from imperialism seems to me a remnant of the "primary contradiction" type of thinking that needs to be dropped. Power is both more plural (a Foucauldian point) and more diffuse (a Gramscian one) than Mathews allows. The recognition of this more complex agenda need not turn attention away from the nation, either in its role as buffer from U.S. imperialism or in its often oppressive domestic role. This kind of (postmodern?) concern was not absent from left-nationalism, though it was not brought clearly into focus.

It is clear from the volume, however, that this intellectual formation has had its day, at least in the form in which it existed. I suggested at the outset that there were three axes in the founding discourse of Canadian Studies: staple theory, cultural nationalism, and the (often disciplinary) interests of the individual researcher. The first two provided the "Canadian Studies" link for the third, and this link has been represented in many of the annual thematic numbers of *Canadian Issues/Themes canadiens*, for example. To say that the discourse has shifted is to argue that the space defined by the intersection of these three axes no longer defines the field within which specific contributions are made. Each of the three axes still exists, of course. It is their timely intersection that has disintegrated. Why? It seems to me that the combined effect of the Free Trade Agreement and NAFTA have produced this disintegration. The coalition against the FTA (at least in English Canada) pulled together in opposition the forces of left-nationalism and many other social groups, such as feminism (NAC), unions, cultural workers, and so forth. When NAFTA came in, no such coalition was in sight. In retrospect, it seems clear that the period prior to the 1988 election was the end of an era. I will not be foolish enough to predict what will come next, but it does seem that, whatever it is, it will have a different shape from before. The polarization in this volume of articles seems to me to reflect a mutual antagonism that has emerged as a result of the fading of the intersection that held together the previous discourse, but rather than organizing the volume around this polarization, I would rather emphasize those articles that articulate themes around the politics of representation which will need to be included in a future discourse of Canadian Studies. It seems to me that the real polarization is between those who would emphasize one social identity *as against others*, and thereby contribute to the falling apart of the nation-space that might protect a plurality of identities, and those for whom the crafting of such a public space is the main issue on the agenda.

What are the axes, or themes, that could intersect to create a new discourse? Couture and Denis emphasize the *productivity of dependent intellectual formations* through the example of Quebec sociology (126). Many of the other contributors similarly focus on the productivity of difference (Bertrand, 66; Greenhill and Tye, 177; Knutson, 188; Leahy, 211–2; Moyes, 309; Sweeny, 344). This theme is thus pervasive and political, and it may be seen as a continuity with the earlier left-nationalist discourse. Couture and Denis also mention, though they do not develop, the notion of *political reason* as produced by Quebec sociology (126), which seems to bear a similarity to Robin Mathews's notion of moral reason (274). This concept may also be seen in continuity with the tradition of the public intellectual in Canadian history, though this tradition did not, it seems to me, enter into the founding discourse as such. There was no theorizing of the public sphere, nor of a particular concept of reason as appropriate to the public – as opposed to science, literature, or disciplinary reason, for example. Joseph Melançon makes an important contribution in this regard when he argues that a domain of knowledge emerges through a system of values that are pre-constituted to meaning-effects within the system (301–2). Specific texts depend upon this pre-institution of value in order to articulate value choices within the discursive field (295). Melançon's axiology would go a long way towards explaining why intellectual interventions, in the absence of a public discursive domain, fail to achieve value effects. While the Canadian tradition valued the public intellectual, it did not theorize the constitution of the public sphere as a domain of knowledge and values upon which such a tradition depended. At the present time, such a radical inquiry is demanded precisely by the loss, or marginalization, of the domain on which public interventions depend.

A third axis is the *problematization of the concept of theory itself*. This is most evident in the remarkable intervention of fiction/theory by Louky Bersianik and Daphne Marlatt. Bersianik proposes an archaeology of the future that requires a revision of philosophical concepts based upon an ontology of women (226–7). Marlatt uses the notion of labyrinth as an articulation of women's reading and writing of theory to unfold a movement towards a centre that returns one to the outside (243–7). In her article on fiction/theory,

Moyes discusses the problematic whereby "I-love-you" might become syn-
chronous with theory (319). These works remind us that the concepts that we
use unreflexively were once crafted by thinkers from the metaphorical extension of experiences into structuring forms. A really radical reflection requires
not only filling old concepts with "our own" meanings, but also crafting new
theoretical forms from our experiences. This is a great task of imagination,
one which will demand that Canadian Studies problematize its own forms of
thought and which might bring it to the important task, addressed but not
completed in this volume, of making Canadian theory.

These three axes – the productivity of dependent formations, political reason, and problematizing the model of theory – suggest a new theoretical formation for Canadian Studies. It seems to me that such a formation would be
able to view the left-nationalist founding discourse as a more specific, or particular, taking up of its own issues. It would also bring into focus elements of
the Canadian tradition not sufficiently theorized by left-nationalism. Further,
it could gather the themes pursued at present under the name of postmodernism into a more general dialogue that might curtail the tendency to set one
social identity against another, and it might congeal into a form of public reason that could say "Canada" without either demanding or rejecting its unity.
We must craft a space for continuing debate that unites us as much by our
disagreements as by unanimity. The Association for Canadian Studies has
done more for this task than any other organization, as its volume well demonstrates, and it has done so in large place because it is not just "of" Canadian Studies but "for" it. This aspect of the issue can never, it seems to me, be
erased. An advocacy, a moral reason committed to the survival of Canada, is
essential. Otherwise, why not take "Canadian" out of the title altogether and
just be the Association for Studies? And is it not left-nationalism that has
articulated this advocacy, up to and including this volume? For all that
postmodernism has added to problematize key issues, has it yet given us
anything crucial on this point?

Conflicting Sovereignties

In a column in the *Globe and Mail* on 12 February 1994[1] Pierre Bourgault pointed out that there are few, if any, voices in English Canada that are currently willing to defend Quebec's right to separation. He is right. He pricked my conscience to speak up and also to explain why it does not often happen. The reason why there is not much enthusiasm in English Canada at this time for defending Quebec's right to independence is that those who did so before were aware that the independence movement in Quebec was a central part of a more widespread movement for social equality and justice. Nowadays, at least from the vantage point of English Canada, it appears to be more like the self-interest of a new business and government elite. It is hard to feel a lot of enthusiasm for such a position.

Nonetheless, Quebec indeed has the right to independence, and it is unconditional, for exactly the reason that Bourgault cites. Quebec was included in Canada by the Conquest. A historical defeat by force of arms can never confer legitimacy on a subsequent polity. This is the reason why, to English Canadians, Quebec never seems satisfied whatever it demands or receives. Because the basic issue is its inclusion in the Canadian confederation by force, every specific issue is always more than a single issue. It is symbolic of an attempt to reverse a historic military defeat. Of course, no single issue, however it is decided, can carry this burden. Thus we always pass on to the next demand with the basic symbolic situation unresolved. The historical fact of defeat could only be overthrown by a free and uncoerced decision to stay (or enter) Confederation by a resounding majority of Quebeckers. But for such a decision to be possible (even if it is not likely), there is an unequivocal prior condition: the *unconditional right to independence* must be acknowledged by all parties. Until such an acknowledgment takes place, no negotiations will really resolve the issue precisely because of the symbolic disequilibrium between the parties. Within the current historical formation, Quebec can never be satisfied, since every particular issue is also symbolic –

really a metonymy, a part standing for the whole – of its forceful inclusion in Canada and is, as such, irresolvable. In English Canada every issue is dealt with as separate, which leads to mounting frustration with Quebec because, whatever is done on an issue-by-issue basis, there is always another issue that comes up the very next day. "They're never satisfied," we say – which is true enough, but we cannot understand why, because the history does not matter to us. It's just old hat.

It is ironic that this is the response in English Canada since we are caught in our own contradictions. On the one hand, there is widespread dissatisfaction with the current organization of Confereration, such as the Senate and the domination of central Canada, as well as more contentious issues, such as free trade and the cutback of social programs. There is a lot of disagreement why, but hardly anybody thinks that the union is working. On the other hand, the response to Quebec is caught in the rut of reasserting the status quo. The dominant cry is: Either accept things exactly as they are or go. Thus the possibility of separation brings forth only boring disquisitions on economic accounting books and dire predictions. Discontent and a reforming spirit with regard to our own complaints never seems to pass over into a balanced or principled response to Quebec's self-assertion. While in Quebec every particular issue is haunted by a larger symbolic history, in English Canada our specific dissatisfactions do not seem to add up to a desire to change the status quo. Our national politics is entirely without vision these days.

Let us look at the independence claims of the Cree in this context. There was a huge outcry in English Canada that Quebec independence was a threat to the self-determination of the Cree. One could not miss the glee at catching Quebec in a contradiction: if independence is good for you, then it is good for them too – which translated into: the federal government will be only preventing Quebec from oppressing the Cree if it forceably retains Quebec in Canada. What a cruel turn of the screw! What about the history of land claims and Aboriginal self-government in English Canada? Is our history any better than that of Quebec? Does it make any sense to contrast small margins when the real issue is the colonial history of the whole of Canada, indeed, the whole of America? The cynical use of the Cree case against Quebec independence was never balanced by an attempt to redress the violent integration of Aboriginal people into Canada. One Conquest played off against another!

It is here that the politics of this country seems to be stuck. There are a multitude of claims for self-government and for the ceding of traditional privilege. But instead of renegotiating them and creating a new, more equal and just, Confederation, national politics is caught in cycles of denial. Instead the claims being opened up, they are denied across the board. If all cannot be free, then none can be. Surely the time has come to explore the other alternative: cease to use conflicting claims for self-government to deny the claims to any one group, but open up as many claims as there are for renegotiation. If Canada is to survive, it can only be through such a general opening up of all claims founded on conquest and violence to renegotiation. Yes, Quebec has the right to separate. But as long as independence claims are posed in terms of maintaining a general status quo, it is hard to have much enthusiasm for them. This country, like all others, was founded on exclusion and violence. We will be stuck where we are now until we begin to craft a new, freely accepted consensus. This is what the constitutional debate should be about. If it becomes so, more voices in English Canada might see the key part that a new relationship with Quebec has in this process. Perhaps, with the cycle of symbolic dependence broken, we might even decide that there are some reasons to stay together.

For a Canadian Philosophy

On 27 September 1988 George Grant died, bringing to an end an iconoclastic intellectual career engaged with national and international political events of the previous fifty years. His defence of Canada's membership in the British empire as a butress against the United States, his famous lament for the defeat of John Diefenbaker's Conservative government, his opposition to the Vietnam War, his positive response to the independence movement in Quebec, his opposition to the testing of the Cruise missile – time after time Grant met the challenge of speaking to the central political currents that have formed the country. For this he was marginalized by the intellectual establishment in Canada. In particular, the guardians of the title "philosopher" refused him the hard-earned recognition of his original contribution to the creation of a truly Canadian philosophy.

I first met George Grant in 1972 when he gave a lecture on "Ideology" at the University of Waterloo. At that time, students were well aware of the dismal failure of almost all our professors to address Vietnam and Canadian complicity in the war, which was the central issue facing us at the time. Many further concerns circled out from this centre: the opposition of the Western governments to self-determination by colonized people in Africa and Asia, the obedient kowtowing of successive Canadian governments to American pressure, the vast inequalities of wealth and power existing within relatively affluent societies, and the key role of universities in providing apologies for this system and technical improvements to sustain it. Only a minuscule proportion of Canada's so-called intellectuals would even discuss these issues, let alone help provide us with the tools that we needed to come to some understanding of the situation and act on it.

That evening George Grant spoke of the colonization of Canadian universities by American professors and their liberal ideology and of the role of so-called value-free social science in maintaining order in an injust society. Most important for us, he connected this general analysis to the horror of Vietnam and the truth it bespoke of the imperialist drive of the American empire. He was willing to call this empire "capitalist," as we insisted, but he also called it "technological." We were less sure of this word, though it did seem to clarify the way in which recent technological advancements were used for destruction, rather than for meeting human needs. To our surprise, we had found a conservative who felt keenly the public responsibility of the philosophical calling, who spoke both passionately and analytically of our subordinate position in Canada and of the global consequences of the American empire. The lecture ended with a discussion of whether conservatives and socialists had more in common than either had with the liberal establishment. I did not realize it then, but this dialogue cut to the root of what is most distinctive in Canadian politics – the centrality of community, ethnicity, and history as against the liberal focus on individuals and their interests.

Grant was always at the centre of discussions such as this. The "Red Tory" appellation, though it was later used widely and loosely, emerged from his example. How many other conservatives, either then or today, would address these radical questions about contemporary society? His conservatism was more like the conservationism of the ecology movement than the Conservative Party. As Grant said, like the Liberals, the Conservatives have bought into the ideology of profit and progress. In the end, he thought himself beyond conservatism too. During his later years he described his goal as "simply to think what we are doing." But the beacon of his philosophical formulations was always directed by his passionate concern for the good life as it could be lived here and now.

What better description of a philosopher? But there have been many who did not think so. In a characteristic gesture, David Gauthier, then (1979) professor and chair of the Department of Philosophy at the University of Toronto, reviewed a volume of essays on Grant entitled *George Grant in Process* for the bulletin of the Canadian Association of University Teachers. He outlined the disparity between professional philosophers who have chosen to concentrate on the tools of thought (such as logical or linguistic analysis) or on the methods of scientific research and those, like Grant, who have directed themselves to the real issues posed by living. Gauthier concluded that Grant avoided the confrontation of his views with the methods of current philosophical analysis, that he was unknown by such professional philosophers, and that therefore he could not be Canada's foremost political philosopher. As Gauthier said, "If he will not speak with the current philosophical tongue, then they will not listen to his lamentation." This quasi-official rejection, the kind of view that has expelled and persecuted genuine philosophical thinking for decades in this country, states that because Grant does not talk to them, he is not a philosopher. Thus the basic criterion for a philosopher is the holding of a position in a university philosophy department – not only a positivist, but a circular and self-serving, definition. No wonder Grant chose to direct his energies elsewhere! That our greatest philosopher has been treated this way is bad enough; that this situation continues to haunt successive generations of Canadians who have attempted to find a philosophical articulation for the politics and history of Canada is inexcusable.

When I began teaching in the Department of Communication at Simon Fraser University in 1981, I had all my students in communication theory read Grant. In lectures there was no difficulty in getting his ideas across. The students all knew that Grant was saying something important and that it went to the heart of what this country is. Certainly, they wanted clarification of what was said and why. Certainly, they wanted to argue with him and to bring their experience to bear on his formulations. This is as it should be – each generation contributing to the dialogue that forges our idea of ourselves. But not for a minute did they doubt his honesty, his clarity and boldness, his grasp of some part of the truth. While the establishment apologists marginalized Grant, it was possible to speak over their heads to students and others who are engaged with passionate thinking about this country and their place in its future.

In Canadian Studies, on the other hand, Grant was lionized. In a sense, his position was a justification of their existence. Yet the forces pushing university and intellectual life to conformity and self-satisfaction are alive and well too. His presence was always unsettling. At a Canadian Studies after-dinner speech at the annual conference of learned societies in Halifax in 1982, Grant addressed the question of what it meant to study ourselves. He quoted Heidegger to the effect that the modern conception of knowledge involves "summoning forth to give its reasons." Bowing to those from outside, mostly the United States, he acknowledged that others could summon us forth and demand our reasons, but he argued that we would not do well to look at ourselves that way. Unlike his writing, which begins with a sure and clear statement of an issue, his speaking voice began slowly, tentatively, clearing a common ground. It gathered direction and conviction, and thundered to a paradoxical conclusion: "My study of Rousseau is a Canadian study." Some were amazed, some outraged, and some carry with them still such characteristic Grantian sayings, which have helped in the forging of intellectual direction and in gathering strength. Grant was four-square against parochialism. He meant: Take up the task to think Canada, put your questions to the past and the future, and put them to the best thinkers. Without their help in bringing our national, binational, multinational, experience to philosophical articulation, we will remain a backwater and will deserve to do so. Argue with Rousseau; argue with Plato; through this dialogue we will make Canadian philosophy.

With his death, there will come a pressure for canonization. He will be respected and quoted, probably at the cost of being read and criticized, which is what every philosopher wants. Let us not forget that George Grant was able only to begin to formulate Canadian philosophy by going outside the canons, by disturbing the boundaries between disciplines and between thought and life. The tradition of philosophical questioning that forges a national tradition is yet to be accomplished in Canada. He began that doing, which will take generations to complete. The future will memorialize him; the past has ignored him; the present needs to continue the dialogue with him.

Let us press against the boundaries, trudge into the wilderness, risk snow-blindness, and bring the bush to thought. That is our solidarity with George Grant – our needing, remembering, and questioning the George Grant trail, leaving some markers as we go our own way. Let them have their chairs of philosophy, their self-congratulation in stuffy rooms. There are many of us who will not forget George Grant.

Notes

CHAPTER ONE

1 Edmund Husserl, *The Crisis of European Sciences and Transcendental Phenomenology*, trans. David Carr (Evanston: Northwestern University Press 1970) 17.
2 Martin Heidegger has explicated the importance of this difference between fate and destiny in "The Question Concerning Technology," in *The Question Concerning Technology and Other Essays*, trans. William Lovitt (New York: Harper and Row 1977) 25, and "Letter on Humanism," in Martin Heidegger, *Basic Writings* (New York: Harper and Row 1977) 241.
3 On this concept of retrospective-prospective thinking, see Martin Heidegger, "Science and Reflection," in *The Question Concerning Technology*, and "The End of Philosophy and the Task of Thinking," in *Basic Writings*.
4 Despite the defence of public philosophy presented here, it must be said that this does not exhaust all of philosophy. In thinking the institution of historical regimes, philosophy escapes the confinement within one that a public philosophy must accept. In this sense it is true that the philosopher has no home or is at home everywhere.
5 My analysis of the contemporary polarization between left-nationalism and postmodernism is presented in appendix 1.
6 The philosophical aspects of this conception of totality have been followed through in my *Dis-figurations: Cultural Criticism and Social Movements in Consumer Society* (London and New York: Verso, forthcoming).
7 The distinction of universalizing from universal was discussed in my first book, *Technique and Enlightenment: Limits of Instrumental Reason* (Pittsburgh: Centre for Advanced Research in Phenomenology; Washington: University Press of America 1984) and is developed in this book through an appropriation and extension of George Grant's concept of particularity.

CHAPTER TWO

1 Max Weber, "Politics as a Vocation," in H. H. Gerth and C. Wright Mills (eds.) *From Max Weber: Essays in Sociology* (New York: Oxford University Press 1976) 77.
2 Weber, "Structures of Power," in ibid., 172.
3 Benedict Anderson, *Imagined Communities: Reflections on the Origin and Spread of Nationalism* (London: Verso 1986) 18–19.
4 Claude Lefort, "The Question of Democracy," in *Democracy and Political Theory,* trans. David Macey (Minneapolis: University of Minnesota Press 1988) 18–20.
5 Peter Alter, *Nationalism,* trans. Stuart McKinnon-Evans (London: Edward Arnold 1985) 9.
6 Anderson, *Imagined Communities,* 26, 30.
7 Ibid., 46. Anderson thus agrees with Innis, McLuhan, and Febvre and Martin that "the book was the first modern-style mass-produced industrial commodity" (38).
8 Weber, "Structures of Power," 172–6; Eric Hobsbawm, *Nations and Nationalism since 1780: Programme, Myth, Reality* (Cambridge: Cambridge University Press 1991) 14–45, 47, 51; Ernest Renan, "What Is a Nation?" in *The Poetry of the Celtic Races, and Other Studies,* trans. William G. Hutchison (Port Washington: Kennikat Press 1970) 70–80; Alter, *Nationalism,* 4–23.
9 Hobsbawm, *Nations and Nationalism,* 5.
10 Renan, "What Is a Nation?" 6.
11 Hobsbawm, *Nations and Nationalism,* 18–19.
12 Michael Ignatieff, "Nationalism and the Narcissism of Minor Difference," *Queen's Quarterly* 102 (1995): 16. See also Hobsbawm, *Nations and Nationalism,* 9, and Alter, *Nationalism,* 9.
13 Abraham Rotstein, "Canada: The New Nationalism," *Foreign Affairs* 55 (1976), and "Is There an English-Canadian Nationalism?" *Journal of Canadian Studies* 13 (1978).
14 Anderson, *Imagined Communities,* 44–6.
15 Karl W. Deutsch, "Peoples, Nations, and Communication," in *Nationalism and Social Communication* (Cambridge: MIT Press 1966) 96, 104.
16 Louis Althusser, "Ideology and Ideological State Apparatuses (Notes toward an Investigation)," in *Lenin and Philosophy, and Other Essays,* trans. Ben Brewster (New York: Monthly Review Press 1971) 154–5.
17 Eric Hobsbawm, "Introduction: Inventing Traditions," in Eric Hobsbawm and Terence Ranger (eds.), *The Invention of Tradition* (Cambridge: Cambridge University Press 1983) 1.

18 Ibid., 13.
19 I am not suggesting that the formation of class as a social identity is not an issue in the Marxist tradition as a whole, but rather that a certain reductionist version of Marxism attempts to avoid this issue and thereby indulges in a simplifying reduction of other social identities. It was certainly a major issue for Marx.
20 See Jill McCalla Vickers, "Sex/Gender and the Construction of National Identities," and Somer Bodribb, "Feminism and Nationalism in Canada: A Discussion," in *Canadian Issues/Themes canadiens* 6 (1984). While it is unclear whether Vickers is *denying* the legitimate reality of national identity or, quite validly, *exploring the connections* between national and family/gender identities, the reductionist feminist assumption becomes clear in Bodribb's commentary where she asks (73), "can we presume that territoriality and a defensive pronatalism are alien to female consciousness? I think we can." Note that the reduction of national identity is a crucial element of its rejection, exactly as in Althusser's text. For an analysis of feminism that elaborates its tendency towards the essentialist claims that are the basis for this reductionism, see Caroline New, "Man Bad Woman Good? Essentialisms and Ecofeminisms," *New Left Review* 216 (March–April 1996).
21 Antonio Gramsci, *Prison Notebooks*, eds. and trans. Quintin Hoare and Geoffrey Nowell Smith (New York: International Publishers 1971) 133.
22 Ibid., 418, 132.
23 Weber, *From Max Weber*, 183–4.
24 Friedrich Engels, "The Tactics of Social Democracy," in Rober C. Tucker (ed.) *The Marx-Engels Reader* (New York: W.W. Norton 1978) 569, 568.
25 Karl Marx and Friedrich Engels, "Manifesto of the Communist Party," in *The Marx-Engels Reader*, 475.
26 Leo Panitch, "The Role and Nature of the Canadian State," in Leo Panitch (ed.) *The Canadian State: Political Economy and Political Power* (Toronto: University of Toronto Press 1979) 5.
27 Karl Polanyi, *The Great Transformation* (Boston: Beacon Press 1971) 132. Emphasis added.
28 Jane Jenson, " 'Different' but not 'Exceptional': Canada's Permeable Fordism," *Canadian Review of Sociology and Anthropology* 26 (1989): 78.
29 Jane Jenson, "Representations in Crisis: The Roots of Canada's Permeable Fordism," *Canadian Journal of Political Science* 23 (1990): 682.
30 See, for example, Daniel Latouche, "Canada: The New Country from within the Old Dominion," *Queen's Quarterly* 98 (1991), and Pierre Fournier, *A Meech Lake Post-Mortem: Is Quebec Sovereignty Inevitable?* trans. Sheila Fischman (Montreal and Kingston: McGill-Queen's University Press 1991) chapter 5.

31 This was always the main reason behind the historically pervasive use of the term "English Canada," as far as I can see. It is thus interesting that it has recently become a problematic term at precisely the point at which the language politics of the country have come to obscure the institutional questions of which they are the expression. The term was used in this way by Kenneth D. McRae in 1964 in "The Structure of Canadian History," in Louis Hartz (ed.) *The Founding of New Societies* (New York: Harcourt, Brace and World 1964) chapter 7.

32 This disparity in the operative concept of language between English Canada and Quebec has been quite widely observed. It has, for example, been made by Charles Taylor in *Reconciling the Solitudes: Essays on Canadian Federalism and Nationalism* (Montreal & Kingston: McGill-Queen's University Press 1993) 56, 101, 164. It suggests the relevance of thinking through the notion of a "medium of communication" within the English Canadian intellectual tradition in such a way as to bring out its implications for institutions, social identity, and politics. This subject is taken up in the next chapter, on the work of Harold Innis.

33 Peter Winch, *The Idea of a Social Science and Its Relation to Philosophy* (London and Henley: Routledge and Kegan Paul 1976) 15–18.

34 Reginald Bibby, *Mosaic Madness* (Toronto: Stoddart 1990), especially 10, 14, 102–4.

35 The special significance of this difference between English and French theoretical traditions for Canadian politics has been noted recently by Philip Resnick in *The Masks of Proteus: Canadian Reflections on the State* (Montreal & Kingston: McGill-Queen's University Press 1990) chapter 10, and *Thinking English Canada* (Toronto: Stoddart 1994) chapter 1, and also by Charles Taylor in *Reconciling the Solitudes*, chapter 3. As one bit of evidence for the German tradition, consider Max Weber's definition of nation in terms of its "normal tendency" to produce its own state in *From Max Weber*, 176.

36 See, as an example of a discourse analysis, my account of the contemporary theoretical discourse of Canadian studies in appendix 1.

37 Jill McCalla Vickers has shown through a citation analysis that Innis and Grant were by far the most cited authors in Canadian Studies publications; see "Liberating Theory in Canadian Studies," in Terry Goldie, Carmen Lambert, and Rowland Lorimer (eds.) *Canada: Theoretical Discourse/Discours théoriques* (Montreal: Association for Canadian Studies 1994) 356, 360.

38 Harold Innis, "Conclusion from *The Fur Trade in Canada*," in David Taras, Beverly Rasporich, and Eli Mandel (eds.) *A Passion for Identity* (Scarborough: Nelson Canada 1993) 18–19.

39 The original essay, which was then elaborated in further works, was R.T. Naylor, "The Rise and Fall of the Third Commercial Empire of

the St. Lawrence," in Gary Teeple (ed.) *Capitalism and the National Question in Canada* (Toronto: University of Toronto Press 1972).

40 Melville Watkins, "A Staple Theory of Economic Growth," *Canadian Journal of Economics and Political Science* 19 (1963): 150–2, and "The Staple Theory Revisited," *Journal of Canadian Studies* 12 (1977): 86.

41 Wallace Clement, "Regionalism as Unequal Development: Class and Region in Canada," *Canadian Issues/Themes canadiens* 5 (1983).

42 See, for example, Wallace Clement, *The Challenge of Class Analysis* (Ottawa: Carleton University Press 1991) 26, 186ff; Leo A. Johnson, "The Development of Class in Canada in the Twentieth Century," in Teeple (ed.) *Capitalism and the National Question in Canada*, and "Independent Commodity Production: Mode of Production or Capitalist Class Formation?" *Studies in Political Economy*, no. 6 (1981); Gordon Laxer, *Open For Business: The Roots of Foreign Ownership in Canada* (Toronto: Oxford University Press 1989).

43 For example, Leo Panitch, "Dependency and Class in Canadian Political Economy," *Studies in Political Economy*, and David McNally, "Staple Theory as Commodity Fetishism: Marx, Innis and Canadian Political Economy"; both in *Studies in Political Economy*, no. 6 (1981).

44 George Grant, *The Empire: Yes or No?* (Toronto: The Ryerson Press 1945) 21.

45 Ibid., 31, 29. It is important to note that Grant, for all of his argument for the British connection, maintained a significant place in his thinking for Canada as formed by the meeting of British and French civilizations. This commitment was maintained throughout his life. He argued in 1945 and later that the survival of French Canadian culture in Canada was due to the British connection. See, ibid., 23.

46 George Grant, *Lament for a Nation: The Defeat of Canadian Nationalism* (Toronto: McClelland and Stewart 1970) 2, 96, xi.

47 Gad Horowitz, *Canadian Labour in Politics* (Toronto: University of Toronto Press 1968) chapter 1. See also Gad Horowitz and George Grant, "A Conversation on Technology and Man," *Journal of Canadian Studies* 4 (1969).

48 Grant always took responding adequately to the exigencies of political action as significant for living the good life. In this he was rare among contemporary philosophers. In the 1970 preface to a reissue of *Lament for a Nation*, after rejecting several criticisms that he regarded as superficial, he referred to the "serious criticism" that his language of inevitability might produce despair in the reader (xi) and went on to discuss it in detail. See my discussion of Grant's politics in appendix 3.

49 Melville Watkins, "Contradictions and Alternatives in Canada's Future," in Robert M. Laxer (ed.) *Canada Ltd.: The Political Economy of Dependency* (Toronto: McClelland and Stewart 1973).

50 Mel Hurtig, "One Last Chance: The Legacy of Lament for a Nation," in Peter C. Emberley (ed.) *By Loving Our Own: George Grant and the Legacy of Lament for a Nation* (Ottawa: Carleton University Press 1990) 56.

51 See especially the essay "Great Britain, the United States and Canada," in *Changing Concepts of Time* (Toronto: University of Toronto Press 1952).
52 Jim Laxer, "Introduction to the Political Economy of Canada" in R.M. Laxer, *Canada Ltd.*, 28–9.
53 D. Drache, "The Canadian Bourgeoisie and Its National Consciousness," in Ian Lumsden (ed.) *Close the 49th Parallel: The Americanization of Canada* (Toronto: University of Toronto Press 1970) 21.
54 Steve Moore and Debi Wells, *Imperialism and the National Question in Canada* (Toronto: Between the Lines 1975) 11. See also Panitch, "Dependency and Class in Canadian Political Economy."
55 Mel Hurtig, *A New and Better Canada* (Toronto: Stoddart 1992) 67.
56 Consider the example of Donald Creighton in this respect. His polemic against the Royal Commission on Bilingualism and Biculturalism argued that it "grotesquely exaggerated the importance of language and culture" by separating culture from "political, economic and financial relations." See "The Myth of Biculturalism," in *Towards the Discovery of Canada* (Toronto: Macmillan 1972) 257.
57 The peculiarly stubborn character of the polarization between political economic and cultural approaches to social and political thought in English Canada was driven home to me when I began teaching in the United States and co-edited a collection of essays on American cultural politics. There was very little discussion, even in its critical reception, of the inclusion of representatives of both groups. The introduction to the volume, which attempted to show the historical and theoretical basis for their integration, did not provoke any polarizing counter-arguments. The U.S. intellectual left was, by way of contrast, much more preoccupied with the hegemonic success of the Reagan-Bush right. See Ian Angus and Sut Jhally (eds.) *Cultural Politics in Contemporary America* (New York: Routledge 1989).
58 Robin Mathews and James Steele (eds.) *The Struggle for Canadian Universities* (Toronto: New Press 1969) 1.
59 Ian Lumsden, "Imperialism and Canadian Intellectuals," in *Close the 49th Parallel*, 327.
60 *The Symons Report* (Toronto: Book and Periodical Development Council 1978) 19–20.
61 David Cameron, *Taking Stock: Canadian Studies in the Nineties* (Montreal: Association for Canadian Studies 1996) 31–2.
62 Rowland Lorimer, "A Personalized Review [of the Cameron Report]," *ACS Bulletin AEC* 18 (1996): 15.
63 One cannot help but notice the fact that there are three axes in this example as there were in the previous example of left-nationalist discourse. I do not want to engage in any general statement as to how many axes are necessary to the constitution of a discourse. I believe, as stated above, that

at least three are required for any reasonably complex discourse. Perhaps I have not investigated thoroughly enough to find a fourth. In any case, I do not want to be accused of being a closet Hegelian, or Christian, because my two examples have three axes. I do not see anything necessary about the number.

64 Paul Litt, "The Massey Commission, Americanization, and Canadian Cultural Nationalism," *Queen's Quarterly* 98 (1991).

65 Harold Innis, "The Strategy of Culture," in *Changing Concepts of Time*, 20.

66 Margaret Prang, "The Origins of Public Broadcasting in Canada," *Canadian Historical Review* 46 (1965): 31.

67 *Vital Links: Canadian Cultural Industries* (Ministry of Supply and Services Canada 1987). All quotes from this document are from 11.

68 This reduction in the concept of culture, often taken even further to refer only to mass media, is the basis for the suggestion that Canada's domination by American mass media does not pose any problems for the survival of the nation. See Richard Collins, "National Culture: A Contradiction in Terms?" *Canadian Journal of Communication* 16 (1991).

69 Tim Buck, "They Are Selling Our Country," in *New Horizons for Young Canada* (Toronto: Labour Progressive Party 1953) 17.

70 Melville Watkins, "The Multi-National Corporation and Canada," *Our Generation* 6 (1969).

71 Melville Watkins, "The Political Economy of Growth," in Wallace Clement and Glen Williams (eds.) *The New Canadian Political Economy* (Kingston and Montreal: McGill-Queen's University Press 1989) 27.

72 Resnick, "From Semi-Periphery to Perimeter of the Core," in *The Masks of Proteus*, 180.

73 Gary Teeple, *Globalization and the Decline of Social Reform* (Toronto: Garamond Press 1995) 63.

74 See the responses by Jorge Niosi and John Warnock to Philip Resnick's essay "The Maturing of Canadian Capitalism" in *Our Generation* 15 (1983).

75 Philip Resnick, *The Land of Cain: Class and Nationalism in English Canada, 1945–1975* (Vancouver: New Star Books 1977) 202.

76 This notion of supplement is taken from Jacques Derrida's work. It refers to an "outside" which is demanded by the incompleteness of the "inside" and which thus shows that the "outside" is not completely outside and that the "inside" is not self-enclosed. Derrida's analysis does not, however, require the other component of the analysis presented here, which is that two factors might each bear a supplementary relation to each other in a mirror-like fashion. This explains the profound strength of the analysis of Canadian political economy based on a synthesis of class and nation. See Jacques Derrida, *Of Grammatology*, trans. G.C. Spivak (Baltimore: Johns Hopkins Press 1976) and *Dissemination*, trans. B. Johnson (Chicago: Chicago University Press 1981).

77 André Gunder Frank, "The Development of Underdevelopment," in *Latin America: Underdevelopment or Revolution?* (New York: Monthly Review Press 1969) 7.
78 Ernesto Laclau, "Feudalism and Capitalism in Latin America," in *Politics and Ideology in Marxist Theory* (London: Verso 1982) 47, 41.
79 Panitch, "Dependency and Class in Canadian Political Economy."
80 This polarization is evident in the Association for Canadian Studies volume on "Canadian theory" based on a conference held in 1992; Goldie, Lambert, and Lorimer (eds.) *Canada: Theoretical Discourse/Discours théoriques.* See appendix 1 for a critique of this polarization and an analysis of the historical moment that it expresses.
81 I use the convention of capitalizing the "Other" when it refers not to the "other" as constituted within one's perceptual-intellectual horizon but as opening to an Other beyond the domination of the self. This convention is a manner of expressing in English the difference between *l'autre* and *l'autrui* in French that is key to the elaboration of this difference by Emmanuel Levinas. See *Beyond Essence, or Otherwise than Being,* trans. Alfonso Lingis (The Hague: Martinus Nijhoff 1981) translator's note to page 21.
82 This conception of totality as a horizon is explicated in more detail in my *Dis-figurations: Cultural Criticism and Social Movements in Consumer Society* (London and New York: Verso, forthcoming).

CHAPTER THREE

1 See Partha Chatterjee, *Nationalist Thought and the Colonial World: A Derivative Discourse* (London: Zed Books 1986), and Gayatri Chakravorty Spivak, "Subaltern Studies: Deconstructing Historiography," in *In Other Worlds: Essays in Cultural Politics* (New York: Routledge 1988).
2 The reference to identity throughout Canadian thought is too extensive to document; however, for policy discussions, see *Vital Links: Canadian Cultural Industries* (Ministry of Supply and Services 1987). For a comparison between Canadian and Australian Studies discussions, see *Australian Studies and Canadian Studies: Reports, Responses, Prospects,* Cultural Policy Studies, Occasional Paper no. 11 (Institute for Cultural Policy Studies, Griffith University 1990). For Latin America, see Leopoldo Zea, "Identity: A Latin American Philosophical Problem," *Philosophical Forum* 20 (1988–89). See also Richard White, *Inventing Australia: Images and Identity, 1688–1980* (Sydney: Allen and Unwin 1981), and Graeme Turner, *National Fictions* (Sydney: Allen and Unwin 1986).
3 Northrop Frye, "Conclusion to *A Literary History of Canada,*" in *The Bush Garden: Essays on the Canadian Imagination* (Toronto: Anansi 1971), and *The Great Code* (Toronto: Academic Press 1982).

4 Lawren Harris, "The Group of Seven in Canadian History," *Canadian Historical Association Report*, 1948, 29.
5 Harold Innis, "A Plea for the University Tradition," *Dalhousie Review*, Innis Papers, University of Toronto Archives, B72–0025/026(01).
6 Donald Creighton, "Harold Adams Innis – An Appraisal," in William H. Melody, Liora Salter, and Paul Heyer (eds.) *Culture, Communication and Dependency: The Tradition of Harold Innis* (Norwood: Ablex 1981) 23; Ian Parker, "Innis, Marx and the Economics of Communication: A Theoretical Aspect of Canadian Political Economy," in ibid., 134–6; Melville Watkins, "Technology and Nationalism," in Peter Russell (ed.) *Nationalism in Canada* (Toronto: McGraw-Hill 1966) 287. Ian Parker also points out that Innis's earlier political economy studies had already paid particular attention to circulation, transportation, and communication.
7 Harold Innis, "An Uneasy Conscience," Innis Papers, University of Toronto Archives, B72–0025/023(19).
8 Marshall McLuhan, Review of *Changing Concepts of Time*, in *Northern Review of Writing and the Arts in Canada*, August-September 1953, Innis Papers, University of Toronto Archives, 1372–0003/037(21).
9 David Crowley, "Harold Innis and the Modern Perspective on Communications," in Melody, Salter, and Heyer, *Culture, Communication and Dependency*, 235.
10 Robin Neill, *A New Theory of Value: The Canadian Economics of H.A. Innis* (Toronto: University of Toronto Press 1972) 93–6, and Crowley, "Harold Innis and the Modern Perspective on Communications," 235.
11 Neill, *A New Theory of Value*, 82–92.
12 James W. Carey, "Technology and Ideology: The Case of the Telegraph," in *Communication as Culture: Essays on Media and Society* (Boston: Unwin Hyman 1988) 203–4.
13 See Edward W. Soja, *Postmodern Geographies: The Reassertion of Space in Critical Social Theory* (London & New York: Verso 1989), and Frederic Jameson, "Cognitive Mapping," in Cary Nelson and Lawrence Grossberg (eds.), *Marxism and the Interpretation of Culture* (Urbana & Chicago: University of Illinois Press 1988).
14 Harold Innis, *The Bias of Communication* (Toronto & Buffalo: University of Toronto Press 1973) xvii.
15 Harold Innis, *The Press: A Neglected Factor in the Economic History of the Twentieth Century* (London: Oxford University Press 1949) 5.
16 Harold Innis, *Empire and Communications* (Toronto & Buffalo: University of Toronto Press 1972) 7.
17 See, for example, *Empire and Communications*, 7, 26–8.
18 Marshall McLuhan, *Understanding Media* (New York: New American Library 1964).

19 Don Ihde, *Technics and Praxis* (Dordrecht: D. Reidel 1979) and *Existential Technics* (Albany: State University of New York Press 1983).

20 Samir Amin, *Eurocentrism*, trans. Russell Moore (New York: Monthly Review 1989) xi.

21 Raymond Williams, "Means of Communication as Means of Production," in *Problems of Materialism and Culture* (London: Verso 1980) 53.

22 Innis, "A Plea for Time," in *The Bias of Communication*, 76. Orality is also counterposed to the "mechanized" in *The Press*, 4, and "A Critical Review," in *The Bias of Communication*, 190.

23 Innis, *The Press*, 4.

24 Innis, *Empire and Communications*, 24, 44, 90, 100; *The Bias of Communication*, 4, 35–6, 50, 100. This account of the contrast of writing and orality also relies on Walter Ong, *Orality and Literacy* (London: Methuen 1982) 31–116, which is a much more comprehensive and systematic comparison than that provided by Innis.

25 At this point we might ask a question. Is oral society as stable as it seems? Or does it simply appear so because it consumes its past? Innis has suggested that orality has a time bias, a stability through time even though it is very local in space. Could it be that oral society simply does not preserve the memory of its instabilities? Also, in reflecting on this question, how could we know oral society as it is, as distinct to how oral society appears to us? In short, how can we answer the reflexive question of appraisal that underlies Innis's work? See Ong, *Orality and Literacy*, 61.

26 Innis, "A Plea for Time," 76.

27 *Empire and Communications*, 56. This analysis of interaction between different media as creating a potential for reflexive awareness is expanded in Marshall McLuhan's conception of "media hybrids" as the source of creative energy. See *Understanding Media*, 57–63.

28 Actually, this characterization refers completely only to Innis's concept of time. He does not criticize the "mathematical substruction" (Husserl) of space in a correlative manner. That he does not do so leads to an impasse in Innis's theory, though it is a productive one insofar as it opens up the critique of colonialism in his work. Space is, we might say, always already colonized in the sense of mathematized and removed from constitutive experience. For this reason, the emphasis on time, connected with the medium of orality, is a critique of empire throughout Innis's work because of its opposition to the term "mechanized." These issues are taken up below.

29 See, for example, Innis, *Empire and Communications*, 25, 170, and *The Bias of Communication*, 60, 76, 92, 96.

30 Innis, "The Problem of Space," in *The Bias of Communication*, 105. This conception is even more central to the work of McLuhan. See, for a selected statement of this pervasive theme, *Understanding Media*, 81.

31 Innis, *Empire and Communications*, 9.
32 Innis, "Industrialism and Cultural Values," in *The Bias of Communication*, 132.
33 Marshall McLuhan, Review of *Changing Concepts of Time* and Introduction to *The Bias of Communication*, vii.
34 Innis, *Empire and Communications*, 9.
35 See ibid., 115, 170.
36 Gayatri Spivak, "Can the Subaltern Speak?" in Nelson and Grossberg, *Marxism and the Interpretation of Culture*.
37 Innis, "A Plea for Time," 61–2.
38 Edmund Husserl, *The Crisis of European Sciences and Transcendental Phenomenology*, trans. David Carr (Evanston: Northwestern University Press 1970).

CHAPTER FOUR

1 George Grant, *Technology and Empire* (Toronto: Anansi 1969) 23–4, 73–4.
2 George Grant, "Ideology in Modern Empires," in John E. Flint and Glyndwr Williams (eds.) *Perspectives of Empire: Essays Presented to Gerald S. Graham* (Thetford 1973) 191. See also Grant, *Lament for a Nation: The Defeat of Canadian Nationalism* (Toronto: McClelland and Stewart 1970) 85–6, 96–7.
3 Alexandre Kojeve, "Tyranny and Wisdom," in Leo Strauss, *On Tyranny* (Ithaca: Cornell University Press 1968). Grant has given an admirable summary of the debate between Strauss and Kojeve in "Tyranny and Wisdom," in *Technology and Empire*, 81–109.
4 Grant, "Tyranny and Wisdom," 93.
5 Karl Marx, "Economic and Philosophic Manuscripts of 1844: Critique of the Hegelian Dialectic and Philosophy as a Whole," in Karl Marx and Friedrich Engels, *Collected Works*, vol. 3 (New York: International Publishers 1975) 332–42; George Grant, "In Defence of North America," in *Technology and Empire*, 30–1. See my account of Grant's relation to the New Left in appendix 3.
6 Grant, *Lament for a Nation*, 15.
7 George Grant, "Canadian Fate and Imperialism," in *Technology and Empire*, 72.
8 George Grant, *Philosophy in the Mass Age* (Toronto: Copp Clark 1966) ix; "Intellectual Background: Conversation," in Larry Schmidt (ed.) *George Grant in Process* (Toronto: Anansi 1978) 64–5; "Tyranny and Wisdom," 99; *Time as History* (Toronto: CBC 1969) 52; *Philosophy in the Mass Age*, 43–9; *Technology and Empire*, 19–23; *English-Speaking Justice* (Sackville: Mount Allison University 1974) 81–2.
9 Grant, *Philosophy in the Mass Age*, 5.

246 Notes to pages 82–90

10 Ibid., 10–13. Despite Grant's rejection of Marxism as an insufficient understanding of moral freedom (ibid., 69–71), these are the two conditions that Marx saw as internal contradictions of the capitalist epoch which give rise to revolutionary consciousness. This agreement results from the influence of Hegel.

11 Ibid., 98.

12 Ibid., 110.

13 George Grant, "An Ethic of Community," in Michael Oliver (ed.) *A Social Purpose for Canada* (Toronto: University of Toronto Press 1961) 20–1.

14 Immanuel Kant, *Groundwork of the Metaphysic of Morals*, trans. H. J. Patton (New York: Harper Torchbooks 1964) 85.

15 Ibid., 88 and 96.

16 Grant, *Philosophy in the Mass Age*, 39.

17 Ibid., vii.

18 *Canadian Dimension* 3 (1966): 59.

19 Grant, *Technology and Empire*, 32; cf. 132–3.

20 Grant, *Time as History*, 18. From this perspective the work of Charles Norris Cochrane on the Augustinian origins of the concept of will in Western thought is of primary importance. See *Christianity and Classical Culture* (Oxford: Oxford University Press 1980).

21 Grant, *Time as History*, 48; *English-Speaking Justice*, 169; "Philosophy: Conversation" in Schmidt, *George Grant in Process*, 144.

22 This is why Arthur Kroker's characterization of Grant as "the Nietzsche of the New World" is mistaken. It is similar to the influence that Grant had in motivating English Canadian political theorists to read Heidegger: it was often forgotten that Grant was, in fundamentals, always a critic of Heidegger. He regarded Heidegger and Nietzsche as symptoms of modernity, not as adequate critics. See Arthur Kroker, *Technology and the Canadian Mind: Innis, McLuhan, Grant* (Montreal: New World Perspectives 1984).

23 Grant, "Revolution and Tradition," in *Tradition and Revolution*, Frank Gerstein Lectures, ed. Lionel Rubinoff (Toronto: Macmillan 1971) 93–4. See also *Time as History*, 51, where Grant points out that any genuine encounter with Asia must be from some "high recognition of what we inevitably are" in the West.

24 George Grant, *Royal Commission on National Development in the Arts, Letters and Sciences* (Ottawa: Edmond Cloutier, King's Printer 1951) 122. See also *Philosophy in the Mass Age*, 7; *Time as History*, 11; *English-Speaking Justice*, 94–5.

25 Grant, *English-Speaking Justice*, 1.

26 I have not raised the question here of whether Heidegger's Nietzsche interpretation is adequate since it is accepted as such by Grant. Heidegger regards Nietzsche's doctrine of the will to power as the consummation,

247 Notes to pages 90–102

rather than the overcoming, of nihilism. See Martin Heidegger, "The Question Concerning Technology," in *The Question Concerning Technology and Other Essays*, trans. William Lovitt (New York: Harper and Row 1977) 104–6.

27 George Grant, "Knowing and Making," in *Proceedings and Transactions of the Royal Society of Canada*, 4th ser., 102 (1974): 63. See, for example, Grant's rejection of the term "technology" in "Revolution and Tradition," 85, n. 1.

28 Grant, *English-Speaking Justice*, 88.

29 George Grant, "The Computer Does Not Impose on Us the Ways It Should Be Used," in Abraham Rotstein (ed.) *Beyond Industrial Growth*, (Toronto: University of Toronto Press 1976) 122.

30 Grant, *English-Speaking Justice*, 72. See also "Philosophy: Conversation," 145.

31 Heidegger, "The Question Concerning Technology," 27.

32 Martin Heidegger, "Plato's Doctrine of Truth," in William Barrett and Henry D. Aiken (eds.) *Philosophy in the Twentieth Century* (New York: Random House 1962) 3: 265.

33 Grant, *Time as History*, 2; *English-Speaking Justice*, 90–1.

34 Martin Heidegger, "The Onto-Theo-Logical Constitution of Metaphysics," in *Identity and Difference*, trans. Joan Stambaugh (New York: Harper & Row 1969) 61.

35 Plato, *Republic*, 509b, Paul Shorey translation.

36 Grant, *Time as History*, 52.

37 Grant, *English-Speaking Justice*, 91. Cf. "Philosophy: Conversation," 144–5, and "The Computer ...," 124.

38 Grant, *English-Speaking Justice*, 60–73; "In Defence of North America," 18–25.

39 Grant, *English-Speaking Justice*, 26.

40 Ibid, 70, 84.

41 Martin Heidegger, "Letter on Humanism," trans. Edgar Lohner, in Barrett and Aiken, *Philosophy in the Twentieth Century*, 3: 276.

42 In a very similar argument, Arthur Kroker has suggested that the focus on "moral economy" is characteristic of Canadian thought. See "On Moral Economy," *Canadian Journal of Political and Social Theory* 1 (1977).

43 See Gary Snyder, "The Place, the Region and the Commons," in *The Practice of the Wild* (San Franscisco: North Point Press 1990), and, for an overview of the concept in environmental politics, Carolyn Merchant, *Radical Ecology: The Search for a Livable World* (New York: Routledge 1992) 217–22.

44 It is an important point of historical interpretation whether the primacy of will begins with Socrates and Plato (as Nietzsche claims) or with Augustine (which would confine it to the Christian tradition), or whether it can be pushed back even further to the pre-Socratics (as Heidegger seems to suggest). The role of Augustine has been emphasized by the classic work

of Charles Norris Cochrane, *Christianity and Classical Culture*, and it has been argued by Arthur Kroker in "Augustine as the Founder of Modern Experience: The Legacy of Charles Norris Cochrane" *Canadian Journal of Political and Social Theory* 6 (1982), that this work establishes Augustine as the founder of modernity.

45 To say so is not merely to comment on Grant's contradiction but also to indicate an inadequacy of this formulation: there is no distinction in it between religious and mythical accounts of the Whole and the philosophical account that grounds Plato's justice. In Grant's formulation, the originality of the philosophical formulation of world-views is collapsed back into religion.

46 H. and H.A. Frankfort, "The Emancipation of Thought from Myth," in *Before Philosophy* (Harmondsworth: Penguin 1959) 247–8.

47 Lynn White Jr, "The Historical Roots of Our Ecologic Crisis," in *Machina ex Deo: Essays in the Dynamism of Western Culture* (Cambridge: MIT Press 1968) 86, 89–90.

48 Grant said somewhere – I believe it was in his seminar on technology at McMaster University, which I attended in the winter term of 1973 – that his conception of Anglicanism was that variant closest to Hinduism. This remark was made in the context of the commitment of Western Christianity to the centrality of will since Augustine. I do not know what it means.

49 It also raises the important question of whether such an immanent and participatory ontology can preserve philosophy, since philosophy emerges through the separation of internal from external that Heidegger has diagnosed as the inception of the metaphysics which results in technology. He thus announces the end of philosophy in favour of what he calls "thought." I cannot address this question here, though I have argued elsewhere that the gnoseological orientation that emerges from this origin of philosophy is, nonethless, not constitutive of philosophy as such. Even so, to the extent to which philosophy is the love of knowledge and not its possession, it may be supposed that philosophy would indeed disappear if the participatory ontology in question did not allow for or require radical questioning of the relation of human action to Being. See Ian Angus, *Dis-figurations: Cultural Criticism and Social Movements in Consumer Society* (London and New York: Verso, forthcoming) chapter 6.

50 On this anti-modernism, see Hans Hauge, "George Grant's Critique of Modernity: Canadian Refractions of Continental Ideas," *Canadian issues/ Themes canadiens* 12 (1990), and Jery Zaslove, "Herbert Read and Essential Modernism: The Loss of an 'Imago Mundi,'" *Collapse*, no. 1: 166–78.

51 This is Hauge's critique of Grant, which is taken over by Jill Vickers in "Liberating Theory in Canadian Studies," in Terry Goldie, Carmen Lambert, and Rowland Lorimer (eds.) *Canada: Theoretical Discourse/Discours théoriques* (Montreal: Association for Canadian Studies 1994) 364. It con-

sists in a simplification to one side of the polarity and a rejection based on this simplification. It is indeed the case that a straightforward archaizing anti-modernism contains a propensity towards a regressive politics. It might be argued that Heidegger's undifferentiated romantic anti-modernism was key to his embrace of Naziism. In his later life Grant pondered repeatedly the meaning of Heidegger's Nazi affiliation, which I believe he regarded as emblematic of the failure of twentieth-century philosophy at its highest moment, but I do not know of any final interpretation at which he may have arrived. Grant may thus have failed to get enough perspective on the Heideggerian aspect of his own thought to analyse Heidegger's failure sufficiently, but he did not necessarily share the failing. Similarly, Grant may never have defined accurately the "truth" brought forth by modern technology, but he never doubted that there was such a truth, which he referred to with characteristic pungency by saying, "I have six children. How could I be against penicillin?"

CHAPTER FIVE

1 Arturo Andres Roig, *Teoria y critica del pensamiento latinoamericano* (Mexico: Fondo de Cultura Economica 1981) 18. My translation.
2 Leopoldo Zea, "Identity: A Latin American Philosophical Problem," *Philosophical Forum* 20 (1988–89): 33.
3 Leslie Armour, "Canada and the History of Philosophy," in Terry Goldie, Carmen Lambert, and Rowland Lorimer (eds.) *Canada: Theoretical Discourse/Discours théoriques* (Montreal: Association for Canadian Studies 1994) 35.
4 Northrop Frye, "Conclusion to *A Literary History of Canada*," in *The Bush Garden: Essays on the Canadian Imagination* (Toronto: Anansi 1971), and *The Great Code* (Toronto: Academic Press 1982).
5 Lawren Harris, "The Group of Seven in Canadian History," in *Canadian Historical Association Report*, 1948, 38.
6 For an example of a discussion that is stuck in this false dichotomy, see Robert J. Brym, "The Great Canadian Identity Trap: Implications for the Comparative Study of Class and Power," *Canadian Journal of Sociology* 14 (1989).
7 J.M.S. Careless, " 'Limited Identities' in Canada," in *Careless at Work* (Toronto: Dundurn Press 1990).
8 Zea, "Identity: A Latin American Philosophical Problem," 41.
9 Harold Innis, *The Idea File of Harold Adams Innis* (Toronto: University of Toronto Press 1980) 6.
10 This issue is discussed more extensively in appendix 1.
11 Leopoldo Zea, *La filosofia en Mexico* (Mexico: Libro Mexico Editores 1955) 2: 251. My translation.

12 George Grant, "Canadian Fate and Imperialism," in *Technology and Empire* (Toronto: Anansi 1969) 73.

13 Gianni Vattimo, *The Transparent Society*, trans. David Webb (Baltimore: Johns Hopkins University Press 1992) 22.

14 Leopoldo Zea, "El descubrimiento de America y la universalizacion de la historia," in Leopoldo Zea (ed.) *El descubrimiento de America y su impacto en la historia* (Mexico: Fondo de Cultura Economica 1991) 6. My translation.

15 Roig, *Teoria y critica del pensamiento latinoamericano*, 22. My translation.

16 This is the convention of capitalization used by Levinas's translator Alfonso Lingis to indicate in English the difference between *l'autre* and *l'autrui* in French. See Emmanuel Levinas, *Beyond Essence, or Otherwise than Being*, trans. Alfonso Lingis (The Hague: Martinus Nijhoff 1981) translator's footnote to page 21.

17 Chief George Watts, "Economics for Future Generations," *Pro-Canada Dossier*, no. 29: 43. Chief Watts is perfectly clear that this statement does not refer to all individuals within Canada (42), but to Canada itself as a social identity distinct from individual identities. Thus one can agree with it, as I do, without taking it as a personal credo and, indeed, doing one's part to change this unfortunate reality.

18 Daniel Latouche, "Canada: The New Country from within the Old Dominion," *Queen's Quarterly* 98 (1991): 329.

19 Pierre Fournier, *A Meech Lake Post-Mortem: Is Quebec Sovereignty Inevitable?*, trans. Sheila Fischman (Montreal and Kingston: McGill-Queen's University Press 1991) 74.

20 Latouche, "Canada: The New Country from within the Old Dominion," 323; Christian Dufour, *A Canadian Challenge / Le défi québécois* (Lantzville, BC: Oolichan Books 1990), 150.

21 Fournier, *A Meech Lake Post-Mortem*, 79; Latouche, "Canada: The New Country from within the Old Dominion," 325; Dufour, *A Canadian Challenge*, 151.

22 Philip Resnick, *Thinking English Canada* (Toronto: Stoddart 1994) xi.

23 Carl Berger, "The True North Strong and Free," in Peter Russell (ed) *Nationalism in Canada* (Toronto: McGraw-Hill 1966).

24 Cole Harris, "The Myth of the Land in Canadian Nationalism," in ibid.

25 Margaret Atwood, *Survival* (Toronto: Anansi 1972) 30.

26 Frye, "Conclusion to *A Literary History of Canada*," 220, and Robert Kroetsch, "Canadian Writing: No Name is My Name," in David Staines (ed.) *The Forty-Ninth and Other Parallels* (Amherst: University of Massachusetts Press 1986).

27 Melville Watkins, "Technology and Nationalism," in Russell, *Nationalism in Canada*, and Arthur Kroker, *Technology and the Canadian Mind: Innis, McLuhan, Grant* (Montreal: New World Perspectives 1984).

28 George Grant, "In Defence of North America," in *Technology and Empire*.

251 Notes to pages 115–23

29 Harold Innis, "Conclusion from *The Fur Trade in Canada*," in David Taras, Beverly Rasporich, and Eli Mandel (eds.) *A Passion for Identity* (Scarborough: Nelson Canada 1993) 24–6.

30 George Grant, *Lament for a Nation: The Defeat of Canadian Nationalism* (Toronto: McClelland and Stewart 1970) chapter 6.

31 For an overview of Watson's influence, see A.B. McKillop, *Contours of Canadian Thought* (Toronto: University of Toronto Press 1987) chapter 7, and John A. Irving, "One Hundred Years of Philosophy in Canada," in *Philosophy in Canada: A Symposium* (Toronto: University of Toronto Press 1952).

32 Grant, *Lament for a Nation*, 15.

33 Ibid., 45–6, 74–6.

34 Gad Horowitz, *Canadian Labour in Politics* (Toronto: University of Toronto Press 1968) 23 (emphasis in original).

35 Herschel Hardin, *A Nation Unaware* (Vancouver: J.J. Douglas 1974) 50.

36 Robin Mathews, *Canadian Identity* (Ottawa: Steel Rail 1988) 62.

37 Philip Resnick, *The Land of Cain: Class and Nationalism in English Canada, 1945–1975* (Vancouver: New Star Books 1977) 176.

38 George Grant, "Foreword" to James Laxer and Robert Laxer, *The Liberal Idea of Canada: Pierre Trudeau and the Question of Canada's Survival* (Toronto: James Lorimer and Co. 1977) 12.

39 Dufour, *A Canadian Challenge*, 149–50, and Latouche, "Canada: The New Country from Within the Old Dominion," 323, 327, 329.

40 Fournier, *A Meech Lake Post-Mortem*, 74–9.

41 The procedure of deconstruction that I am explaining and using here is indebted to Jacques Derrida's work, which is undoubtedly the most influential in propounding deconstruction as an approach to contemporary philosophy and human sciences. The deeper influence in this work, however, is that of the phenomenological tradition of Heidegger and Husserl. See Jacques Derrida, *Margins of Philosophy*, trans. A. Bass (Chicago: University of Chicago Press 1982), *Writing and Difference*, trans. A. Bass (Chicago: University of Chicago Press 1978), and *Of Grammatology*, trans. G.C. Spivak (Baltimore: Johns Hopkins University Press 1976).

42 The theme of the end of philosophy is discussed in my *Dis-figurations: Cultural Criticism and Social Movements in Consumer Society* (London and New York: Verso, forthcoming) chapter 6.

43 This is a defect of the otherwise excellent history by Leslie Armour and Elizabeth Trott, *The Faces of Reason: An Essay on Philosophy and Culture in English Canada, 1850–1950* (Waterloo, Wilfrid Laurier University Press 1981).

44 Martin Heidegger, "The End of Philosophy and the Task of Thinking," in *On Time and Being*, trans. Joan Stambaugh (New York: Harper Torchbooks 1972).

45 Martin Heidegger, *Identity and Difference*, trans. Joan Stambaugh (New York: Harper & Row 1969) 61.

46 Edmund Husserl, "The Origin of Geometry," appendix 6 to *The Crisis of European Sciences and Transcendental Phenomenology*, trans. David Carr (Evanston: Northwestern University Press 1970) 360.

47 Frederick Jackson Turner, "The Significance of the Frontier in American History," in *Frontier and Section: Selected Essays of Frederick Jackson Turner* (Englewood Cliffs: Prentice-Hall 1961) 38, 62.

48 Michael A. Weinstein, *The Wilderness and the City: American Classical Philosophy as a Moral Quest* (Amherst: University of Massachusetts Press 1982).

49 See Morris Zaslow, "The Frontier Hypothesis in Recent Historiography," *Canadian Historical Review* 29 (1948), and George F.G. Stanley, "Western Canada and the Frontier Hypothesis," *Canadian Historical Association Report*, 1940. Geoffrey Blainey claims that the frontier was not characteristic of Australian history either, but rather the concept was of distance; see *The Tyranny of Distance* (Melbourne: Sun Books 1966).

50 Frye, "Conclusion to *A Literary History of Canada.*" Frye does not distinguish, as this essay does, between wilderness, frontier, and border. Thus he says that in the U.S., one could move out to or retreat from the frontier, whereas in Canada the frontier was all around (220). Rather, wilderness was all around, and a border was constructed to civilize it. Keeping it outside leads to the garrison mentality; this essay attempts to voice the other possibility of taking inside, which Frye calls "mythic resolution," that also haunts Canadian literature (241–2).

51 See, for a similar argument, Patricia Marchak, "Political Economy in and out of Time," in Goldie, Lambert, and Lorimer, *Canada: Theoretical Discourse/Discours théoriques*, 262.

52 Harold Innis, "A Defence of the Tariff," included as an appendiz to Robin Neill, *A New Theory of Value: The Canadian Economics of H.A. Innis* (Toronto: University of Toronto Press 1972) 150.

53 Heidegger, *On Time and Being*.

54 I believe that this is what Heidegger calls the "earth" that is beneath, as it were, the necessary unfolding of earth into a plurality of "worlds." See Martin Heidegger, "The Origin of the Work of Art," in *Poetry, Language, Thought*, trans. Albert Hofstadter (New York: Harper and Row 1971).

55 The order that is wilderness is normally called ecology, or ecosystem, today. It is an order that is not subjected to human purpose. See Stan Rowe, *Home Place: Essays on Ecology* (Edmonton: NeWest Press 1990), and Max Oelschlager, *The Idea of Wilderness* (New Haven: Yale University Press 1991).

CHAPTER SIX

1 Gilberto Giminez, "Apuntes para una teoria de la identidad nacional," *Doxa: Cuaderno de ciencias sociales* 4 (1993/94): 67, and Eric J. Hobsbawm, "Nationalism and Ethnicity," *Intermedia* 20 (1992): 15.
2 Hilda Sabato, "Pluralismo y nacion," in *Punto de vista* 12 (1989).
3 The tradition of collective rights in English Canada normally traces its origins to Loyalism and the conservative Canadian rejection of the American Revolution. However, it has been pointed out by Leslie Armour, in *The Idea of Canada and the Crisis of Community* (Ottawa: Steel Rail 1981) and "History, Community, Ethnicity and the Thrust of Technology in Canada," in Ian H. Angus (ed.) *Ethnicity in a Technological Age* (Edmonton: Canadian Institute of Ukrainian Studies 1988), that French Canadians and also later immigrants shared the pre-Enlightenment communitarian bias of the Loyalists. Also, as Harold Innis and others have pointed out, the "public enterprise culture" of the Canadian state is based on a conception of public collective goals; see, for the economic history that grounds this case, the classic summary in the concluding chapter to Harold Innis, *The Fur Trade in Canada* (Toronto: University of Toronto Press 1970), and, for a contemporary extension of this thesis, Herschel Hardin, *A Nation Unaware* (Vancouver: J.J. Douglas 1974). I by no means deny that this tradition of collective public rights has always coexisted in Canada with the individual rights characteristic of the United States nor that in recent years it has been under considerable attack from the neo-liberal ideology of the recent Conservative Party; see, in this connection, Robin Mathews, *Canadian Identity* (Ottawa: Steel Rail 1988) chapter 4. I do claim, however, that collective rights have been historically important and are, even today, a significant minority tradition. It is within this tradition that the politics of multiculturalism in English Canada properly belongs.
4 In Australia, for example. See Peter Putnis, "Constructing Multiculturalism: Political and Popular Discourse," *Australian Journal of Communication*, no. 16 (December 1989).
5 Gad Horowitz, "Mosaics and Identity," in Bryan Finnigan and Cy Gonick (eds.) *Making It: The Canadian Dream* (Toronto: McClelland and Stewart 1972) 467–8.
6 Reginald Bibby, *Mosaic Madness* (Toronto: Stoddart 1990) 10, 14, 102–4.
7 Chantal Mouffe, "Feminism, Citizenship and Radical Democratic Politics," in *The Return of the Political* (London: Verso 1993) 83.
8 Compare the first, sixth, and seventh paragraphs of the act. The first quotation is from the sixth paragraph, where the connection is attempted. The statement by Trudeau was made in the House of Commons on 8 October 1971 in the context of accepting the recommendations of the Royal Commission on Bilingualism and Biculturalism, which led to the later devel-

opment into multiculturalism. These documents are available as appendices to Angie Fleras and Jean Leonard Elliot, *Multiculturalism in Canada* (Scarborough: Nelson 1992).

9 This dual usage is a theme in the collection, Angus, *Ethnicity in a Technological Age*, and is commented upon in the introduction.

10 See George Grant, "Canadian Fate and Imperialism," in *Technology and Empire* (Toronto: Anansi 1969) 68, and Armour, *The Idea of Canada and the Crisis of Community,* chapter 6.

11 Sabato, "Pluralismo y nacion," and Putnis, "Constructing Multiculturalism: Political and Popular Discourse." In this connection it is interesting that Gordon Laxer, in addressing the fact that the Canadian economy has never been able to escape the staples trap of foreign ownership as other countries have done, turns to the absence of popular nationalism as the only factor that seems specific and unique enough to provide an explanation. See *Open for Business: The Roots of Foreign Ownership in Canada* (Toronto: Oxford University Press 1989), especially chapter 4.

12 Ian Angus, "Oral Tradition as Resistance," in Manoly R. Lupul (ed.) *Continuity and Change: The Cultural Life of Alberta's First Ukrainians* (Edmonton: Canadian Institute of Ukrainian Studies 1988).

13 Neil Bissoondath, *Selling Illusions: The Cult of Multiculturalism in Canada* (Harmondsworth: Penguin 1994) 211; see also 110, 118, 133, 224.

14 Quoted by Michael Valpy in his column, *Globe and Mail*, 8 February 1995.

15 CBC television news special on multiculturalism, 28 September 1994.

16 For one example of the continuum on which we have apparently come "too far," see Bibby, *Mosaic Madness*, 105.

17 Bissoondath, *Selling Illusions*, 212, 110, 211.

18 This statement should not be taken to suggest that I oppose such recognition for French Canada/Quebec, or for Aboriginal people. It suggests rather that the conditions of such recognition are different in these cases than they are for ethno-cultures within English Canada, precisely because the presumption of English as the language of everyday commerce and politics is not possible. The reason for this circumstance, stated generally, is that these groups were included into Canada by military force, not immigration, and thus it poses different – and in a certain sense more radical – issues for the self-consciousness of English Canada. It is for this reason that I refer to them as "external determinants" of English Canada and to ethno-cultures as "internal determinants." This external-internal difference is historically based and decidable by the distinction between voluntary and involuntary inclusion, a distinction which may be psychologically dubitable, but which is politically essential. See appendix 2.

19 Jurgen Habermas, "Citizenship and National Identity: Some Reflections on the Future of Europe," *Praxis International* 12 (1992): 7. See, for an example of Taylor's position to which Habermas refers, *Reconciling the*

Solitude: Essays on Canadian Federalism and Nationalism (Montreal & Kingston: McGill-Queen's University Press 1933) 56.

20 Habermas, "Citizenship and National Identity."

21 Ibid.

22 Michael Ignatieff, *Blood and Belonging: Journeys into the New Nationalism* (Toronto: Viking 1993) 14–19, 116.

23 Charles Taylor, "The Politics of Recognition," in *Multiculturalism and "The Politics of Recognition"* (Princeton: Princeton University Press 1992) 43.

24 Ibid., 58 and 59.

25 Taylor, *Reconciling the Solitudes*, 56

26 Taylor, "The Politics of Recognition," 59; *Reconciling the Solitudes*, 129–30, 152.

27 Taylor, *Reconciling the Solitudes*, 182–3

28 Ibid., 183.

29 Ibid., 198.

30 Taylor, "The Politics of Recognition," 60; cf. 43 and *Reconciling the Solitudes*, 138.

31 Taylor, "The Politics of Recognition," 67.

32 Ibid., 71.

33 Ibid., 72.

34 Ibid., 73. Taylor's view is thus anti-Rousseau in that it allows for and fosters individual and social differences and anti-Kant in its defence of collective goals. See ibid., 50, 57.

35 While a certain genetic sense of "first mine, then the other" still remains with regard to the rearing of babies in the ethno-culturally defined home and their subsequent introduction to others, this approach has now receded to the point where it occurs at least as early as school-entering age and probably in fact a lot earlier. The us/them experience has faded, even as a genetic component, to such a degree that it cannot be the starting point for multicultural theory. For adults, of course, the multicultural context has even become the primary experience in the context of which one retreats, as it were, to preserve and develop ethno-cultural identity. In this sense, it is first and foremost a *critical* tendency.

36 See Taylor, *Reconciling the Solitudes*, 191, and chapter 6; "The Politics of Recognition," 38.

37 George Grant, *Lament for a Nation: The Defeat of Canadian Nationalism* (Toronto: McClelland and Stewart 1970) 85.

38 On the concept of language in English Canada, see Taylor, *Reconciling the Solitudes*, 55, 164; with regard to the interpretation of Meech Lake as a confrontation between collective rights and procedural rights, see ibid., 150, 161–2, 165, 177–9, 194, and "The Politics of Recognition," 53–55, 60. I do not deny that this opposition is part of the issue, only that it is a simplification that tends to throw all other trends in English Canada to the dogs

in order to defend Quebec's distinctness. Such an approach may be all
right for an intellectual in Quebec, but it is completely unacceptable for
one based in English Canada. It would pose for us the same dilemma that
we have had with regard to the United States for many years: either defend an attachment to Canada on entirely parochial grounds or accept
submergence into the "universality" of the American empire. George
Grant's work is an attempt to find a way out of this unsatisfactory alternative, and for this very reason, it is key to rethinking a commitment to collective rights in English Canada.

39 George Grant, "Canadian Fate and Imperialism," 73.
40 A.J. Parel regards Grant's vision of Canada as inherently opposed to multiculturalism for this reason – that it undermines the commitment to the
nation. But this argument rests on the presumption that I am attempting
to unearth and displace – that ethno-cultural allegiances necessarily compete with national ones. In my view, the rethinking of the relation of particular and universal towards which Grant's work orients us should lead
to criticism of the common-sense assumption that identity is a zero-sum
game. See Parel, "Multiculturalism and Nationhood," in Yusuf K. Umar
(ed.) *George Grant and the Future of Canada* (Calgary: University of Calgary
Press 1992).
41 Jean-Paul Sartre, *Being and Nothingness*, trans. Hazel E. Barnes (New York:
Philosophical Library 1956) 79, 81. Emphasis in original.
42 These two inflections are also confused in the work of Ernesto Laclau and
Chantal Mouffe, where the Lukacsian rhetoric of "it is no accident that"
based on a Hegelian conception of totality is reversed into a rhetoric of
"non-necessary, or contingent, connections" to such an extent that the investigation of the possibility of a new concept of totality which does not
assume such an inherent necessity is hindered. See Laclau and Mouffe,
Hegemony and Socialist Strategy (London and New York: Verso 1985)
chapter 3.
43 Richard Rorty, *Contingency, Irony and Solidarity* (Cambridge: Cambridge
University Press 1989) 33; see also 41, 61, and passim.
44 Ibid., 189; see also 45.
45 Ibid., xv.
46 Ibid., 60. The possibility that a language may be a mode of action in the
world with characteristics that carry it beyond contingency is therefore
ruled out by Rorty. His claims do not follow directly from the linguistic
turn in philosophy and the human sciences, but from a specific theory of
language.
47 Ibid., 190. As, interestingly, so does Sartre; see *Being and Nothingness*, 413–
5.
48 Michael Ignatieff, "Nationalism and the Narcissism of Minor Differences," *Queen's Quarterly* 102 (1995): 21.

49 The distinction between universal and universalizing goes back to
Kant's *Critique of Judgment* and has been used and developed by many
twentieth-century thinkers in order to theorize the intermediate realm –
"aesthetic," according to Kant; "political," according to Hannah Arendt
– in which judgments have a claim upon others but cannot be shown
to be universal and necessary. Interestingly, Max Horkheimer and Hans-
Georg Gadamer also began from this part of Kant's work to explicate
the type of judgments pertaining to critical theory and hermeneutics.
I think that this fact indicates something fundamental about twentieth-
century philosophy. See Hannah Arendt, *The Life of the Mind*, vol. 1,
Willing (New York: Harcourt, Brace, Jovanovich 1978) appendix "Judging"; Max Horkheimer, *Kants Kritik der Urteilskraft als bindeglied zwischen
Theoretischer und praktischer Philosophie* (Stuttgart: Verlag von W. Kohl-
hammer 1925); Hans-Georg Gadamer, *Truth and Method* (New York:
Crossroad 1975); Ian H. Angus, *Technique and Enlightenment: Limits of
Instrumental Reason* (Pittsburgh: Centre for Advanced Research in
Phenomenology; Washington: University Press of America 1984)
chapters 4 and 5.

50 This account suggests that the further the practices of a (sub)culture are
from one's own, the greater the moral weight of the postulate of equal
worth. In the case of Aboriginal people and Quebec this suggests that it is
precisely the greater distance of these "external determinants" from English Canada that warrants insistence on respect.

51 For a rigorous formulation of this reversible relation of context and content, see Vernon E. Cronen, Kenneth M. Johnson, and John W. Lanna-
mann, "Paradoxes, Double Binds, and Reflexive Loops: An Alternative
Theoretical Perspective," *Family Process* 21 (1982).

52 Mouffe, "Feminism, Citizenship and Radical Democratic Politics," 84–5.

53 Parel, "Multiculturalism and Nationhood," 142.

54 The concept of totality implied by this notion of context is the phenomenological one of "horizon," rather than the Hegelian one of "totality of
determinations" or the empiricist one of a mere aggregate. Hegelian totality is open to positive knowledge and thus reduces philosophy to science,
whereas phenomenological totality is continuously reformed by and
through its contents. That this distinction is little appreciated in contemporary social theory leads to the current tendency to abandon a concept
of totality rather than reform it. I have discussed the concept of totality
though the phenomenological problematic of theme/horizon in *Dis-
figurations: Cultural Criticism and Social Movements in Consumer Society*
(London and New York: Verso, forthcoming).

55 Tom Murphy and I spoke with James Peggy MacDonald, prior to an after-
noon of drinking Scotch and singing, about the history of Gaelic in Cape
Breton in August 1974. This story is from his personal experience.

56 Manoly R. Lupul, "Ukrainians: The Fifth Cultural Wheel in Canada," in Angus, *Ethnicity in a Technological Age*.

57 Leslie Armour, "History, Community, Ethnicity, and the Thrust of Technology in Canada," in ibid., 171.

CHAPTER SEVEN

1 G.W.F. Hegel, *Philosophy of Right*, trans. T.M. Knox (Oxford: Oxford University Press 1969) preface, 13.

2 The concept of diversity as the basis for an ecological theory that involves both social justice and the integrity of natural systems first became important in the Canadian intellectual landscape through the Science Council of Canada report no. 27, *Canada as a Conserver Society* (Hull: Supply and Services Canada, September 1977) 30–4.

3 George Grant, "Canadian Fate and Imperialism," in *Technology and Empire* (Toronto: Anansi 1969) 73.

4 See, especially, George Grant, "A Platitude," in *Technology and Empire*.

5 C.B. Macpherson, *The Political Theory of Possessive Individualism* (Oxford: Oxford University Press 1962).

6 The suggestion that the new radicalism had some common ground with elements of conservatism was around in the 1960s, but it did not go anywhere, at least theoretically, but perhaps precisely into the new social movements. See appendix 3.

7 Diego Martin Raus, "Acerca de la constitucion de identidades sociales," *Doxa: Cuadernos de ciencias sociales* 4 (1993–94): 63. My translation.

8 Jean L. Cohen and Andrew Arato, *Civil Society and Political Theory* (Cambridge and London: MIT Press 1992) 2.

9 Karl Marx, *On the Jewish Question*, in Robert C. Tucker (ed.) *The Marx-Engels Reader* (New York: W.W. Norton 1978) 43.

10 Ibid., 46.

11 Ibid. Italics removed.

12 Published under the title "Marx on the History of His Opinions" in ibid., 4.

13 Karl Marx, "Contribution to the Critique of Hegel's *Philosophy of Right*," in ibid., 64.

14 Karl Marx, *The Holy Family*, excerpted in ibid. as "Alienation and Social Classes," 133.

15 Marx, "Contribution to the Critique," 64. Italics removed.

16 Douglas M. Brown, *Towards a Radical Democracy* (London: Unwin Hyman 1988) 42.

17 Ibid., 61.

18 Karl Polanyi, *The Great Transformation* (Boston: Beacon Press 1971) 252.

19 Harold Innis, "The Penetrative Powers of the Price System," in *Essays in Canadian Economic History* (Toronto: University of Toronto Press 1979)

20 See, for example, Leo Panitch, "Dependency and Class in Canadian Political Economy," and David McNally, "Staple Theory as Commodity Fetishism: Marx, Innis and Canadian Political Economy"; both in *Studies in Political Economy*, no. 6 (1981).

21 Karl Marx, *Capital*, vol. 1, trans. Ben Fowkes (New York: Vintage Books 1977) 174, n. 34; see also 153, 174, 242, 251, 256, 651–2.

22 Polanyi, *The Great Transformation*, 234.

23 Gordon Laxer, "Social Solidarity, Democracy and Global Capitalism," *Canadian Review of Sociology and Anthropology* 23 (1995): 305. For a similar strategy for Latin America, see Jorge Castaneda, *Utopia Unarmed: The Latin American Left after the Cold War* (New York: Vintage Books 1994).

24 Samir Amin, *Delinking: Toward a Polycentric World*, trans. Michael Wolfers (London and New Jersey: Zed Books 1985) 52.

25 Ernesto Laclau and Chantal Mouffe, *Hegemony and Socialist Strategy* (London and New York: Verso 1985) 127–34.

26 Alain Touraine, *Critique of Modernity*, trans. David Macey (Oxford and Cambridge: Blackwell 1995) 235.

27 Michel Henry, *Marx: A Philosophy of Human Reality*, trans. Kathleen McLaughlin (Bloomington: Indiana University Press 1983) 283.

28 See Martin Heidegger, "The Age of the World View," in *The Question Concerning Technology and Other Essays*, trans. William Lovitt (New York: Harper and Row 1977), and Edmund Husserl, *The Crisis of European Sciences and Transcendental Phenomenology*, trans. David Carr (Evanston: Northwestern University Press 1970).

29 In this sense, industrial capitalism is the epoch of a separation of ideology from material conditions, such that ideology comes to determine material conditions, and therefore its overcoming cannot be formulated simply within the opposition of ideology and material conditions that defines the epoch. Rather, a new understanding of praxis – indeed, of Being – is required. See, in this connection, Michel Henry, "The Concept of Being as Production," *Graduate Faculty Philosophy Journal* 10 (1985), and *Marx: A Philosophy of Human Reality*.

30 Marx, *Capital*, 1: 133.

31 Ibid., 1: 128.

32 Karl Marx, *Critique of the Gotha Program*, in Tucker, *The Marx-Engels Reader*, 530.

33 Karl Marx, *Economic and Philosophical Manuscripts of 1844*, in ibid., 105.

34 Stanley Moore, *Marx versus Markets* (University Park: Pennsylvania State University 1993) 76.

35 Ibid., 60–5.

36 For a description of new social movements in these terms, see Castaneda, *Utopia Unarmed*.

37 Marx, *Capital*, 1: 163.

38 Gianni Vattimo, *The End of Modernity*, trans. Jon R. Snyder (Baltimore: Johns Hopkins University Press 1988) 172, 177.

39 World Commission on Environment and Development, *Our Common Future* (Oxford: Oxford University Press 1987) 43, 44.

40 I by no means want to ignore or underestimate these issues. However, they are the contemporary form of the traditional issue of inequality *within human society*. My present concern is with what is new in the ecological movement – the linking of human society to non-human nature – and I therefore do not deal with these issues explicitly. This does not mean that they are unimportant, only that they are addressed by a traditional socialist politics that needs, of course, updating but no fundamental theoretical reorientation.

41 Jim MacNeill, Pieter Winsenius, and Taizo Yakushiji, *Beyond Interdependence: The Meshing of the World's Economy and the Earth's Ecology* (Oxford: Oxford University Press 1991) 20.

42 Stan Rowe, *Home Place: Essays on Ecology* (Edmonton: NeWest 1990) 118.

43 The clarification of terminology that I am suggesting here is not shared by all commentators. Neil Evernden rejects the use of the term "ecology" because it is limited to the quantitative and non-ethical precepts of the normal scientific paradigm. He uses the term "environmentalist" to refer to "one who expresses a sense of value in nature and is moved to assert the reality of this experience to others." This is almost exactly the reverse of the usage that I propose. I do not see that it is necessary to confine ecology to its scientific definition, however, even though some confusion is possible in this regard. While Evernden's usage is clear on this issue, it nevertheless obscures the point that I am making – that environmental concern may be "humanistic" in exactly the sense that he wants to reject. Terminology differs, but the underlying issue is the same. See Neil Evernden, *The Natural Alien: Humankind and Environment* (Toronto: University of Toronto Press 1985) chapter 1; the quotation above is from page 6.

44 The debate between deep and social ecology now constitutes a very large literature. See the summaries in Carolyn Merchant, *Radical Ecology: The Search for a Livable World* (New York: Routledge 1992) chapters 4 and 6, and Andrew Dobson, *Green Political Thought* (London: Unwin Hyman 1990) chapter 2.

45 Arne Naess, "The Shallow and the Deep, Long-Range Ecology Movement: A Summary," *Inquiry*, 1973, 16, 95. See also Arne Naess, *Ecology, Community, and Lifestyle*, trans. David Rothenberg (Cambridge: Cambridge University Press 1990) chapter 7.

46 Gary Snyder, "Tawny Grammar," in *The Practice of the Wild* (San Francisco: North Point Press 1990) 70.

47 Gary Snyder, "Ancient Forests of the Far West," in ibid., 138.

48 Martin Heidegger, *Being and Time*, trans. John Macquarrie and Edward Robinson (New York: Harper and Row 1962) 84.

49 This phrase is not, to my knowledge, generally current in phenomenological studies of the self, but it has been fruitfully used by Neil Evernden to bridge these studies as a whole with the concerns of environmental thought. See *The Natural Alien*.

50 Of course, this quick example does not document the experience in question, nor argue its relevance adequately. However, the phenomenological accounts of embodiment in tools and of the self do provide this documentation, though I do not think that these two thematics have been properly linked as yet. See Don Ihde, *Technics and Praxis* (Dordrecht: D. Reidel 1979) and *Existential Technics* (Albany: State University of New York Press 1983); Herbert Spiegelberg, *Steppingstones: Toward an Ethics for Fellow Existers* (Dordrecht: Martinus Nijhoff 1986) 29–86.

51 Not only do the initial and terminal relations to practical life need to be rethought in a critique of industrialism, but also the understanding of thought that is so designed. I have pursued a critique of the instrumental concept of reason that emerges from this late-Renaissance origin in *Technique and Enlightenment: Limits of Instrumental Reason* (Pittsburgh: Centre for Advanced Research in Phenomenology; Washington: University of America Press 1984).

52 This is the theoretical basis for George Grant's reading of Heidegger, which has exerted so much influence in recent years. It suggests, to put it schematically, that the role of the "turning" in Heidegger's thought is similar to the relation between conservatism and the new conservationism that this essay begins to work out. A critique of Grant's "humanism" such as that which I have proposed in chapters 4 and 5 is central to this task.

53 See Heidegger's discussion of these metaphors in order to argue that such dwelling is exactly the sense in which "Being-in is the formal existential expression for the Being of Dasein, which has Being-in-the-World as its essential state." *Being and Time*, 80.

54 Martin Heidegger, *Identity and Difference*, trans. Joan Stambaugh (New York: Harper & Row 1969) 28.

55 Naess, *Ecology, Community, and Lifestyle*, 14.

CHAPTER EIGHT

1 This conception of totality is defended in my *Dis-figurations: Cultural Criticism and Social Movements in Consumer Society* (London and New York: Verso, forthcoming) chapter 5.

2 See my analysis and critique of the contemporary theoretical impasse between postmodern approaches and left-nationalism in appendix 1.

3 I do not mean to imply by this conception that philosophy is entirely exhausted in the task of thinking destiny, though it cannot sidestep it; but a full elaboration of the practice of philosophy is beyond the objectives of this book. For part of what is left out by this characterization, see *Dis-figurations*, chapter 6.

4 The notion of the "step back" as a continuation of the phenomenological reduction is developed in Martin Heidegger, *On Time and Being*, trans. Joan Stambaugh (New York: Harper and Row 1972).

APPENDIX ONE

1 Edited by Terry Goldie, Carmen Lambert, and Rowland Lorimer (Montreal: Association for Canadian Studies 1994). Page references to this book are included in the main text.

2 This, of course, will not exclude Innis's work from having different effects when brought into another related, but not identical context. The recent appropriation of Innis in Australia, for example, is developing his work in interesting directions. See the special issue on Harold Innis in *Continuum: The Australian Journal of Media and Culture* 7 (1993).

3 One may well be sceptical of Wein's assertion that the initially mean-spirited (387) and unattractive (386) components of economic contractarianism can be overcome within it, culminating in a preference for institutions of peace, order, and good government (387). However, this is an unexamined assertion within his article, and I will not examine it here. Another aspect of this issue is the narrow range of the philosophies compared by Wein. His focus solely on social-contract theories of justice means that it is a long jump from the discrepancy he describes to the theoretical culture of the two countries in general. Are most of the theories of justice in Canada contract theories, for example? If most philosophical theories are such, might not this be an example of the extent to which the culture of university philosophy departments has lost touch with the political culture of Canada? Not only is the relation between theory and social order complex, but it is important to respect the degrees of mediation between the two.

4 And as philosophers know, the way in is itself part of philosophy. I would argue that this is true of Plato and is constitutive of the discourse called "philosophy," though this is not the place for that argument. I believe that it was also true of George Grant's version of the relation between perenniality and entry. For him, all truly philosophical themes are perennial, but nonetheless we have to discover them for ourselves. He sees it this way because of his Platonism. Armour's Hegelianism pushes him towards viewing it as a choice between two opposed interpretations.

5 By virtue of her contribution to this volume, Marchak might better be called an ex-left-nationalist. When she describes political economy as having abandoned left-nationalism for French regulationist theory, it is ambiguous whether she herself endorses this move (260–2), though her concluding reformation of political economy certainly seems to do so (262–7). Mathews clearly interprets her as having abandoned the left-nationalist tradition (275). Marchak's turn to globalism seems to have some resonances to postmodernism, even though she rejects such a direction (264–5).

6 The two other places where the issue between postmodernism and left-nationalism is addressed directly are, significantly, from within the left-nationalist literary camp. Dean documents the controversies between Mathews and other literary critics such as Frye, Atwood, Keith, Koetsch, and Woodcock (154–63), and Mathews offers some trenchant criticisms of Linda Hutcheon and Lorraine Weir (279–81, 283). One might mention also that Cavell discusses the views of Frye on space before proceeding to his own post-colonial theory (78–82), but Frye cannot be included in the left-nationalist camp, and the other authors (Innis, McLuhan, Gould, Harris, McGregor) are only mentioned by Cavell, not discussed in any detail.

7 Had her research gone any further, Vickers might have noticed, for example, that my book on George Grant has not been discussed or mentioned in any of the recent collections of essays on his thought. Also, an obituary that I wrote was initially of interest to the *Globe and Mail*, but was later rejected when the editors had seen its content. It later appeared in the *Canadian Journal of Political and Social Theory* and is included here as appendix 3. It should be obvious to any undergraduate that it is not talking about George Grant that makes one part of the establishment, but what one has to say about his work.

8 I am emphasizing this point, in part at least, as a self-criticism. I also wrote an essay suggesting that the space of the nation needed to be empty in order for internal differences to be recognized. This was, as I am indicating now, a superficial posing of the issue and has been rectified in the chapter on multiculturalism in this book. See "Oral Tradition as Resistance" in Manoly R. Lupul (ed.) *Continuity and Change: The Cultural Life of Alberta's First Ukrainians* (Edmonton: Canadian Institute of Ukrainian Studies 1988).

9 In Mathews's essay he does precisely this with regard to the specific authors he discusses: he documents significant absences with regard to the theme of imperialism. But the leap from these specific cases to the general claim is not directly addressed.

10 Or even a single text. The selectivity of Vickers's choice of sources is indeed remarkable. For example, she refers exclusively to George Grant's *Canadian Forum* article against abortion when discussing him (358, 366).

While this article is certainly part of his work and could well be discussed in a critique, to refer to it as if it were the only, or the most significant, of his works is an amazing distortion. Why not mention Grant's defence of the Quebec independence movement or his opposition to Cruise missile testing? Or perhaps even read some of his books and refer to them?

11 I admit to being white and male – as Vickers probably guessed through the same "methodology" that she guessed the ethnicity of writers in journals from their names (356), and as others have probably noticed first-hand.

12 This term is taken from Gayatri Spivak. It suggests that any *actual* discourse, at least one involved in political intervention, requires the postulation of one (or some) of its terms as natural even when they are "really" not so. For my part, I do not think that this usage solves the problem, but that it rather reveals an inadequacy of deconstructionist theory – an inability for it to theorize, rather than merely refer to, a key component of precisely the strategic domain to which it is addressed. But, in any event, it demonstrates an awareness of the issue at hand.

13 See in this connection the essay by Madhu Kishwar, "Why I Do Not Call Myself a Femininist," in *Manushi* 61 (1990), and the statement by Ofelia Schutte that "the specific structure of domestic work in Latin America is a clear case where class oppression supercedes gender oppression" in "Philosophy and Feminism in Latin America: Perspectives on Gender Identity and Culture," *Philosophical Forum* 20 (1988–89): 73.

14 For a volume that retains a commitment to Canada and yet thematizes the problems of internal diversity, see the special issue, edited by Robert Schwartzwald, of *The Massachusetts Review* (vol. 31, no. 1–2): *an/other Canada, another Canada? other Canadas.*

APPENDIX TWO

1 Because this analysis is of a contemporary political mood – one that one hopes will change – it should be pointed out that this comment was written in early 1994, shortly after the column was published.

Index